Also by Gerry Stoker

THE NEW POLITICS OF BRITISH LOCAL GOVERNMENT *(editor)*

MODELS OF LOCAL GOVERNANCE: Public Opinion and Political Theory *(with W. Miller and M. Dickson)*

HOLISTIC GOVERNANCE *(with Perri 6, D. Leat and K. Setzler)*

THEORIES AND METHODS IN POLITICAL SCIENCE Second Edition *(co-edited with D. Marsh)*

TRANSFORMING LOCAL GOVERNANCE

BRITISH LOCAL GOVERNMENT INTO THE 21ˢᵗ CENTURY *(co-edited with D. Wilson)*

WHY POLITICS MATTERS: Making Democracy Work

RE-ENERGIZING CITIZENSHIP: Strategies for Civil Renewal *(with T. Brannan and P. John)*

Governance Theory and Practice

A Cross-Disciplinary Approach

Vasudha Chhotray
School of International Development,
University of East Anglia, UK

Gerry Stoker
Professor of Governance,
University of Southampton, UK

First published 2009
Published in paperback 2010 by
PALGRAVE MACMILLAN

Palgrave Macmillan in the UK is an imprint of Macmillan Publishers Limited, registered in England, company number 785998, of Houndmills, Basingstoke, Hampshire RG21 6XS.

Palgrave Macmillan in the US is a division of St Martin's Press LLC, 175 Fifth Avenue, New York, NY 10010.

Palgrave Macmillan is the global academic imprint of the above companies and has companies and representatives throughout the world.

Palgrave® and Macmillan® are registered trademarks in the United States, the United Kingdom, Europe and other countries.

ISBN: 978–0–230–54676–9   hardback
ISBN: 978–0–230–25039–0   paperback

This book is printed on paper suitable for recycling and made from fully managed and sustained forest sources. Logging, pulping and manufacturing processes are expected to conform to the environmental regulations of the country of origin.

A catalogue record for this book is available from the British Library.

A catalogue record for this book is available from the Library of Congress.

10   9   8   7   6   5   4   3   2   1
19   18   17   16   15   14   13   12   11   10

Printed and bound in Great Britain by
CPI Antony Rowe, Chippenham and Eastbourne

Contents

List of Tables

Acknowledgements

We are very grateful to Damian Tobin for his co-authorship of Chapter 7. We thank our family and colleagues for their support. Thanks should particularly go to Andy Hindmoor and Tony Payne for their comments on earlier drafts of parts of the book. The financial support of the Economic and Social Research Council (ESRC) provided us both with the time and resources to write this book. It came in the form of professorial fellowship from January 2004 (ref no: RES-051-27-0067) provided to Gerry Stoker. We thank the ESRC for their support and the time and opportunity it has provided.

1
Introduction: Exploring Governance

Twenty years ago nobody would have written this book. Governance has moved in the last two decades from the status of a lost word of the English language to a fashionable and challenging concept in a range of disciplines and research programmes. But after two decades of publication and debate it seems appropriate to ask: has it been worth it? We must quickly add, lest the reader throws the book down immediately, fearing they are about to waste their time, that our answer is a definite and clear affirmative: governance theory offers a valuable and challenging dimension to our understanding of our contemporary social, economic, and political world. The substantive chapters that follow will give able support to demonstrate the truth of that statement.

In this book we offer a cross-disciplinary focus in order to generate, ultimately, a multi-disciplinary synthesis. The concluding chapter of the book attempts to draw out some general lessons from our governance tour. The key disciplines investigated in Part I of the book are politics, economics, development studies, international politics and socio-legal studies. Each of the disciplines we examine moves to a focus on governance, in order to deal with issues of central importance to that discipline, and each has spawned a substantial literature. But core insights also come from the application of governance in particular settings to specific challenges. There have been extensive research programmes into the practice of governance in specific fields and functions. Chapters in Part II of the book explore in detail, insights stemming from the large literature generated by research into corporate governance, participatory engagement, and environmental management.

The fact that governance emerged as an issue across a large range of disciplines and research programmes cannot, we argue, be put down to the fact that social scientists are just dedicated followers of fashion, jumping on whatever research programme or conceptual discussion that happens to be passing. Rather, we argue that the rise in interest in governance reflects changes in our society, and researchers' attempts to come to grips with the new empirical phenomena and practices that they are observing. The twin forces that mark out this era of change over the last few decades, we suggest, are globalisation and democratisation. These are the implications of our growing interdependence in a context where the expectations of citizens to influence the decisions that affect them have increased the pressure on established systems of collective decision-making, and brought forth demands for new forms of governance. Governance has become a focus of academic and practical discourse because traditional literatures and ways of explaining were inadequate to the task. The world has changed and the rise of governance seeks to an attempt to understand the implications of these changes, and how they might best be managed.

Governance seeks to understand the way we construct collective decision-making. Its introduction as a term into our debates, coincided with a sense that existing models were failing to capture what was happening, and not providing an appropriate framing of key issues for reformers. In both political and economic spheres, the established ways of making collective decisions have come under challenge. The basic unit of political organisation, the nation-state has been challenged by the complexity of social problems, the strength of organised interests, and the growing internationalisation of interdependencies (Benz and Papadopoulos, 2006). The basic unit of the economy – the firm – has found itself the focus of new consumer demands, complex regulatory calls for ethical and social responsibility, and its institutions have to operate in an increasingly global market (Mallin, 2003). Much of the governance literature is about capturing the response to that changing world.

Collective decisions have still to be made by states and governments at all levels, and policy and strategic objectives have to be established by firms. Governance asks how these tasks can be undertaken with effectiveness and legitimacy. In the past, elections could be seen as giving governments the mandate and the state had the resources of finance, knowledge, organisation, and authority, to ensure that social coordination was achieved. Similarly, firms dealt with their businesses in relatively autonomous way sanctioned by the traditions and legal requirements of their national setting. Both states and firms now face challenges to their legitimacy and effectiveness that require them to consider alternative ways of making decisions.

In this introductory chapter we first seek to define the core features of the topic and move on to focus on the impact of democratisation and globalisation in changing the context for collective decision-making. An outline of the remainder of the book is then provided.

Defining the scope of governance theory

Governance theory is about the practice of collective decision-making. A regular complaint across all literatures is that governance is often vaguely defined, and the scope of its application is not specified. These protests are particularly keenly expressed in our home discipline of political science. Most reviews on the development of a governance perspective start with the comment that governance has been used in a variety of ways in the political science literature (for example Kjaer, 2004; Pierre and Peters, 2005; Jordan *et al.*, 2005) and note some difficulty with definition and focus in using the concept. According to Pierre and Peters (2000:7) the concept of governance 'is notoriously slippery' and Schneider (2004:25) comments that the conceptual vagueness of the term is the 'secret of its success'. As Kohler-Koch and Rittberger (2006:28) put it bluntly despite decades of work 'there is still confusion about the conceptualization of the term'. We recognise the validity of these concerns and the dangers that we add by our interdisciplinary focus.

To address anxieties over the scope and coverage of the term governance, we offer the following basic definition. *Governance is about the rules of collective decision-making in settings where there are a plurality of actors or organisations and where no formal control system can dictate the terms of the relationship between these actors and organisations.* There are four elements about this definition that are worth dwelling on a little bit more. First, we should clarify what we mean by rules. The rules embedded within a governance system can stretch from the formal to the informal. Decision-making procedures generally find expression in some institutional form and can be relatively stable over time, although not necessarily unchanging. Indeed one reason for growing interest in governance is precisely because established institutional forms of governance appear under challenge, and new forms of governance appear to be emerging. In studying governance we are interested in both the formal arrangements that exist to structure decision-making and the more informal practices, conventions and customs. In short we are most often interested when it comes to governance in what Ostrom (1999:38) refers to as 'rules-in-use', the specific combination of formal and informal institutions that influences the way that a group of people determine what to decide, how to decide, and who shall decide: the classic governance issues.

The concept of 'collective' is the second element in the definition that is worth dwelling on. Collective decisions are, rather obviously, decisions taken by a collection of individuals. But crucially although we can normally express our preferences through various mechanisms by way of the agreed decision-making processes, the outcomes of the process are then imposed (Stoker, 2006a: Ch 4). You are not guaranteed what you want even in a system of formally democratic governance. Collective decisions involve issues of mutual influence and control. As such governance arrangements generally involve rights for some to have a say, but responsibilities for all to accept collective decisions.

Thirdly, we should dwell on what we mean by decision-making. Decision-making can be strategic but it also can be contained in the every day implementation practice of a system or organisation. Deciding something collectively requires rules about who can decide what, and how decision-makers are to be made accountable. Governance frameworks can focus on collective decision-making in societal systems or internal processes within organisations. Governance can be concerned about collective decision-making on global issues, and concerned about the rules governing a local executive or administrative body. It is important to recognise these macro and micro elements of the governance debate and distinguish between them. But equally it can be noted that micro and macro perspectives are connected to one another and although most of the literature we review tends to take a more macro perspective, we consider that both perspectives offer something of value.

The final element in our definition of governance that deserves further attention, is the idea that in governance 'no formal control system can dictate' the relationships and outcomes. Or put another way: governance is a world where 'no one is in charge'. Monocratic government – governing by one person is the opposite of governance, which is about collective governing. Authority and coercion are resources available to some in governance arrangements but never in sufficient quantity or quality to mean they can control the decision-making process. The characteristic forms of social interaction in governance rely on negotiation, signals, communication and hegemonic influence rather than direct oversight and supervision.

Governance theory is interested not just in offering explanation, it also seeks to provide advice. It has the character of being both concerned with 'what is' and 'what might be'. The study of governance is focused not just on aiding a better understanding of part of our world, but it also has a concern with how the functioning and operation of that world could be made better. The interdependence of our lives makes constructing mechanisms for collective decision-making an essential and significant human activity. We need to understand the changing ways in which the governance challenge is being met, and whether there are ways in which the way we meet that challenge can be improved. With all governance mechanisms there are input and output challenges to be met. Are the right interests involved in decision-making? Does the governance arrangement help the delivery of better outcomes?

The construction of governance regimes matters to the well-being of our societies. The world recognises that the under-development of Africa is in part down to failures in national and international governance regimes. It is increasingly aware that if environmental issues are going to be resolve then global governance issues around the making of binding collective decisions will need to be resolved in order to resolve issues of global warming. Equally there is much intervention and policy premised on the idea that the performance of public services, for example, could be enhanced by better governance arrangements within and between the agencies involved. The operation of multi-national and powerful companies in a globalised world raises major issues about how they make decisions and how they might be held to account for some of those decisions. So governance matters but choosing what options are best is not a technical matter but an issue of values and politics.

The processes of governance then demand to be understood analytically and empirically as a set of practices, rather than through the lens of a 'wish-list' of principles to be followed. We do not lay out a set of normatively-derived governance principles for all social systems or organisations. Although lists of such governance principles can be found elsewhere and do provide some valuable food for thought (Hyden *et al.*, 2004; Kaufmann and Kraay, 2007). Our general purpose in this book is to better understand the diverse strands of governance theory in order to advance our understanding of governance practice in a range of settings. Governance theory, we claim, helps to better frame an understanding of how the processes of collective decision-making fail or succeed in our societies. We aim through our cross-disciplinary lens to push that process of understanding further forward.

Governance scholars are interested in how governance arrangements are chosen (intentionally or unintentionally), how they are maintained or how they are changed. But governance is not a science with clear causal pathways to be identified, nor can it be adequately captured by laws, statutes or formal constitutions. Governance is a practice. We examine these issues of translating governance into a practice in Part II of the book when we look at how governance theory has led to developments in the practice of corporate, participatory, and environmental, governance. Moreover, it is an intensely human activity and is not undertaken by super beings that are all-seeing and all-knowing. Governance is undertaken by human agents who are defined by bounded rationality – limited by their information processing capacities – and constrained by conflicting power positions and perceptions.

Two things flow from this statement. First governance is a political activity; it is about coordination and decision-making in the context of a plurality of views and interests. Conflict and dissent provide essential ingredients to a governance process. Given human society, as it has been and as it might reasonably be expected to be in the future, people will make judgements about what is right for themselves and for others, and that there is no reason to assume that those judgements will be shared. Equally it is clear that as humans we need to find ways to act together, to engage in collective action, to resolve the problems and challenges of living together. John Dunn (2000:73) defines politics as 'the struggles which result from the collisions between human purposes: most clearly when these collisions involve large numbers of human beings'. Politics informs governance in that it provides the raw material both to construct governance arrangements and the focus of much governance activity when it is operating.

The second factor to flow from our assertion that governance is an intensely human activity is that its existence to some extent is explained by the limits of our human capacities. If we are all-seeing and knowing and could faithfully predict each other's behaviour then the frameworks and rules of governance would be unnecessary. We could exchange views and resolve conflicts without resort to institutions and practices that simplify our choices, limit our areas of focus, push our understanding in certain directions and provide rules of thumb or heuristics so that we have a rough idea about what to do in different settings. Governance exists in part because it provides us with effective ways to cope with the limitations of human cognition and understanding. It provides architecture for choice in the context of our bounded rationality (Jones, 2001).

Governance arrangements are brought to life by decision-makers that are boundedly rational. Decision-makers, as it were, have to deal both with the external environment and their inner world, their cognitive architecture. The inner world helps them to focus on some things and ignore others and it is driven by habits of thought, rules of thumb, and emotions. Rationality is 'bounded' by this framing role of the human mind. Insights from social psychology and cognitive studies suggest that actors develop various coping techniques and heurists to deal with the challenges they face. Some are seen as providing effective ways of coming to a judgement – 'better than comprehensive rationality' – and others are seen as having in-built pathologies or weaknesses (Bendor, 2003). One of the characteristics of an effective governance mechanism is that it steers actors and the organisations they lead to certain types of desired behaviour in the context of bounded rationality. Governance at its best brings into play what Dunn calls 'the cunning of unreason' (Dunn, 2000).

The driving force behind the explosion of interest in governance is a sense that changes in the practice of governing our societies are being driven by powerful and relatively novel forces. Indeed governance systems are seen as particularly under pressure in all sectors of society as changes in the economic, political, social and ecological context place new demands on existing arrangements. The greatest of these forces for change is relatively easy to identify in the literature drawn from politics, international relations and development studies, the spread of global economic and social links, and the rising power of democratisation.

Explaining the rise of governance theory

Two developments, over the last three decades, have provided the backcloth to the surge in interest in governance. The first is the extent and degree of globalisation. The second is the spread of basic institutions of democracy and more generally the triumph of the democratic ideal. These are significant changes in our world and constitute defining features of our historical era. Although governance theory obviously touches on themes visited by previous scholars, what makes the current governance turn new is the context for the current debate: a context defined by substantial social and economic change.

Something fundamental is happening to our economies and the umbrella term 'globalisation' is a good one to capture what is going on. There has been a strong trend towards a world of more rapid world-wide communication, closer connections between peoples and organsations and a greater sense of interconnectedness. Economies appear to be more interconnected, patterns of migration have taken on powerful and challenging directions, environmental pressures on the world's resources seem to be both more intertwined and more pressing than in the past and the speed and pace of communication and the sharing of ideas and practices throughout the world appears to be offering new opportunities but also threats. But the importance, meaning and impact of globalisation are a matter of dispute (Scholte, 2005). Some writers suggest that the forces of globalisation are so powerful that they are sweeping away all efforts at human steering. If that was the case then governance theory and practice would be pointless. But our view is that globalisation has fundamentally changed the context for governance but not removed its prospects completely.

We live in a world where there is a significant further development towards a global market in which patterns of production and consumption are organised by transnational companies and other related organisations, operating across national boundaries. Global finance markets and patterns of international trade in turn influence the shape of national economies. In the industrialised countries these forces are experienced in terms of sweeping changes in the economy with old style industrial jobs declining and new style service and high-technological jobs emerging. Consumers in these countries observe an increasing amount of goods coming from outside their national boundaries as their economies are brought into the grip of a global market to a greater degree than before. In the non-industrialised parts of the world consumers face new economic demands and some new opportunities. But so far at least, globalisation has presented little scope to redress the disparity between rich and poor countries; indeed it may have worsened the position of some poor countries. However, as Andrew Gamble (2000:46) points out: 'Acceptance that there is something called globalization, or at least that there are certain trends towards a global market, is not the end of the argument but the beginning of it, since there are so many ways in which states and groups can adjust to these changes'. Globalisation does not provide an end to argument but rather a new starting point to it. There remains space for governance solutions to emerge.

Another reason why governance prospects are opened, rather than diminished, by social and economic developments, is that what we have seen is as much a process of regionalisation as pure globalisation. As Colin Hay (2007:139) argues 'the world economy is regional and triadic...but it is neither global nor globalizing'. In a purely descriptive sense, globalisation is not the dominant experience of the last three decades in economic terms; rather we have seen the reinforcement and development of three powerful economic blocks. The triads are: North America, Europe and South-East Asia. Developments in economics and society in these areas, have met with a governance response, most obviously in the case of the European Union. In short the regionalisation of our economies has created space for regional governance.

Democratisation presents the other great force for change in our world. Although in 1974 less than three in ten nations in the world could be classified as democratic, 20 years later in 1994 that number had grown to six in ten and at the beginning of the 21st century most of these newly established democracies have survived and joined by a few more recruits (Diamond, 2003). But it is not just the spread of the basic institutions of liberal democracy that is historically unique about the current period; it is that the idea of democracy has gained a certain universal appeal. As Nobel Prize winning academic Amartya Sen (1999:5) points out:

> In any age and social climate, there are some sweeping beliefs that seem to command respect as a kind of general rule – like a 'default' setting in a computer program; they are considered right *unless* their claim is somehow negated. While democracy is not yet universally practiced, nor indeed uniformly accepted, in the general climate of world opinion, democratic governance has now achieved the status of being taken as generally right.

Democracy is a universal value not because everyone agrees with it. Democracy is a tougher concept than that. It has been hard fought over, and won respect because it expresses a fundamental human right to have a say. It can afford, through the power it gives individuals and communities, some protection against exploitation, and finally because sharing experiences and thoughts can help us find solutions to intractable problems. The rise of democracy requires space for governance and lays out conditions for governance practice. The spirit of democracy can even be seen as having had an impact on the world of corporate governance, with some evidence of greater assertiveness from shareholders (Daily *et al.*, 2003) and a sense that non-shareholder stakeholders – employees, customers, suppliers – have some right to have a say in the decision-making of firms.

The literature of politics and international relations on governance might be seen as reacting directly to the impact of these twin forces of globalisation and democratisation, and the rather different world they are helping to create. The pressures created by these forces obviously create new dynamics and changed governance practices that have emerged as a focus of attention. The governance debate in development studies also reflects the intensive impact of these twin forces to a degree both because of the willingness of an increasingly international-ised world to intervene in the governance structures of developing countries, and the strengthening of internal democratic capacity within these countries that leads to demands for different forms of governing. The studies of participatory and environmental governance offered in this book, are framed by the impact of at least one of the twin forces of globalisation and democratisation. The effects of globalisation and democratisation are not easily demonstrated in the case of literatures from economic institutionalism, corporate governance and socio-legal studies, but they constitute a significant framing context for debates in those disciplines.

A cross-disciplinary tour of governance

Our goal then, is to draw on the rich insights of those engaged in studying and debating governance across a range of disciplines and research programmes. But before offering an overview of the remainder of the book a brief note on terminology is necessary and appropriate here. Our starting point is cross-disciplinarity, a generic term to refer to productive interchange between different disciplines. Our end point is multi-disciplinary in that we seek to combine in overall synthesis, insights from different disciplines, in order to illuminate governance theory. But we make no claims to interdisciplinarity in that we attempt no deep integration and merger of different disciplines. Our approach 'is to let each discipline do its best in its own terms and using its own methods in the first phase, and then to use the results from each dis-cipline to develop an overall analytical synthesis' (Kanbur, 2002:483). We are making no broad claims about the advantages of breaking down disciplinary boundaries in the development of the sciences in general, and social sciences in particular except for the general and defendable claim that different disciplines, because of their different approaches may well have something to learn from one another, and may, illuminate issues neglected or over-looked within one discipline. Some larger claims for the virtues of working across disciplines are assessed in the context of governance theory in the conclusion of this book. For the present we simply want to hold onto the claim that there is value in working across disciplines.

This claim about the value of working across disciplines will be pursed throughout the book. It should however, be conceded immediately, that disciplines themselves are not necessarily coherent or solid bodies of knowledge. Rather there is an element of chaos in disciplines (Abbott, 2001) in which debates between contending schools often reflect the recycling of core ideas and follow a similar pattern across a range of disciplines. Moreover there are shared methodologies and theories between disciplines. The history of each discipline is complex, so it is important to be cautious in presenting disciplines as if they were coherent wholes that can be contrasted.

In this book what we can offer to do is compare the way that different disciplines from within the humanities, and more particularly the social sciences, have treated the concept of governance. In particular we have chosen to focus on those disciplines that have seen governance used as a trigger to new thinking and new developments. Governance is a term sometimes used in mainstream legal studies but not in a way that expresses innovative approaches to the subject. We concentrate in this book on the challenge from socio-legal studies to that mainstream approach. Another approach not covered in this book is cybernetics, which might be described as the study of the abstract principles of organisation in complex systems. Cybernetics focuses on how systems use information; it models, and seeks to control actions, in order to steer towards and maintain their goals, while counteracting various disturbances. In a broad sense it could be seen as offering a governance frame. It is an approach that crosses many disciplines and is beyond the scope of our investigation (but see Heylighen and Joslyn, 2001). In short, our claim is not to provide a comprehensive review but in our selection of disciplines and programmes of work focused on governance we have identified the main areas where the arrival of a governance turn has made an impact.

The starting point for our study of governance is with the discipline that is closest to home for us. It is the discipline of political science, given its prime focus on decision-making that is collectively defined and enforced. As Chapter 2 makes clear for political scientists, governance is predominantly a system level concept. There has been much less focus on governance arrangements within organisations, governmental or otherwise. The focus has been predominantly macro, in that governance theory has been about explaining how governing decisions are made across societies or systems. These governance systems are seen by political scientists as driven by networks, rather than hierarchies. There is a common recognition that the relationships in increasingly complex systems of governing are not necessarily hierarchical in nature, or determined by the authority and capacity of state actors. The governance turn for political scientists is the story of discovering networks which itself is premised on the 'discovery', or perhaps 'rediscovery', of forms of collective decision-making, based on negotiated interaction between a plurality of public, semi-public and private actors. To make something happen, to achieve an outcome, with only minor exceptions, requires the engagement of a range of actors and it cannot be delivered by the simple passing of a law, or an edict from those in formal authority in any social system. Negotiation in networks is the key governance activity. This argument does not rule out the possibility of state steering of governance, nor does it assume that the state is no longer a powerful actor. Rather it takes as its starting point the idea that governing is operating in a different context. The governance turn for political scientists signalled an increased awareness of the multi-layered nature of decision-making with local, national and supranational institutions intertwined in, often complex and overlapping, collective decision-making challenges.

Chapter 3 establishes that whereas political scientists started with formal institutions and under the influence of governance moved to networks, economists started with free-floating individuals, and used the governance turn to get themselves into institutions. The dominant paradigm in economics is premised on analysing the voluntary exchanges between individuals in conditions of scarcity. The key mechanism is the market that provides the demand and supply signals to ensure that, for example, consumers and suppliers can each maximise their utility and achieve a position of equilibrium. The most common conception of the market in the literature of economics is as an 'institution free zone' where in addition ideologies and ideas have no part to play. Information-rich individuals make choices under a variety of conditions and constraints but all individuals tend to make the same type of rational calculation so their behaviour is predictable to a large degree. Little scope for a focus on governance would seem to be present within the ambit of this way of viewing the world.

In a reaction against the 'hyper-individualism' of the dominant paradigm, economics literature began to emphasise the role of institutions as the humanly devised constraints that shape human interaction. This has opened up the option of a turn to governance. The idea was not to overthrow established economics however, but to provide a complement to it. Choice remains central to the perspective of institutional economics but it is choice made in the context of rules that shape and governs what is decided. The idea of governance as rules in operation is the dominant approach from institutional economics but has attracted a lot of support from other disciplines.

Chapter 4 argues that in international relations literature the governance debate is first and foremost a challenge to a realist understanding of the way the world works. Although for realists, international relations is about intergovernmental relations – the negotiations and the agreements and disagreement of states – the governance turn saw, in contrast, how international systems and non-state actors play their part in achieving global order. Problems such as AIDs, terrorism, currency crises and global warming are not confronted by states acting on their own or by any single agency of world government. Rather they are dealt with in a governance system involving a range of actors and the coordination of states but also other collectivities. 'Some of the systems are formalized, many consist essentially of informal structures, and some are still largely inchoate, but taken together they cumulate to governance on a global scale' (Rosenau, 2000:172). The international relations literature identifies several new sites of governance. First, there is an emerging global architecture of governance with not only the United Nations but also a role for the World Bank, the International Monetary Fund, the World Trade Organisation, the Bank for International Settlements, the Organisation for Economic Cooperation and Development (OECD), the G8 and other bodies. Second, there is the emergence of a pattern of multi-level governance, in which regions of the world organise their social and economic affairs of which the European Union is one of the more prominent and developed but where patterns of international cooperation can be observed elsewhere. Finally, the international relations literature spends much effort dwelling on what Murphy (2000: 794) refers to as 'global-level "private" authorities that regulate both states and much of transnational economic and social life'. These authorities include private bond-rating agencies and global oligopolies engaged in reinsurance, accounting and high-level consulting that provide a shared framework of options and ideas for all governments and many private actors to operate in. There are also global and regional cartels in industries as diverse as mining and electrical products and the power available to large-scale suppliers of computer software and internet suppliers. Finally there is the hegemonic power of economists who establish and maintain a dominant wisdom about the way that economies should be run.

Chapter 5 examines that the development studies literature starts with unlike other disciplines a 'project of governance', aimed at promoting a particular type and form of good governance. The definitive statement came from the World Bank in 1992 and argued for a governance system that would deliver clear accountability in political decision-making, a strong legal framework, and transparency in the way that government and business conducted their affairs. These ingredients were held to be required for effective development. These ideas about the virtues of good governance became widespread and part of the everyday discourse of development practice. But what marks out development studies is the range of studies that have used the prominence of the governance debate to raise a range of critical and analytical perspectives on the topic.

Chapter 6 explores literature within the socio-legal perspective. Governance, within the socio-legal frame, is an overarching concept to describe the complex and multi-faceted social processes – official and unofficial, intended and unintended, visible and invisible – that together mediate social behaviour and conduct. So the socio-legal perspective shares with other disciplines that governance is concerned with establishing social order. However it rejects the idea that the law can, in an unambiguous way, lay out a set of rules for people to follow. More broadly it questions the idea of governance as an instrumental idea. The socio-legal understanding is that social behaviour cannot be rationally and consciously directed, changed or engineered, and to this extent, governance is not a goal to be pursued but rather a description of social reality.

Part II of the book moves from a focus on disciplines to the application of governance theory to various practices, and begins in Chapter 7 with a review of the literature on corporate governance. Broadly, that literature is dominated by work that takes an economistic perspective and concentrates on the tension between managers of corporations and shareholders in those corporations. The literature has a very practical purpose in that it aims to provide advice about the most effective forms of governance but appears to be unable to offer definitive evidence one way or another. The chapter then examines alternative approaches to assessing corporate governance that focus more attention on the resources that board construction can bring to the successful operation of corporations. The chapter concludes with a broader comparative examination of the development of corporate governance forms.

Chapter 8 explores the issue of participatory governance. It argues core debates are played out within two disciplines in particular, that of politics (including political sociology) and development studies (where economic institutionalism has been influential). For the former, the notion of participation has been a vital part of discussion on the democratic ideal and a commitment to civil society organizations. The development studies tradition offers a more jaundiced take. The explosion of interest in 'community-based' participatory development has aroused concerns over the nature and legitimacy of participation. Participatory governance is a unique area of practice in that older theoretical conundrums within politics have been re-enacted within the multi-disciplinary arena of development studies. The chapter moves to explore the issue of power in participatory governance and criticises those development institutions that continually act to strip participatory governance of politics, presenting it as an apolitical phenomenon that can be easily designed by technocrats and planners. The third section of the chapter asks whether participatory governance can produce more effective governance.

Chapter 9 sets out to understand key strands of thought within environmental governance. It explores the transformation in values and outlines major epistemological developments which have shaped current perceptions of the environment. A second section presents an overview of contemporary discourse on environmental governance and focuses attention on three issues: the nature of the environment and its governance as a 'global' issue, environmental governance as a collective action problem eliciting institutional responses from states, markets and communities, and the tense environment of the governance dialogue between the developed and the developing world. The final two sections again examine issues of power in environmental governance and the issue of whether effective mechanisms of governance can be identified.

The broad message we wish to communicate at this stage of our book is the fruitfulness and value of the governance literature. In what follows we note how governance theory addresses a perceived inadequacy in each of the disciplines and opens up opportunities to examine new and changing forms and practices of governing. In our discussion we also note some of the shortcoming, inadequacies, omissions and confusions that have dogged the governance but argue that none is so problematic as to lead to a wholesale rejection of the governance perspective. Our aim in this introduction is to have done enough to convince the reader that the more detailed exploration undertaken in the remainder of the book is a journey worth taking.

2
Governance in Public Administration and Political Science

The emergence of governance theory from the early 1990s onwards has been one of the core developments in public administration and more broadly, for that part of political science orientated towards the study of policy-making. By 1999 George Fredrickson was able to make the bold claim that:

> Public administration is steadily moving ...toward theories of cooperation, networking, governance, and institution building and maintenance. Public administration, both in practice and in theory, is repositioning itself to deal with the daunting problems associated with the disarticulation of the state. In short, a repositioned public administration is the political science of making the fragmented and disarticulated state work (Fredrickson, 1999:702).

Not all governance scholars from public administration, let alone political science, would be willing to accept the idea that their goal was, or should be, to make a disjointed state work, as Fredrickson suggests, but most would go along with the claim that new thinking about governance has been introduced into the discipline because of shifts in the context for governing. The way of thinking about public administration and politics has changed in recognition of the changed conditions and practices of governing. The governance paradigm is about the central importance of how the interaction of government and non-governmental actors are guided and directed in collective decision-making. That interaction is not driven by the state's use of its power and authority to command compliance but by its capacity to steer using a complex set of hard and soft governing tools and by network relationships that reflect the dynamic of power dependencies between the actors (Stoker, 1998). The task for this chapter is to ask what new insights this relatively recent governance revolution has achieved for the discipline of public administration and politics in general.

Globalisation and the spirit of democratisation, as noted in Chapter 1, helped to create conditions where the search for new methods of governing became a strong and near universal trend in advanced industrial societies and beyond. Salamon (2001:1611) refers to the emergence of new governance as a revolution:

> The heart of this revolution has been a fundamental transformation not just in the scope and scale of government action, but in its basic forms. A massive proliferation has occurred in the tools of public action, in the instruments or means used to address public problems. Where earlier government activity was largely restricted to the direct delivery of goods or services by government bureaucrats, it now embraces a dizzying array of loans, loan guarantees, grants, contracts, social regulation, economic regulation, insurance, tax expenditures, vouchers, and much more.

Alongside government developing new tools, governance has become about managing networks in both the input processes and output practices of governing networks of deliberation and delivery. According to Rhodes (1997a:53) 'governance refers to self-organizing, interorganizational networks'. He goes on to argue that these networks are driven by 'the need to exchange resources and negotiate shared purposes' and that they are subject to a complex dynamic and are not directly accountable to the state but that the state may be able to 'indirectly and imperfectly steer network'. This new practice of governing has emerged in different forms and with varied strength in a wide range of particularly western industrial democracies. But it should not be assumed that all countries are following the same reform path, far from it, as the careful study of comparative public management reform trends by Pollitt and Bouckaert (2004) indicates. Yet many countries have been adventurous in different ways in developing new styles of governing. Students of public administration have been playing catch up with policy-makers and practitioners who have been innovating in a multitude of complex and diverse ways to meet their societies' challenging problems.

The first section of this chapter looks at how the governance paradigm has helped to encourage scholars to reshape their understanding of public administration and policy-making. As in other disciplines the governance paradigm emerges as a challenge to perceived weaknesses at the heart of the discipline. But perhaps more than others the stimulus for rethinking has as much been driven by changes in what governing means in our complex societies, as well as by internal reflections within the discipline. There has been in practice a hollowing out of the nation-state, and governance theory has stepped forward to help us understand the forces and dynamics realised by that development. The second section of the chapter looks at how different methodologies and theories have been developed in response to the governance challenge. It looks at network, delegation, social interpretative theories bounded rationality and cultural institutionalist theories. No new grand consensus has emerged as a result of just over a decade's worth of work and the third section of the chapter outlines those areas where there are major debates about the implications of a governance paradigm for the public administration and political organisation of society. It examines the concept of metagovernance and that of governance failure. It also addresses two fundamental questions in the discipline: the role of government in governance and the degree to which governance undermines or supports democratic accountability in public decision-making. What emerges is a picture of how governance has opened up a new terrain in public administration and political studies but has yet to establish a firm or fully coherent new position.

Challenge to the discipline of politics and public administration

The starting point for the emergence of the governance turn in political science and public administration is the idea that there has been a hollowing out of the state. At the domestic level the state has become fragmented. This is as a result of managerial changes such as the introduction of semi-independent government agencies and the greater use of arms-length bodies of all types to deliver policies, programmes and services (Rhodes, 1997a: Ch5). But the domestic drive towards fragmentation also reflects pressure from new political forces promoting local and regional devolution. At a supra-national level the pressure has also led to a plurality of decision forums with policy and practice choices being made at the level of European Union, or through other regional level agreements between nation states or even at the international level through various organisations (Benz and Papadopoulos, 2006).

Given the dynamics that were driving an interest in governance it is the case that the strongest developments in governance theory and usage came in those parts of the discipline that were dealing with public policy and administration and multi-level governance. As Simon Bulmer (forthcoming) observes in the case of European Union studies there was often a complex dynamic between practice and theoretical reflection in the process that led towards a governance turn.

[T]he emergence of governance as a theme in UK and Irish research on the EU governance did not come about in my view as a deliberate 'turn' but rather as a consequence of several inter-related developments: the emergence of a European Union political system; the growth in comparative politics analysis of the EU; broader developments in the political science discipline; and the advocacy of new institutionalism and policy networks as vehicles for understanding EU governance.

The focus of governance reflects debates about the EU and about how it should organise its decision-making and develop its policy procedures, but also recognition among scholars of the importance of institutions in the way that they shape what policy actors can and cannot do and operate in a range of formal and informal ways.

The governance turn in EU studies might be seen as leading to a new governance perspective that according to Hix (1998:54) focuses on governing as 'multi-level, non-hierarchical, deliberative and apolitical governance, via a web of public/private networks and quasi-autonomous executive agencies'. This understanding is contrasted with a more hard-nosed perspective that sees politics as involving a clash of interests driven by the self-seeking behaviour of a range of actors. As argued in Chapter 1 and developed in Chapter 10 there is nothing inherent in the governance perspective that argues for an apolitical understanding of the dynamics of policy-making or a vision of politics without power and it would be a mistake to view the new focus on governance as tied to an apolitical or managerial understanding of dynamics of social interaction. Bulmer (forthcoming) suggests that most EU scholars have been happy to combine a focus on a new dynamic with an understanding of 'old' politics in their analysis, and identifies a range of valuable contributions that deal with issues of multi-level governance (Hooghe and Marks, 2001), the role of policy networks in the European decision-making (Peterson and Blomberg, 1999) as well as other elements in an emerging supra-national governing system. According to Kohler-Koch and Rittberger (2006:33) 'the "governance turn" in EU studies resembles developments in both the field of policy analysis and in IR. First, it has an elaborate process dimension that explores the patterns, instruments and conditions of policy formulation and implementation and the diversity of actor constellations. Second, it reflects the different aspects of "system transformation" (at both EU and national levels) and its likely impact on problem-solving capacity and democratic accountability'.

The most distinctive contribution of EU studies has come through its discussion of multi-level governance. Another prominent feature of EU governance is its multi-level nature. As Kohler-Koch and Rittberger (2006:34) explain multi-level governance takes the line that decision-making capacity is not the monopoly of the governments of the Member States but 'is diffused to different levels of decision-making – the subnational, national and supranational levels'. Hooghe and Marks (2001:4) comment that:

> while national arenas remain important arenas for the formation of national government preferences, the multi-level governance model rejects the view that subnational actors are nested exclusively within them. Instead, subnational actors operate in both national and supranational arenas ... National governments ... share, rather than monopolize, control over many activities that take place in their respective territories

The distinctive contribution of EU studies is the way that the governance emphasis on multiple decision centres is understood in the context of a complex set of exchanges at and between different territorial levels including both government and non-governmental actors.

In the spheres of policy studies and public administration the governance turn again reflects that the world has changed, as well as pressures for new theoretical insights. Governance theory has been defined by its capacity to provide 'a reference point which challenges many of the assumptions of traditional public administration' (Stoker, 1998:18). The first plank of the alternative perspective is to recognise that public administration's brief stretches beyond multiple government institutions to those drawn from the community, voluntary and private sectors. The role of these non-governmental agencies in delivering public services and programmes is an important part of the focus provided by the governance perspective. The second focuses on how responsibilities that might in the past have been defined as exclusively the domain of government are now shared between government and a range of non-governmental actors. According to Salamon (2001:1611):

> The upshot is an elaborate system of third-party government in which crucial elements of public authority are shared with a host of non-governmental or other governmental actors, frequently in complex collaborative systems that sometimes defy comprehension, let alone effective management and control. In a sense, the 'public administration problem' has leapt beyond the borders of the public agency and now embraces a wide assortment of 'third parties' that are intimately involved in the implementation, and often the management, of the public's business.

A third element in rethinking is a greater emphasis on the fragmented nature and condition of the state. According to Sorensen (2006), alongside those theorists that stressed how societal forces were gaining ground, were those that focused on the hollowed out and disjointed nature of the state. They were clear that the state did not act as a unitary body but rather as a complex set of linked but divided institutions. Sorensen (2006:100) further argues:

> In the 1990s and 2000s, the two theoretical paths... met in a joint effort to develop a new theory of governance. The starting points for this theoretical endeavor are (a) that the state has become a differentiated, fragmented, and multicentered institutional complex that is held together by more or less formalized networks and (b) that the dividing line between state and society is blurred because of the fact that governance is often produced by networks involving both public and private actors.

Governing in these circumstances involved a capacity to work through networks both within and without the state. Governance theory then points to a redefinition of the terrain of institutions and actors that should be a focus of attention. A complex and more diverse set of organisational bodies and actors lie at the heart of public administration as redefined by the governance perspective. While traditional public administration concerned itself with the challenges of managing the political/administrative dichotomy in individual organisations and the making of policy, budget and practice within those organisations; the governance perspective argues that it is the complex set of relationships between the organisations and actors that also needs to be a focus of attention.

The governance perspective emphasises the idea that these organisations can no longer be linked together through a simple hierarchical chain. Modern governing faces an extremely demanding set of power dependencies (cf. Stoker, 1998). Power dependence implies that organisations committed to collective action are dependent on other organisations and cannot command the response of each other but rather have to rely on exchanging resources and negotiating common purposes. Thus for example even a nation state, the most powerful of all actors in public administration, needs to be able to operate at an international level and at the same time encourage action they favour at the regional, local or neighbourhood level. In all of these settings they cannot command; although especially within its boundaries they may be able to dominate the exchange. However, even in these settings, the costs of seeking to impose control may be felt through the emergence of malign unintended consequences or incapacity to achieve control except in a narrow range of issues.

Interdependence means according to Salamon (2001:1611) the development of new tools of governing and the recognition that success in public administration is achieved in new ways. He argues that governments gain partners but lose direct control in the world of governance:

> A variety of complex exchanges thus comes into existence between government agencies and a wide variety of public and private institutions that are written into the operation of public programs. In these circumstances, the traditional concerns of public administration with the internal operations of public agencies – their personnel systems, budgetary procedures, organizational structures, and institutional dynamics – have become far less central to program success. At least as important have become the internal dynamics and external relationships of the host of third parties – local governments, hospitals, universities, clinics, community development corporations, industrial corporations, landlords, commercial banks, and many more – that now also share with public authorities the responsibility for public programs operations.

Moreover, the governance perspective tells political scientists more than ever before that collective action intentions are not always matched by prescribed outcomes. Power dependencies, and the opportunistic behaviour they allow, add to complexity and encourage uncertainty of outcome. Governance implies a greater willingness to cope with uncertainty and open-endedness on the part of policy-framers.

Government suggests an emphasis on certainty and proscribed and mandated outcomes; governance instead draws much more attention to unintended consequences and outcomes.

Governing is concerned with the processes that create the conditions for ordered rule and collective action within the public realm. The governance perspective challenges the dominant Weberian-influenced perspective that rests on viewing governing as a tight cluster of connected institutions. It offers a contrasting organising framework built around a wider, looser set of organisations joined through a complex mix of interdependencies. To understand the politics and management of this world requires us to look beyond a tight core of institutions based around bureaucracy and political parties and a limited elite form of democracy. Governance frames issues by recognising the complex architecture of government. In practice there are many centres and diverse links between many agencies of government at neighbourhood, local, regional and national and supranational levels. In turn, each level has a diverse range of horizontal relationships with other government agencies, privatised utilities, private companies, voluntary organisations and interest groups. Moreover, whereas the Weberian model offers one solution to the coordination challenge in a complex setting, the governance perspective recognises there are at least four governing mechanisms beyond direct provision through a bureaucracy. The bureaucratic form solves the problem of organising in a complex world by dividing tasks into manageable parts and then connecting the actors responsible for individual tasks through a hierarchical structure of command. Complex tasks of cooperation do not necessarily always require the imposition of a hierarchical chain of command in an integrated organisation. There are other options: regulation at arm's length, contracting through the market, responding to interest articulation and developing bonds of loyalty or trust. Recognition of this wider array of governance mechanisms enables the processes of modern governing to be better understood.

Governing by regulation from a governance perspective is about one public organisation aiming to shape the activities of another (Hood *et al.*, 1998). It is oversight at arm's length, in that there is not a direct or command relationship. Crucially the relationship rests on a level of legitimacy for the regulator to act as an overseer. Regulation, however, is not through a Weberian hierarchical chain of command but rather through a process of challenge and exchange. Hence, what at first can appear to be a contradiction in governance, a growth in oversight by higher levels of government of lower governmental levels and various agencies, is best understood as the rolling out of a governing technique in the context of complex architecture of governance. Regulation can be a soft form of governance where the regulated agency or organisation is not commanded to do something but acts with autonomy, within prescribed limits, and is held to account against the achievement of certain goals or outcomes.

A second coordinating mechanism is provided by the market and associated incentives (see Savas, 2000). The coordination task of achieving a complex activity is achieved through the invisible hand of appropriate incentives being provided to individuals so that their self-interested behaviour contributes to collective goals. Market or quasi-market mechanisms provide a common way of achieving the appropriate incentives. A government agency under such a mechanism retains the role of arranger but the responsibility for producing the service rests within another agency that 'earns' the right to do so through competition. Introducing competition is vital and requires a conscious governance strategy to create the conditions in favour of a market-like system. Options may take a wide variety of forms from the familiar contract with a private or voluntary sector producer to 'market-like' competition between public sector producers. The government agency achieves effective coordination through the specification of the service, the selection of the best producer and by monitoring and oversight of their performance. The presence of competition both keeps the performance of producers up to scratch and encourages innovation among producers as they seek to sustain or enhance their position in the market.

A third coordinating mechanism is that provided by interest articulation most of which takes place through policy networks that provide the crucial framework for including in some interests and excluding others. As Rhodes (1997a:9) comments:

> Policy networks matter: they are not an example of otiose social science jargon. All governments confront a variety of interests. Aggregation of those interests is a functional necessity. Intermediation is a fact of everyday life in government.

Rhodes goes on to identify a variety of different forms of policy network, some of which are more closed than others. All provide a way of bringing together interests that are central to the process of governing. By including these interests, by negotiating with them and understanding their positions governments then have a better chance that policy, once adopted, will have the desired effect because it has had the engagement and support of these interests.

A fourth governance mechanism can be identified that stands in contrast to the others that are simply variations of standard political tools for managing conflicting interests by recognising that politics in governance often involves the search for the identification of shared goals. Herbert Simon pointed out in his classic *Administrative Behaviour* (1945, 1997) that people in organisations often make decisions based on their identification with the goals of their organisation or more broadly out of attachment to the organisation itself. Their choices are driven not by self-interest but their judgement of what is seen as most important to the organisation and its values. Understanding the mission of different institutions and how to appeal to the mission-driven individuals in those bureaucracies is a vital part of governance (Wilson, 1989). The governance perspective applies the logic of this position to relationships between actors in different organisations or more generally between the state and actors in civil society. The building of effective partnership is often seen as an attempt to develop a positive-sum political game so that in the midst of complexity and diversity a common sense of purpose and a capacity to govern can emerge (Stoker, 1995; Stoker, 2000a). If a loyalty bond can be established, then actors in organisations, and beyond them, can behave in a way that enables governing tasks to be met just as effectively, if not more effectively, than those driven by oversight, market-like incentives and voice-based challenges. The potential in this vision of collaboration is considerable (Sullivan and Skelcher, 2002) but sometimes although there is agreement between partners, a dynamic of mutual trust does not always emerge. Many partnerships are a marriage of convenience. However, when trust and loyalty do come to the fore they provide a powerful governance force.

Realism, rather than optimism, is the dominant tone of much of governance literature in public administration and political science. Stoker (1998) suggests that for each step towards a governance-style in collective action and decision-making there is a corresponding dilemma or difficulty. As suggested already, the greater the power independencies between the various actors, then the greater the possibility of unintended consequences. Although collaboration may be fruitful and effective, it can deteriorate into blame avoidance and an unwillingness to take responsibility. More generally the emergence of governance has led to the identification of three related fears. First, given the complexity of the relationships that are often involved in governance, a significant problem of accountability would appear to come to the fore. As Bovens (1998) argues, given a situation where there are many hands involved in achieving an outcome, it can become difficult and challenging to allocate responsibility for success, or more particularly, failure. And failure there will be, indeed, the dynamics and character of governance failure (Jessop, 2000) has been a specific focus of study. Finally, there is a nagging concern that governance can provide a legitimate form of governing. 'There is a divorce between the complex reality of decision-making associated with governance and the normative codes used to explain and justify government' (Stoker, 1998:19). A democratic deficit is seen as a potential defining feature of the governance era. We will return to these issues in the concluding section of the chapter.

Making governance work: five theoretical threads

There is no one theory of governance in political science and public administration. Rather it is a field where scholars have used a variety of theoretical lenses to examine what is going on, so it is important when reviewing the literature to be clear about what criteria you are using to select theories to study in more depth. Pierre and Peters (2000:37), in their treatment of the field, note the development of a very wide range of perspectives 'some of which are even mutually contradictory'. In the short review offered by Pierre and Peters the works of public management, rational choice and Marxism all get a mention. Sorensen and Torfing (2007) suggest a focus on theories that are associated with new institutionalism and therefore a concern with the way that institutions shape and are shaped by governance. The selection offered in this section of the chapter reflects our concern with the practice of governance. We focus on the major theoretical pillars in thinking about governance that take the issue of constructing and maintaining governance arrangements as central to their concerns. We examine five groups of theories that draw attention to, first, the management of networks as key to governance; second, to perspectives that focus more on the dynamic of delegation and the creation of appropriate incentive regimes to steer governance; third, on social theories that look at how interests are articulated, communicated and conditioned by a governance discourse and how identities and trust might be built; and fourth, on theories that operate around the concept of bounded rationality as the core condition and starting point for the human action that drives governance. Finally we examine the contribution of cultural institutional theory. As will become clear there are some parallels between these theoretical threads and the different broad types of governance mechanism identified in the previous section of the chapter.

Network management theory

One axiomatic statement provided by the governance perspective is that governing is about the operation of networks of a complex mix of actors and organisations. As Rod Rhodes (1997a) argues, initial work on policy networks – that focused on policy-making in particular sectors of economy and society – gave way to a wider appreciation of the way that networks are central for many of the elements of governing, including implementation (Hill and Hupe, 2002), to the extent that many academics began to take the view that 'governance is about managing networks' (Rhodes, 1997a:52). The theory around the management of networks that has emerged has been useful and insightful with descriptive and practitioner arms, although it does have certain limitations in terms of the depth of causal explanation and clarity.

So what is it that governments do when it comes to steering networks? Kickert *et al.* (1999) and Klijin *et al.* (1995) identify two broad types of management strategy: game management and network structuring. The first refers to the management of relations within an existing network and the second refers to attempts to change the structure or participants in a network. The first type can often involve government in the search for compromises to create the conditions for joint decision-making. For example, a government body could call together all the relevant interests in order to agree to a new form of regulation and in doing so bring about a beneficial outcome that is recognised as such by all those interests. The second type of intervention is more 'hands-on' and involves changing relations between actors, shifting the pattern of resource distribution and seeking to encourage a major change in policy direction. New players are brought into the network and given legitimacy and resources that provide them with the opportunity to influence the decision-making process and push for different outcomes that would otherwise have emerged. In such a case a government agency might, for example, bring a group of biology trained conservationists into an argument between residents and developers over the regeneration of an urban park in order to get more expert input and a more wildlife friendly outcome.

Kooiman (2003) makes a set of distinctions that in many respects parallel those discussed above. He refers to 'first-order' governing that deals with day-to-day management of networks and to 'second-order' that focuses on shifting the institutional conditions for governing. The first might be seen as playing the game according to established rules and the second more about setting the rules as different institutional arrangements will favour different interests. But Kooiman goes on to identify a further category of 'third-order' meta-governance. He suggests in a rather abstract way that meta-governing 'is like an imaginary governor, teleported to a point "outside" and holding the whole governance experience against a normative template' (Kooiman, 2003:170). It is difficult to be sure what is meant by meta-governance in his work but it appears to rest on debates about the best underlying principles for a governance system and judgements about how any governance practice is living up to these principles. The point is that government needs to step back and take a look at the overall state of the governing arrangements of networks.

This concern about managing networks has grown into one of the key sub-fields of the governance literature and there has developed a debate around the concept of meta-governance. The interest is in the way governments provide the ground rules and the context in which governance takes place (Bell and Park, 2006). Sorensen (2006:100–1) suggests that 'meta-governance' is a term best reserved to describe any 'indirect form of governing that is exercised by influencing various processes of self-governance'. She goes on to argue that meta-governance is 'an umbrella concept for the fragmented plurality of toolkits for regulating' networks. A careful review of the literature on managing networks leads her to identify certain regularities or patterns in the tools that are observed and practiced by different writers. Although as she notes it is not possible to offer a comprehensive guide Sorensen does offer a useful framework to identify four main ways in which networks might be managed. They are:

1. Hands-off framing of self-governance
2. Hands-off storytelling
3. Hands-on support and facilitation
4. Hands-on participation (Sorensen, 2006:101)

The last two forms of intervention identified by Sorensen are similar in many ways to the direct forms of intervention identified in the earlier work on network management. They involve state actors in game management by supporting and facilitating exchange between network members or more actively joining the exchange in order to promote particular interests or a particular outcome. What is more novel about Sorensen's list is the identification of hands-off forms of network management.

The first of these hands-off forms – framing – captures a broad range of activities. It includes facilitative legislation to give networks a general sense of direction but that leaves its constituent organisations free to define their own paths and mechanisms for achieving these goals. It also covers incentive-based measures that encourage organisations to cooperate in a particular way. Crucially the state in both cases is acting in a hands-off way. It is guiding and not dictating.

Formal goal setting and incentive structures are not the only way of influencing networks. You can influence networks through narrative as much as through the harder tools of legislation and finances. Drawing on insights from Foucault (see Chapter 6) and the work of March and Olsen (1989, 1995) on the construction of democratic governance through the development of identities and norms Sorensen suggests that storytelling is a second tool on network management. She explains:

> Through storytelling, it is possible to shape images of rational behavior through the construction of interests, images of friend-enemy relations, and visions of the past and possible futures for individuals and groups and for society at large. Hence, storytelling represents a forceful hands-off means of influencing the formation of political strategies among a multiplicity of self-governing actors without interfering directly in their strategy formulation (Sorensen, 2006:101).

The essence of the insight here is that networks can be influenced and encouraged to view and understand their world in certain way and through that activity they can be managed. But in order to effectively manage networks argues Sorensen, managers and more particularly politicians need to learn new skills of leadership.

The argument that what is required is new capacities in order to operate the world of network management is developed by several other writers who seek to practitioner-oriented advice and theory. Salamon (2001:1611) refers to the need to develop enablement skills to replace those of traditional inside bureaucracy management skills.

> Unlike both traditional public administration and the new public management, the 'new governance' shifts the emphasis from management skills and the control of large bureaucratic organizations to enablement skills, the skills required to engage partners arrayed horizontally in networks, to bring multiple stakeholders together for a common end in a situation of interdependence.

He identifies three core sets of skills. The first is activation skills, getting the relevant players involved in helping to resolve problems. This role might involve getting enough 'buy-in' from various participants in a scheme to promote environmental improvement or, on a more hard-nosed basis, ensuring that there is a dynamic market in producers of care services for the elderly that can be established. In both cases a key requirement for the manager in the context of network management is coaxing engagement by participants and more broadly constructing an environment suited to the search for public value in which they can operate (Stoker, 2006b). A second skill set identified by Salamon is the capacity to orchestrate in order to help the various elements of any network more effectively to work with each other. There are skills of diplomacy, communication and bargaining often involved in achieving coordination (Rhodes, 1997b). Finally Salamon (2001:1611) suggests that what is required is a modulation skill set.

> Urban economic development specialists have referred to this as enoughsmanship – the provision of just enough subsidy to get private parties to make investments in rundown areas they might avoid, but not so much as to produce windfall profits for doing what the developers would have done anyway. Inevitably, as we have seen, third-party government leaves substantial discretion over the exercise of public authority and the spending of public funds in the hands of a variety of third parties over which public officials have, at best, limited control. In these circumstances, the central challenge for public managers is to decide what combination of incentives and penalties to bring to bear to achieve the outcomes desired.

A key element of the last skill set is to remain sufficiently independent of the process in order to provide the appropriate checks and balances. In many respects it is the hardest of the skill requirements and demands a sophisticated capacity for judgement and understanding of the position of other interests.

The ability to mange networks is a key theme in several management-oriented works (Kettl, 2002; Sullivan and Skelcher, 2002; Goss, 2001; Moore, 1995; Stoker, 2006b) and Goldsmith and Eggers (2004:21–2) argue that for all types of public institutions 'the skill with which the agency manages networks contributes as much to its successes and failures as the skill to which it manages its own public employees'. They go on to note that managers' key tasks include having to align goals among partners; averting communication breakdown; and overcoming data deficits and capacity shortages. The authors go on to provide a lot of insights about how to construct partnerships that can be sustained and how to overcome some of the dilemmas and tensions created by network public administration. But above all, the key is a shift in the way that governing is conceptualised so 'the idea of government based on programs and agencies will give way to government based on goals and networks. ...public employees ...will view their role as working out how to add maximum public value by deploying and orchestrating a network of assets' (Goldsmith and Eggers, 2004:181).

Managers are urged to ask if whether the public intervention that they are directing is achieving positive social and economic outcomes; whether it is meeting the challenge of public value (Moore, 1995). They do not have to directly provide anything themselves necessarily. But even if acting directly, the assumption in network management is that the outcomes are checked by stakeholders or more broadly consumers or citizens. The touchstone for network-based governance is a different narrative of public action that points to a motivational force that does not rely on rules or incentives to drive public service reform but rests on a fuller and rounder vision of humanity. People are, it suggests, motivated by their involvement in networks and partnerships, that is, their relationships with others formed in the context of mutual respect and shared learning (Stoker, 2006b).

Network management theory has been successful in pointing to a different way of doing the business of public administration. As a description of new ways of working, as a source of ideas for managers and politicians, management network theory has considerable strengths. Yet it has been argued that 'network' is used in much of this literature as a metaphor (Dowding, 1995) that enables writers to capture a sense of a different form of governance, but the network concept and how best it should be analysed, remains somewhat problematic and unclear. As Marsh and Smith (2000) argue in terms of policy outcome, it is unclear how much explanation is down to the existence of a particular network, and what it is about that network that delivers certain outcomes. They suggest that a number of elements need to be taken into account if we are to understand the impact of networks: the context in which the network operates, the network structure (for example how tight or loose it is) and the skills and resources available to different network actors in their attempts to influence outcomes. The interaction of these different elements is the key to understand how networks influence policy.

Looking more at the impact on public administration Provan and Milward (2001:415) argue that despite the promise of networks, the absence of rigorous assessments mean that it is still 'premature to conclude that networks are effective mechanisms for addressing complex policy problems'. They suggest that the overall effectiveness of networks needs to be judged against three broad questions, each offering a different level of analysis. First, does the network deliver outcomes that are valued by society and its representatives? Second, does it deliver sustainable relationships among a set of partners? Third, does it enable individual agencies to survive and continue to construct their futures in a way that is beneficial to them and wider societal interests? In short, does it work for the community, as a network and for its participants? The answer to each of these questions may be different but as Provan and Milward suggest this challenge should not put analysts off the task of judging the performance of networks rather than simply advocating them as the new way of governing.

Theories of delegation

If network theories argue that the key governance task is to manage networks effectively, then delegation theorists argue that key to effective governance is getting the structure of delegation right. When incentives are appropriately aligned then the desired outcome can be achieved is the basic assumption of delegation theorists. As Bertelli (2006:10) comments 'delegation is at the heart of new governance reforms' as powers and responsibilities are shared between a range of agencies and as understanding how delegation works could provide a key element in understanding the operation of governance. The style of theorising tends towards the formal rather than the informal in contrast to network management theory. Moreover the emphasis is on generating insights from parsimoniously specified models that are subject to empirical testing insofar as that is possible in 'real world' settings.

Theories of delegation start from a premise that is shared with principal–agent theory (see Chapter 3) that the boss (or principal) is engaged in a 'non-cooperative' game with a subordinate (the agent). The boss can either delegate or not and the agent can either shirk or work; or to be put it less pejoratively 'the subordinate can either act in a way that is good for the boss or not' (Bendor *et al.*, 2001:236). Table 2.1 captures the four possible outcomes given that set of assumptions.

Given that the model is about finding the conditions under which the boss achieves her ends then the next assumption made in the model is that the boss prefers the agent to work towards objectives in alignment with the boss's wishes. This assumption plainly makes a lot of sense. The agent, however, may or may not prefer to have discretion, that is, being on the receiving end of delegation is not necessarily

Table 2.1   A typology of delegation

Boss Delegates	Outcome A:	Outcome B:
	Agent Works	Agent Shirks
Boss Controls	Outcome C:	Outcome D:
	Agent Shirks	Agent Works

considered to be more attractive than being subject to control. This slightly less intuitively plausible assumption is justified, it is claimed, because in some settings the subordinate may not want to take responsibility for fear of being held responsible for the outcome. So what is the basis of any deal? Why should the agent want to help out the boss? Well the answer given in delegation theory is that it is because the subordinate wants to avoid the option of control-shirk. The assumption here appears to be that outright conflict between agent and subordinate would be considered untenable and unsustainable by both. So for everyone's point of view the aim is avoid outcome C and from the boss's point of view the goal is to achieve outcome D or A and at a pinch accept outcome B, if time constraints or lack of relevant information prevent a more optimal solution. Even then, a deal might be difficult to strike where, for example, the outcome of a project is unclear. The boss may delegate in order to avoid the blame and the agent may work hard in order to get the credit, but if the boss sees that happening and takes back control in order to claim credit, then the agent may shirk and so on and so forth.

Thinking formally about the dynamisms of delegation in this manner helps to indicate why achieving effective delegation in the world of governance can be difficult. Starting with the classic principal agent assumptions of non-cooperation between principal and agent and then recognising that the power to direct is in the hands of the boss but a possible information advantage in the hands of the agent as they are the person with direct involvement, it is possible to see delegation as a delicately balanced game. The issue becomes: 'is the gain produced by delegating the decision to a more informed party worth the loss produced by having someone with different preferences make the choice?' (Bendor *et al.*, 2001:242). This stripped down version of the model can then have several 'what ifs' added to it. What if the agents started to volunteer to take on delegated tasks – how would that affect the game? What if there was a more intense conflict between boss and agent would the boss ever be able to delegate? What if there were multiple agents (some of whom might be tempted to free ride) or multiple principals that might have some, but potentially cross-cutting, scope to control the agent?

But delegation theory does not just stop there and it would be disappointing if it did. As well as signalling the complexity of delegation arrangements, it also identifies a number of ways in which delegation can be effectively managed. One option, of course, is for the principal to impose sanctions after the event once something has gone wrong and the agent has stepped out of line. The delegation literature is clear about how costly this method is, in that it requires a lot of monitoring effort in the context of information asymmetry, and could be potentially damaging to the reputation of both principal and agent in the future.

But there are other ways in which control can be exercised other than extensive monitoring and oversight. One option that appears to have stood up well in delegation studies is what Bendor *et al.* (2001:259) refer to as the ally principle – that a boss prefers subordinates who resemble herself ideologically'. Where such over-arching selection procedures cannot be put in place there are other ways to constrain the discretion of agents. McCubbins *et al.* (1987) suggest that principals often engage in 'deck-stacking' in order to increase the likelihood of agents choosing outcomes they prefer. They use administrative rules to set broader rules of the game: how the agency can make a decision, which interests it needs to consult and the speed at which it can be allowed to make decisions. The principal's control can further be enhanced by installing recall mechanisms to ensure that if an agency makes a decision that is out of line with the principal's thinking, it has to reconsider. Thus, an agency can be given quite broad legislative remits (and also have the advantage of flexibility) but an environment can be created in which they are more likely to make decisions in tune with the perspective of the principal.

A key message from delegation theory is that if political principals lack the time and resources to supervise their permanent appointees, they can regulate bureaucratic discretion through their access to rule-making institutions. Bureaucrats, on the other hand, usually must work with the system as they find it. Epstein and O'Halloran (1999) and Huber and Shipan (2002) in careful empirical work emphasise the choices legislators face when designing delegation systems. In particular, the tightness, or otherwise, in the framing of legislation is seen as the way politicians seek to exercise control over bureaucracies. If politicians give bureaucrats freedom of manoeuvre through the vagueness of statues, officials may 'adopt policies that they prefer and do little to serve the interests of politicians' (Huber and Shipan, 2002:222). Alternatively, the right amount of restriction over discretion can deliver desired outcomes for the politicians; but they must be careful not to tip their design of statutes to encourage non-compliance. The evidence presented suggests that politicians in the United Congress have not too bad a record at developing the right sort of delegation mechanisms for different agencies. If the argument applies to political-bureaucratic relationships generally, as well as in the context of the US Congress and in key western European legislatures, politicians should be free to organise political institutions in their interests, revealed by the particular schemes of delegation that appear in various contexts across the world, whether at the national, state or local levels (Huber and Shipan, 2002:10).

There is one particularly interesting variation identified in the literature in which the key objective for the principal is to set up an agency that will not be seen as 'kow-towing' to their interests and whims. The aim of this game is to establish credible commitment (see Bendor *et al.*, 2001:259–265), a propensity to act in a certain way and to keep acting that way as time unfolds. The most well known example is that of delegating control over the money supply and interest rates to an independent decision-making body to insulate it from short-term political interests. It is given responsibility to set the money supply levels and interest rates for the long-term health of the economy. The principal creates an insulated form of delegation that keeps her away from the decision, but still does a job for her in that it delivers a credible commitment that decisions are going to made in the long-term public interest. Another factor in the principal's thinking might be to install a decision-making procedure that cannot be easily unravelled by political opponents when they gain power at the expense of the currently dominant principal. Thus, for example, a highly independent environment protection commission might be set up – free from day to day political lobbying – in order to ensure that even when out of power the principal could be reassured that environmental issues will have a strong promoter and protector. There are of course costs in such a strategy – in that a rigid and inflexible agency might result in being unable to adapt to new demands and circumstances.

In summary, much of the delegation literature is relatively optimistic about the possibility of 'smart' design solutions to the problem of how to delegate effectively and thereby keep a complex system of governance under the direction and influence of political principals. The implication of the literature is that democratic politicians can if they delegate deliberatively and responsibly see 'the will of people' as they interpret it put into practice despite the complexities of modern governance. The formal nature of theorising enables a number of hypothetical or simplified solutions to be explored but what is not so clear as even its advocates concede is that the method enables the effective exploration of real-world institutions and decision settings with all their contradictory and confused practices and their context of past decisions and present commitments (Bendor *et al.*, 2001:266–267). Does delegation theory really allow for the sheer messiness and multiple interpretations and understandings that characterise action and inaction in the world of governance?

Social interpretive theories

The sense that the world is not easily controllable and that the design of governance arrangements is not a straightforward task pervades the last broad school of thought to be examined in this chapter. Social interpretive theory differs from the delegation literature not as is sometimes suggested (March and Olsen, 1989), because it takes institutions seriously – that it is a characteristic shared between the two schools – rather the key difference is that it develops a more complex and nuanced perspective on how individuals and groups respond to the challenges and difficulties of governance. While delegation theory assumes that people respond rationally to a given set of incentives created by institutional rules that are universally perceived and understood, the social interpretive literature takes as a starting point that people interpret the world differently and that social and political communication is far from straightforward and is rather the greatest challenge of governance. As Janet Newman (2001:6) argues, to understand governance requires an emphasis on 'the way in which social arrangements are constructed as a result of the production of meanings and the repression, subordination or coordination of alternative meanings'.

Bevir (2003) criticises institutionalist approaches such as those developed by delegation theory because they assume that you can develop procedures or rules to steer the behaviour of subordinates. A principal may construct a rule Y for people in position X and expect behaviour Z as a result. But 'people who are in a position X might not grasp that they fall under rule Y, or they might understand the implications of rule Y differently from us, and in these circumstances they might not act in a manner Z even if they intend to follow the rule'

(Bevir, 2003:206). In particular, the model builders of delegation theory start with the assumption that people are self-interested, but then make further assumptions as to what might be in someone's self-interest in a particular context. These arguments are made to sound natural, obvious and even self-evident, but all they are simply guesses by the analyst. Bevir (2003:206) comments that 'we cannot blithely assume that bureaucrats understand and judge their institutional context as we do'. Without exploring people's beliefs and perceptions there cannot be any adequate explanation.

Bevir (2003:200) argues for 'a narrative approach ...that unpacks human actions in terms of the beliefs and desires of actors'. To explain people's actions you need to invoke their beliefs and desires by exploring the ways in which they understand their location, the norms that affect them and their values. But importantly he notes 'people cannot have pure experiences, their beliefs are saturated with contingent theories' (Bevir, 2003:205). Political scientists have the task of understanding these beliefs and desires and this is best done by interpreting them 'by relating them to other theories and meanings' (Bevir, 2003:205). People live and work in the context of traditions and these traditions prompt them to adopt certain meanings and when dilemmas occur they may modify their traditions and beliefs. In summary Bevir (2003:211) 'encourages us to understands governance in terms of a political contest resting on competing webs of belief and to explain these beliefs by reference to traditions and dilemmas'.

Above all, as Bang (2003:7) emphasises, it is important to view governance as a 'communicative relationship'. Governance, in particular, calls to attention relationships that are not articulated through formal authority. Governance relationships in the context are seen as driven by processes of exchange between governed and governors that are going to have to be open, developed and reflexive. Relations between state and citizen and between citizens are in a state of constant ambiguity and new more engaging and flexible forms of governing will have to be developed. For the social interpretative school, all social life is negotiable and governance, if it is to be effective and legitimate, will have to self-consciously take that form. 'A more interactive, negotiable, dialogical and facilitative authority is ...needed to help people in governing themselves' (Bang, 2003:8).

The bounded rationality school

The 'bounded rationality' school is one of the least developed in its application to governance issues, but we argue it has much to offer.

The school is strongly associated with the work of Herbert Simon drawing on crucial insights that come from the cognitive psychology (Simon, 1985). The school has expanded to include a wider understanding of the practices and heuristics involved in human decision-making (for a brilliant over-arching review see March, 1994). Bendor (2003) suggests that while some studies indicate how well humans cope with decision-making challenges; others (see in particular the work of Tversky and Kahneman, 1986) concentrate on systematic flaws in human judgement. Some heuristics are seen as providing effective ways of coming to a judgement – 'better than comprehensive rationality' – and others are seen as having in-built pathologies or weaknesses (Bendor, 2003). Jones (2001) follows in the footsteps of Simon by exploring not only psychological insights into decision-making but also the role of social institutions in correcting and channelling the decision-making of humans. It is his work, in particular, that helps us to recognise the importance of this perspective for our understanding of governance.

The thinking of the bounded rationality tradition starts with the same assumption as rational choice – that the people are goal-oriented, but accept, like social institutionalists, that goals may reflect selfish but also other motivations, where it is distinctive in its understanding of the process of selection that individuals go through. The strongest objection to the micro-foundations of the rational choice school from the perspective of bounded rationality is that they are 'behaviorally flawed' (Jones 2001:208). Effective analysis requires micro-foundational assumptions that are not 'off-base' and an understanding of how humans develop adaptive responses framed by complex institutions (Jones, 2001:208). Rational choice theorists – such as those discussed above in the examination of delegation theory, give agents fixed preference rankings and argue that incentives will steer their choices given the desire to maximise their utility. Bounded rationality suggests that the process of choosing what to do is more complex because there is a fundamental human problem in processing information, understanding a situation and determining consequences given the limits of our cognitive capacities and the complexities of the world we operate in. 'Humans are goal directed, understand their environment in realistic terms, and adjust to changing circumstances facing them. But they are not completely successful in doing so because of the inner limitations. Moreover, these cognitive limitations 'make a major difference in human affairs – in the affairs of individuals and in the affairs of state and nation' (Jones, 2001:27). Decision-making is conditioned by the framing features of the human mind and the organisational context in which people operate in complex ways.

The possibility of using this tradition as a counter-weight to the rational choice school in research has been recognised by several writers including Moe (1984), Jones (2001) and Bendor (2003). It is at the level of critique that the approach currently has most to offer. Again, reflecting on the work on delegation theory discussed earlier in the chapter, the bounded rationality approach would argue that the approach is erected on an insecure platform. Delegation theory drawing on its rational choice roots assumes that incentives shape human action in a straightforward way: the opportunities and con- straints in the task environment determine an individual's effort towards goal accomplishment. That is why incentives work – and why a combination of 'targets-and-terror' should deliver for reformers. The trouble is, as Herbert Simon (1997) and other theorists of bounded rationality point out (Jones, 2001), for individuals to respond in the manner required by the theory, assumes that decision-making on the part of humans is a rational response to external stimuli. The decision- maker, it is postulated, comprehensively perceives the environment and weighs up options against her preferences in the context of incen- tives and constraints, and chooses the option that maximises her pref- erences. However, the advocates of the bounded rationality model argue that that is a misleading picture of decision-making. Decision- makers, as it were, have to deal both with the external environment and their inner world, their cognitive architecture. The inner world helps them to focus on some things and ignore others and it is driven by habits of thought, rules of thumb, and emotions. Rationality is 'bounded' by this framing role of the human mind. Insights from social psychology and cognitive studies suggest that actors develop various coping techniques and heuristics to deal with the decision from challenges they face.

As Jones (2001:194) argues 'a major reason that institutional reforms fail to perform as well as expected is that designers do not pay enough attention to how the incentives they create or alter are likely to be per- ceived by participants in the institution'. Bounded rationality prin- ciples tells us that agents will selectively search based on incomplete information and partial ignorance and terminate that search before an optimal option emerges and choose instead something that is good enough. To understand the behaviour of such a decision-maker it is necessary to know what they know, what they want and what they can compute. We need considerable empirical information about the decision-maker and cannot assume a response on the back of assumptions about their capacity for rational calculation is driven by a set of ranked and fixed preferences. This is not to say that the behaviour of agents needs to be judged as irrational. On the contrary, they are rational in the sense that their behaviour is generally goal-oriented and usually they have reasons for what they do (cf. Simon, 1985). It is just that their rationality may be very different to that of the principal and rests on the interaction of their cognitive structure and the context in which they are operating.

The bounded rationality school provides a number of insights into governance failure and why steering by government in the context of governance is a challenging task. First, the perceptions of actors of their task and role are not easy to change. They are likely to be defined in different ways according to previous definitions of the problem space which has been essential in enabling them to selectively attend to the management of tasks and meet the challenge of information overload. These perceptions of what to care about and what not to care about are reinforced in the rules and operating procedures of organisations and people may have developed an emotional attachment to them and a loyalty to their part of the organisation. These attachments can block reform efforts. Finally, in coping with past reform programmes agents may have developed heuristics that are undermining or distorting of reform messages.

There is the potential for the school to move beyond critique to a stronger sense of what could guide institutional processes in the context of governance. Models of how humans behave matter, because they inform not only the thinking of social scientists, but also those of policy-makers.

> Nothing is more fundamental in setting our research agenda and informing our research methods than our view of the nature of the human beings whose behavior we are studying. It makes a difference, a very large difference, to our research strategy whether we are studying the nearly omniscient Homo economicus of rational choice theory or the boundedly rational Homo psychologicus of cognitive psychology. It makes a difference to research, but it also makes a difference for the proper design of political institutions (Simon, 1985: 303).

The bounded rationality framework draws to attention three understandings. First, the challenge of communication comes to fore in a world where 'can' and 'do' regularly misunderstand one another rather than a world where communication is cost and problem free. Second, bounded rationality argues that information processing practices and heuristics will need to be addressed rather than the issue of information asymmetry in any governance arrangement. Third, bounded rationality accepts that individuals can be minded to cooperate with others rather than automatically behave in a self-interested and egotistical manner.

Could bounded rationality provide a better framework for thinking through policy and governance arrangements or reform programmes? Its message is interpreted by some (Ostrom, V., 1997) to be that all humans are fundamentally flawed decision-makers and we need to design institutions with extensive checks and balances and very limited spans of responsibility set within a framework of limited government. That is not a path we find either attractive or inherent to the adoption of a bounded rationality frame. What the framework suggests is that people are flawed, but often still effective decision-makers. If you add to that point the understanding that humans are naturally inclined to cooperate, at least as much as they are to hinder one another, then scope for effective governance is wide. Reformers would focus on how interventions could shape how attention is paid and to what issues; how the problem space is represented, defined and understood by actors; the role of heuristics in controlling the search for alternatives and options for action and the impact of emotional attachment and loyalty on the framing of the decision-making environment. The major challenge is responding to the impact of our limited cognitive architecture as both reformers and active decision-makers in the governance arena.

Cultural institutional theory

The cultural institutionalist school we argue also has much to offer to our understanding of modern governance (Hood, 2000; Perri 6 *et al.*, 2002; Verweij and Thompson, 2006). The school may offer the prospect of incorporating insights neglected by rational choice but at the same time appears capable of offering sufficient 'analytical efficiency' (Grendstad and Selle, 1995:6) to provide a guide to institutional design. The starting point of cultural institutional theory is to recognise, as rational choice theory does, that individuals are active, creative thinkers but it sees them as more deeply affected by their social context than rational choice allows. People are not only influenced by social relations that permit or constrain their choices but they adopt socially influenced principles to guide those choices; principles that can be 'used for judging others and justifying' themselves to others (Douglas, 1982:190). Social relations and justifying cosmologies or world views are central to the context for individual decision-making. Social relations and world views combine together in ways of life or cultures.

From the perspective of cultural institutional theory people's interests are the product of social relations and the 'origins of their preferences may be found in the deepest desires of all: how we wish to live with other people and how we wish others to live with us' (Wildavsky, 1987:4). As a result 'preference formation is much more like ordering *prix fixe* from a number of set dinners or voting the party ticket. Only those combinations that are socially viable, that can cohere because people are able to give them allegiance, to share their meanings, may be lived' (Wildavsky, 1987:4). People's preferences and their management strategies to realise these preferences, are shaped by ways of life. Bounded rationality work allows for the development of schemas and heuristics, tacit theories about the world and the way it works, which are used by individuals to ease decision-making in the context of a complex environment and a corresponding complex array of strategic responses. But cultural institution theory sees these decision-facilitating devices as not purely cognitive but also as socially influenced: 'mental activity is embedded in and justifies social relations' (Thompson *et al.*, 1990:58). People use cultural biases to help them to determine for people what they want, who to blame, when to take risks, when to be apathetic, all central concerns of the governance dynamic. As Thompson *et al.* (1990:59) comment:

> These cultural biases – the shared meanings, the common convictions, the moral markers, the subtle rewards, penalties, and expectations common to a way of life – that become so much a part of us are constantly shaping our preferences in ways that even the brightest among us are only dimly aware.

Crucial to delivering analytical efficiency cultural institutionalists argue that only certain cultures – combinations of social relations and world views – occur sufficiently regularly in human society to suggest that they are sustainable. 'What makes order possible is that only a few conjunctions of shared values and their corresponding social relations are viable in that they are socially liveable' (Wildavsky, 1987:6). To specify what those combinations are cultural institutional theory, following the pioneering work of Mary Douglas (1982:190), uses the concepts of group and grid to specify 'a full array of possible social structures'. The question underlying the concept of group is: who am I? The question underlying the concept of grid: what shall I do? As Wildavsky (1987:6) explains:

> The question of identity may be answered by saying that individuals belong to a strong group, a collective, that makes decisions binding on all members or that their ties to others are weak in that their choices bind only themselves. The question of action is answered by responding that the individual is subject to many or few prescriptions, a free spirit or a spirit tightly constrained. The strength or weaknesses of group boundaries and the numerous or few, varied or similar, prescriptions binding or freeing individuals are the components of culture.

The implications of these insights are spelt in Table 2.2. Social relations repeatedly are institutionalised in a small number of forms, reflecting the limited positions available on the grid/group frame. You either experience a strong membership of a group or you do not. Your world is either subject to a lot of rules and direct regulation or it is not. Grid-group is about you as an employee in a large organisation (a role holder in a hierarchy); you as a hospital patient (a fatalist in the hands of others); you as a consumer (an individual making choices) and you as a church member (you as a communitarian). As the above illustrations indicate, an individual may find himself shaped by diverse social relations in different settings.

What brings home the relevance of cultural institutional theory to governance is its recognition of how these patterns of social relations in which individuals are embedded in help to determine their choices and in turn enable people to make decisions in the context of limited information and extensive complexity. The social framing measured by the grid-group framework provides people with a heuristic, a way of making sense and shaping a response to governance dilemmas. Crucially the social filters provide not just values but also decision rules. These social filters 'enable people who possess only inches of fact to generate miles of preferences' (Wildavsky, 1987:8). People know what to do because they know who they are and where they are located. Rational people support their ways of life. But whereas for rational choice theory there is only one 'rationality', for cultural institutionalists there can be up to four.

Consider the case of an intervention operating in a professional setting, then a governance solution that went with the grain of the dominant institutional way of working and thinking might be more

Table 2.2   Four commonly occurring cultures in institutions

Grid/Constraints: STRONG
Social relations are conceived as if they were principally involuntary, driven by numerous rules and prescriptions.

	Fatalist	Hierarchical	
G r o u p B o n d s	Social structure: isolate; casual, shallow ties, occasion-bound networks Value stance: personal withdrawal (from others, social order, institutions), life seen as beyond the control of the individual, the best that can be done is to cope, to find ways of surviving.	Social structure: centrally controlled and managed, roles and functions extensively classified Value stance: affirmation by rule-following and strong incorporation of individuals in social order with designated functions and roles.	G r o u p B o n d s
W E A K	**Individualistic** Social structure: open, configurations characterised by weak ties; system emerges spontaneously from individual action Value stance: affirmation by personal entrepreneurial initiative, responsibility lies with the individual.	**Communitarian** Social structure: enclave, strongly bonded and enclosed, built on fellowship, inward-looking, respect for all members Value stance: affirmation by peer group, shared criteria and procedures for knowing and deciding.	S T R O N G

Grid/Constraints: WEAK
Social relations are conceived as if they were principally voluntary, less rules and restrictions

effective. The professional setting can be taken as strongly influenced by the 'communitarian' framing of social relations with a social structure built on fellowship and inward-looking, respect for all members and a value stance that rests on affirmation by peer group. Thus rather than impose rigid rules or set about giving professionals individual incentives to change, you might instead seek to incorporate some members of the professional group in your project and then let their leadership create followers and adherents among the professional group. One illustration of this tactic might be the way that leading doctors have been appointed as for example anti-cancer 'tsars' in the UK's NHS to promote best practice and more effective forms of treatment. In this way the inherent culture of a social setting is turned to the advantage of top-level hierarchical decision-makers and may aid them in achieving their over-arching goals.

One of the most useful insights offered by cultural institutional theory is that it enables the analyst to be clearer about the variety of governance options available in any one setting. Table 2.3 provides an illustration. Moreover the grid-group framework can be given another twist, like a microscope in a laboratory, magnifying its focus to examine each of the quadrants in more depth (Hood, 2000). Table 2.4 provides an application of this technique to look at governance strategies in the hierarchical frame. The approach could also be extended to apply to the other quadrants. As a heuristic device it is valuable in

Table 2.3 Governance responses: insights from cultural institutional theory

	Grid Constraints: STRONG		
Group Bonds: WEAK	**Fatalist** Governance by Lottery: multiple overlapping initiatives and experiments; randomized to surprise	**Hierarchical** Top-Down Governance: contracts, inspection, regulation and oversight	**Group Bonds: STRONG**
	Individualistic Governance by Incentives: markets, information-sharing, trust, micro-benefits and polycentric structures	**Communitarian** Governance by Networks: power dependency, shared values and closure	
	Grid Constraints: WEAK		

Table 2.4 Hierarchical governance responses: a classification

	Grid Constraints: STRONG		
Group Bonds: WEAK	**Fatalist** Contrived randomness in inspection and regulation	**Hierarchy** Centrally-controlled rules, contracts, targets, plans and performance assessment	**Group Bonds: STRONG**
	Individualistic Rewards and sanctions, incentive-driven career progression, competition, and performance related pay	**Communitarian** Charismatic Leadership: bosses that create loyal followers, champions and social entrepreneurs	
	Grid Constraints: WEAK		

suggesting ways of governance that might be appropriate in particular settings. Moreover as Hood (2000) argues cultural institutional theory offers the designer a wider or fine grained selection of governance tools. But more than that as a design principle cultural institutional theory holds that that a sustainable governance system needs to have a requisite variety of coordination mechanisms drawing on each of the solidarities or cultural forms outlined above. We will return to this issue in the concluding chapter of the book.

Governance debates in political science and public administration

There are a number of debates about the implications of governance that occur in the political science and public administration literature. Below we examine three: the role of government in governance, the concept of governance failure and the challenge of achieving accountability or more broadly democratic credentials for the practice of governance.

Governance without government?

Rhodes (1997a) and Sorensen and Torfing (2007) can be seen as representative of the governance without government perspective. Their focus is on identifying how established forms of governing have come under challenge. For Rhodes (1997a:46) the phase 'governing without Government' is used explicitly to refer to changes in processes and practices of governing. The approach establishes that governing relies on actors from both within, but also beyond, government and that the complexities of inter-organisational relations thereby created leads to a 'distinctive managerial style based on facilitation, accommodation and bargaining' (Rhodes, 1997a:57). Sorensen and Torfing (2007) examine the emergence of networks which they see as constituted by stable, negotiated interaction between relatively autonomous actors. All these writers, while emphasising the role of relatively autonomous networks of societal-based actors in collective decision-making, still give credence to a governmental role in steering or providing a meta-governance framing by political representatives and governmental officials. In many respects the phase 'governing without government' is used for rhetorical purposes by these authors in order to emphasise the changed conditions of governing.

The above line of defence is not sufficient for those taking a stronger line about government still being a powerful actor, and who reject the idea of governing without governance as empirically unsustainable (Marinetto, 2003; Bell and Park, 2006; Jordan *et al.*, 2005). These writers provide compelling empirical evidence to counter the idea that networks engaged in governing activity operate regularly without some sort of input from government. Other writers point to the complexities of new modes of governance operating in the shadow of hierarchy with government exercising oversight in different sectors of EU decision-making, for example, in a variety of ways and with different levels of control (Heritier and Lehmkuhl, 2008).

Jordan *et al.* (2005) approach the topic with care through a simple typology of governance forms based on the selection of goals and means (see Table 2.5). Strong government would see strong steering of both goals and selection of means by government. In contrast, strong governance would see self-organising societal groups directing both goals and means. What Jordan *et al.* (2005:492) found in their study of European environmental policy instruments in nine jurisdictions is that all had, on balance, shifted from a position of 'government' to one of 'governance' with respect to their use of (environmental) policy instruments. However, the total distance travelled along the continuum by the nine jurisdictions has been surprisingly modest. Furthermore, the overall pattern of change 'has been spatially, temporally and sectorally highly uneven'. Very few cases of the pure strong governance case were found to be present by Jordan *et al.* (2005) and although there is only one study, in one policy area, their work is more than enough to create doubts over any loose claims about governance without government.

All the major reviews of the governance literature including those by Pierre and Peters (2000), Kettl (2002), Kjaer (2004) and Jacob and Sorensen (2007) agree that governance involves not networks that are self-governing, standing free and alone but rather networks of organisations that are guided and steered by government. In short, there are few analysts that seriously propose that governance occurs without government, but there is a difference of emphasis between those that

Table 2.5   **A simple typology of government and governance**

	Government determines goals	**Society determines goals**
Government selects means	Strong government	Hybrid
Society selects means	Hybrid	Strong governance

Adapted from Jordan *et al.* (2005:484)

see governance through the eyes of government steering, and those that see it in a less structured way. The two perspectives are best seen as opposite sides of a coin rather than in conflict with one another (cf. Pierre and Peters, 2005).

The nature of governance failure

As Bob Jessop reminds us 'markets, states and governance all fail. This is not surprising. For failure is a central feature of all social relations' (Jessop, 2000:30). But what counts as failure in governance? There are at least two possibilities. The first expression of failure may be the absence of a process of engagement and re-engagement among partners. To put it the other way around, when asked for their criteria of success, partners often cite the numbers of meetings held and the continuing existence of a process of dialogue and negotiation as a positive measure. So a lower tier of governance failure would be the breakdown of ongoing reflection and negotiation among partners. However, it appears slightly bizarre to leave the issue there. The reflection and negotiation must ultimately be about achieving some social purpose. The higher tier of governance failure must be based on an assessment of its capacity to produce more effective long-term outcomes than could have been produced using markets or imperative coordination by the state. It is necessary to consider not only the doing of governance – either by coalition-building or by government steering and pulling policy levers – it is also necessary to consider the impact of governance.

Governance failure could occur for a multitude of reasons because, as Sorensen and Torfing (2007:96) comment, 'network governance relies on precarious social and political processes and takes place in an uncontrollable political and economic context'. The features of governance that make it particularly prone to failure include the high transaction costs in developing partnerships and networks failure, a discrepancy between the temporal or spatial horizons of the various actors and the weakness or lack of capacity for those charged with the task of meta-governance, providing the steering to the system.

Some actors may enter the governance relationship with a very localist perspective, for others the boundary is regional, for still others it may be international. Reconciling these different spatial perspectives is complicated. In the same way with respect to time-scales what is short-term to some will appear like an eternity to others. Governance arrangements are in general about encouraging a longer-term time horizon but the perception of 'long-term' for a community group, politician or multinational company is likely to vary to such a degree that governance failure may result. Electoral considerations may encourage politicians to break apart complex governance arrangements for short-term advantage. But generally governance learns to cope with politics.

Conflict between partners is not an inherently undermining factor as far as governance is concerned. A never-ending series of conflicts is characteristic of market societies, and these conflicts can be managed as long as they are divisible, that is conflicts over actors getting more or less. Such conflicts lend themselves to compromise and the art of bargaining. Yet they are never resolved 'once and for all' and so the scene is always set for the next round of negotiation. The cumulative experience of managing numerous such conflicts is at the heart of an effective governance system. What can be disabling to governance and a cause of failure is conflict that is not divisible. Conflicts which are driven by matters of religion, race, language or ideology, which have an 'either-or' character and present considerable difficulties to governance (cf. Hirschman, 1995: Ch. 20). They are not inherently irresolvable but in so far as they figure strongly they are likely to make the compromise and messiness central to governance appear inadequate.

Emphasising the 'improbability of success' (Jessop, 2000:30) for governance should not be read as leading to the conclusion that it is necessary to look elsewhere for salvation. On the contrary, by recognising the incompleteness of any particular governance, the aim is to encourage continued experimentation and learning. Jessop (2000:31) argues that those concerned with governance should deliberately cultivate a 'flexible repertoire' of responses. This in turn involves a commitment to review and re-assessment, to check that mechanisms are achieving desired outcomes and a 'self-reflexive irony in which participants 'recognise the likelihood of failure but proceed as if success were possible'. Rhodes (1997b) comes to similar conclusions in his analysis of governance and argues that government needs to keep on picking up the skills of indirect management and learning.

The challenge of democracy and accountability

According to March and Olsen (1995:161): 'Democratic political systems have generally insisted on an allocation of personal accountability for political outcomes that most modern students of political history would consider descriptively implausible'. This observation captures well the dilemma created by a system of governance in which its essence is the interaction between varieties of actors. The narrative of the democratic basis for governing in modern industrial economies is of informed consent as the basis of governmental authority. Those who hold office in these circumstances have to be active representatives, providing both an account of their (proposed) actions and being subject to enforced accountability for results achieved and outcomes. Accountability, therefore, involves justification and being held responsible. Democratic theory usually demands that someone takes a leadership role in both functions. Governance with its 'problem of many hands' makes the quest for responsibility already demanding under established democratic governance arrangements but in the context of complex organisations it gets even more challenging (Bovens, 1998).

There is much 'wringing of hands' in the governance literature in political science and public administration as writers worry about whether governance can be made accountable. Pierre and Peters (2005:5, 127) are clear that it is necessary for 'those actors delivering governance to society to be accountable for their actions', and warn that 'we still have not developed a model of *political* accountability in a governance perspective'. Rhodes (1997a:21) notes that recent changes in the form of governance has 'led to a chorus of complaints about the loss of democratic accountability', but goes on to argue that although new governance forms challenge existing practices of accountability, they do not undermine the idea of accountability in a democratic society. The challenge is that 'accountability can no longer be specific to an institution but must fit the substantive policy and several institutions contributing to it' (Rhodes 1997a:59). Pierre and Peters (2005: 133) argue contrary to Rhodes and others, they think that accountability even in the context of governance demands a focus on institutions and in particular the institution of the state. For them, the state can be brought back in as the guarantor of the public interest and the key legitimate democratic institution. Its task is to subtlety manage governance processes to address issues of justice and liberty that reflect central political values (Pierre and Peters, 2000, 2005).

The solution offered by Pierre and Peters can be criticised as a bit of 'sticking plaster' affair. They hope that the state can make good the damage done to accountability by governance by imposing state steering on top of governance structures. The problem remains, however, that the state is the state. An institution defined by its monopoly of institutional coercion may learn new techniques but cannot disguise from citizens its essential core. Moreover, in complex settings, attenuated lines of accountability apply whether the governance structure is in network form or directed by central state. Accounts of attempts at state steering (see for example Stoker, 2000a) return continually to the difficulties the state has in presenting itself in a more flexible light-touch mode. But what is at issue is more than failure to learn new tricks. It also reflects a dominant image of the state in the minds of those from business, voluntary and community sectors namely that it is not only prone to bureaucratic rigidities but that it is an agent of coercion and control. As a result there is a fundamental underlying tension between state steering and the form of engagement that could guarantee democratic accountability.

Perhaps we need to re-examine the concept of accountability in a more fundamental way. Bovens (1998, 2006) asks why public accountability is so important and comes up with three answers. The first is accountability is about monitoring and controlling governing processes. Perhaps this is the test that others feel that governance most obviously fails, but as suggested by Rhodes (1997a) in terms of system accountability, within a policy area, governance with its interaction between state and non-state actors may offer at least some form of accountability. But Bovens offers two additional views that take us into territory not already touched on in the discussion in this chapter. Accountability could be viewed as the establishment of systems to prevent the concentration of power and accountability. In a complex world of decision-making holding an individual to account is often an exercise in constitutional fiction given that any individual responsibility for a decision is limited but what accountability demands is that there are checks and balances and practices of power-sharing built into the system of governance. Accountability could again be seen as a system characteristic rather than focused on an individual if it was viewed as demanding that a governance system should have learning capacity built in, in order to ensure that it adjusts and improves as it meets problems. If accountability concerns stay focused on individuals to be held responsible then governance arrangements will often appear to be lacking accountability given their inherent quality of 'many hands'. But if accountability is seen as a quality that can be displayed by at a system level then new forms of governance may score more highly than those of a more established government form precisely because they can involve 'many hands' and so in practice diffuse power and they provide an effective arena for joint learning and reflexive policy practice. These issues are addressed further in the final chapter in the book.

Concluding comment

The governance turn in political science and public administration has set out important lines of investigation that grapple with the central challenges of governing in today's world – especially in the advanced industrial democracies. The strength of the political science literature is the range and variety of its empirical studies. Moreover a variety of theoretical frameworks are on display ranging from rational choice to cultural institutionalism. The debate has shown a capacity to throw up useful new conceptual insights such as the idea of governance failure or the options for meta-governance. Political science and public administration can claim to be the home of the governance turn but the argument of our book is that its debates would be enhanced by a deeper understanding of the governance literature emerging from other disciplines and research programmes.

3
Governance and the New Institutional Economics

New Institutionalist Economics (NIE) offers a seminal contribution to the wider debate on governance. NIE arose as the result of a growing interest among rational choice theorists in explanations for the emergence and change of institutions, specifically the link between individual agency and structural transformation. It presented a theory of institutions in order to extend neoclassical economics, which presumed that a complete set of smoothly functioning markets exists but did not refer to institutions to explain their existence and working. New institutionalism was a reaction against the 'hyper-individualism' of classical economic theory. Its principal offering is that institutions are the rules of the game in society, or more formally, are the humanly devised constraints that shape human interaction. Among its principal architects, Douglass North (1990) emphasised that institutions reduce uncertainty in human exchange, which arises in the first place because human beings have incomplete information and limited mental capacity by which to process information. Institutions help to manage the demands and costs transacting.

The definition of institutions as rules is central to NIE and places governance at its heart. This chapter attempts to highlight the principal intellectual contributions of the NIE to the wider debate on governance today. The first summarises how NIE departed from neoclassical economics. It then maps the intellectual domain of the wide field that now constitutes the new institutionalist economics and identifies the key conceptual issues that it grapples with. The second part focuses on the principal voices within the NIE literature, and discusses their contributions to the notion of governance. The third part examines the main critiques of NIE. The conclusions consider the propositions for institutional reform contained within NIE, for these bear utmost significance for the contemporary practice of governance.

The challenge of new institutional economics

Neoclassical economics rests on a fundamental premise of the individual as a rational being with an 'inviolable' judgement of her own welfare (Bates, 1995). Further, in the neoclassical world, an individual perceives the world as it actually is. It is thus possible to predict the choices that will be made by a rational decision-maker entirely from knowledge of the real world, and without knowledge of the decision-maker's perceptions or modes of calculations, as long as the individual's utility function is known (North 1995:17). This is a world where 'instrumental rationality' of the individual prevails. Ideas, ideologies and institutions do not matter, and economies are characterised by efficient markets (North, 1995).

Further, this 'institution-free' economy is viewed to be in equilibrium. This conception followed the triumphant theoretical codification, following the work of Arrow (1951) and Debreu (1959), of the necessary and sufficient conditions for the existence of equilibrium in a market economy. Arrow and Debreu's work, amongst others, proved the conditions under which it would be feasible for prices in markets to shape the decisions of consumers and firms such that all consumers would maximise their utility and all firms would maximise their profits. As this allocation enables all agents to maximise simultaneously, it constitutes an equilibrium; in addition, it is efficient, i.e. Pareto Optimal. Under the conditions that generate market equilibrium therefore, it would be impossible to improve the utility of any consumer or the profits of any firms without reducing the welfare of another. By extension, insofar as Pareto Optimality constitutes a defensible criterion of social welfare, the Arrow/Debreu conditions render the choices of rational individuals consistent with the social welfare (Bates 1995:28).

The fundamental problem with neoclassical economic theory was that it simply could not account for the realities of individual and collective behaviour, despite its cogent theoretical modelling of the same. Except in those instances where conditions approximating its assumptions exist, such as financial markets, which tend to have many of the characteristics described earlier, neoclassical models struggle to capture the practices of economies (North 1990). Bates (1995) has systematically described the common sources of market failure, which arise when the necessary and sufficient conditions for market equilibrium fail to hold. As a market equilibrium is held as sacrosanct by neoclassical economic theory, the all too common occurrence of 'market failures' prompted the need for fresh theorising on the subject. The sources of market failures typically include production externalities (when the activities of one impose costs on another, and the private decisions of 'rationally maximising agents' fail to promote socially rational outcomes), public goods (when the private choices of individuals create inefficient allocations of resources between private and public goods), imperfect information (the acquisition of information is costly and individuals might therefore choose to be imperfectly informed), hidden action (high information costs limit the ability of people to monitor the choices of others), hidden type (uncertainty not only about prices or choices of others, but also of 'type', i.e. the quality of a good or the capabilities or intentions of another) and unforeseen contingencies (arising from the inability of human beings to foresee future states of the world) (Bates, 1995:29–34). He argues that each of these sources led to the rise of new institutionalist economics, which essentially puts forward the theory that 'when the market fails to arrive at an optimum state, society will, to some extent at least, recognise the gap, and non-market social institutions will arise attempting to bridge it' (Arrow, 1971b; cited in Przeworski, 1991:109). The core of NIE thus is that rational individuals, confronted with the limitations of individually rational behaviour, create institutions that, by creating new incentives or by imposing new constraints, enable them to transcend these limitations.

It should be noted that there is, both within European public finance and American economics more generally, an older institutionalist tradition, which predated and crystallised explicitly into an opposition movement against the neoclassical orthodoxy. The original notion, as developed by John R. Commons (1931, 1937) and Thorstein B. Veblen (1899, 1919) and their followers, was to examine the ways in which collective action could be institutionally embodied and in that form, shape and constrain subsequent individual choice. While the more positive and 'constructive' side of the old institutionalist project was to study the institutions and mechanisms that create and control economic life (such as property law and the rules of courts enforcing them), the more negative aim was to undermine the neoclassical orthodoxy by demonstrating ways in which its idealised notions of 'free markets' misrepresent the institutional reality of any actual economy (Goodin, 1996:7). Further, the most distinguishing aspect of the older institutional tradition is that the notion of individual agents as 'utility-maximising' is regarded as inadequate and erroneous (Hodgson, 2000). This school does not assume a given individual with given purposes or preference functions, and holds onto the idea of 'interactive and partially malleable agents, mutually entwined in a web of partially durable and self-enforcing institutions' (Hodgson, 2000:325). Older institutionalists emphasise both 'upward' and 'downward' causation, in that individuals create and change institutions, just as institutions mould and constrain individuals. In their belief that individuals are socially and institutionally constituted, the older institutionalism is distinct not only from neoclassical economics, but also from the new institutionalist economics.

NIE departs from the old school in that its critique of mainstream neoclassical economics is a largely positive one (Nabli and Nugent, 1989). It has been described as 'a kind of "expanded economics"', which like standard (neoclassical) economics focuses on the choices people make in their lives, but is willing to accommodate a 'richer conception of human motivation and to countenance greater limitations on the rational calculation of individual advantage' (Clague, 1997:16). It abandons the instrumental rationality assumption that is so fundamental to neoclassical economics. Instead, it explicitly considers that individuals make choices on the basis of their mental models, which are in part 'culturally derived', produced through the 'intergenerational transfer of knowledge, values and norms', and in part acquired through experience which is 'local' to their particular environment (North, 1995:18). In consequence, there is no single determinate equilibrium which will obtain, but multiple equilibria can occur. It is this incomplete information and limited information capacity by which to process information that determines the costs of 'transacting'. Further, traditional microeconomic theory was incomplete because it only included production and transport costs, neglecting the costs of entering into and executing contracts and managing organisations. These costs, commonly known as 'transaction costs', account for a considerable share of the total use of resources in the economy. Because a large part of national income is devoted to transacting, institutions, and specifically property rights, transaction costs are the crucial determinants of the efficiency of markets. This insight was the chief contribution of Ronald Coase (1937, 1960), who made the crucial connection between neoclassical economics, transaction costs and institutions. Using this line of thought, Douglass North (1990) among others, argued that institutions are formed to reduce uncertainty in human exchange, precisely to reduce the transaction costs that are disregarded by neoclassical economic theory. Building a theory of institutions thus, on the foundations of individual choices, North argued, was 'a step towards reconciling differences between economics and the other social sciences' (1990:5).

A key theoretical departure of NIE from neoclassical economics was on the issue of cooperation. Neoclassical economic theory is based on the fundamental assumption of scarcity and hence competition. Its harmonious implications come from its assumptions about a frictionless exchange process in which property rights are perfectly specified without cost, and information costs nothing to acquire. What has been missing from this explanation is an understanding of the nature of human coordination and cooperation (North 1990:11). Much of new institutionalism is devoted to addressing this important aspect of individual and collective behaviour. This is the theoretical focus of NIE that makes it particularly relevant for governance.

The new institutionalist economics has come to embody the intersection of a number of different lines of investigation, each interesting in its own right. These include the analysis of behavioural norms, interest group formation, transaction costs, organisation theory, rent-seeking behaviour, the emergence of the rules of thumb for firm decision-making and the determination and effects of property rights, amongst other things. NIE is interdisciplinary in scope and has allowed for the cross-fertilisation of ideas between historians, sociologists, political scientists, psychologists, and of course, economists. Synthesising the field in its entirety is an enormous task and will not be attempted here (a few brave attempts have been made earlier (see for example Harriss *et al.*, 1995; and Clague, 1997). We will try however to map the intellectual domain of the NIE, to obtain a sense of its principal concerns and their relevance to governance issues.

Thus the new institutionalist economics covers a large and impressive domain. Nabli and Nugent (1989) usefully point out that there are two 'branches' of NIE, namely the analysis of transaction costs on the one hand, and the analysis of collective action on the other. Although, equally, they note that the two branches are by no means unrelated. In the following section, we will further substantiate the contributions of the principal proponents of NIE. We will arrange these according to themes as pertinent to the debate on governance today.

Intellectual domain of the NIE and the study of governance

The discussion below looks at how NIE has influenced our thinking about governance by examining the body of work and debates associated with the work of Williamson, North and Ostrom. In addition we examine the work on principal-agent theory.

Williamson and transaction cost economics: firm-level governance

Basic economic analysis concentrated on studying the functioning of the economy in the framework of an institutional structure which was taken as given. An offshoot of this approach was that the existence of firms seemed self-evident. This changed drastically with Coase's (1937, 1960) seminal intervention highlighting the importance of transaction costs, in addition to production and transport costs, in influencing the efficiency of markets. Coase also demonstrated that the power and precision of analysis may be enhanced if it is carried out in terms of rights to use goods and factors of production instead of the goods and factors themselves. He demonstrated how the definition and distribution of these 'property rights' among individuals by law, contract clauses and other rules determines economic decisions and their outcomes. Thus, in this analysis, every type of firm is comprised of a distinctive contract structure and thereby a specific distribution of rights and obligations, i.e. property rights. Coase, in his later work, extended his firm-level analysis to argue that property rights constitute a basic component in the institutional structure of an economy. He then came to the important conclusion that it is the fact that transaction costs are never zero, which indeed explains the institutional structure of the economy, including variations in contract forms and many kinds of legislation. In his later work *The Problem of Social Cost* (1960), Coase postulated that if a property right is well defined, if it can be transferred, and if the transaction costs is an agreement which transfers the right from one holder to another are zero, then the use of resources does not depend on whether the right was initially allotted to one party or the other (except for the difference which can arise if the distribution of wealth between the two parties is affected). In other words, all legislation which deals with granting rights to individuals would be meaningless in terms of the use of resources; parties would 'agree themselves around' every given distribution of rights if it is to their mutual advantage. Thus, a large amount of legislation would serve no material purpose if transaction costs are zero.

Using Coase's contribution as its starting point 'Transaction Cost Economics' (TCE) has developed, described as an interdisciplinary undertaking drawing from law, economics and organisation. Here, the firm is regarded as a 'governance structure' and not a production function, as was assumed in neoclassical economics. Further, the transaction is the basic unit of analysis, whereas neoclassical orthodoxy was concerned with composite goods and services. Its principal proponent Oliver Williamson (1975, 1979), explains that TCE is concerned with the institutions of governance, such as markets, hybrids, hierarchies and bureaus that operate at the level of individual transactions. Williamson, taking the cue from Jon Elster's dictum that 'explanations in the social sciences should be organised around (partial) *mechanisms* rather than (general) *theories*, described institutions as the 'mechanisms of governance' (1996:5). The principal insight of TCE is that while the concept of transaction costs is a useful one, such costs are difficult to measure and a more plausible analytical approach is to 'look at the issue of governance comparatively, so that the costs of one mode of governance are always examined in relation to other alternative feasible modes' (Williamson, 1996:45). In this analysis, transactions, which differ in their attributes, are aligned with governance structures, which differ in their competence, so as to affect a 'discriminating – mainly a transaction cost – economising' result.

Williamson expounds that the study of governance, more generally, is concerned with the identification, explication and mitigation of all kinds of contractual hazards. These hazards can be attributed to the twin behavioural assumptions from which TCE works: bounded rationality (i.e. behaviour is *intendedly* rational but only *limitedly* so) and opportunism (self-interest seeking with guile). It is concerned with the feasibility and efficacy with which governance structures serve to mitigate hazards, and investigates into the attributes that cause different governance structures to mitigate hazards differently. It asks why one form of economic organisation (e.g. hierarchy) is unable to replicate the mechanisms found to be efficacious in another (e.g. the market).

Further, it considers property rights and contracts to be both difficult and costly to define and enforce, believing thereby that Coase (and others like Alchian (1959, 1961) overstated the case for property rights. It thus advocates a 'comparative contractual approach' as opposed to a 'pure property rights approach put forward by Coase (Williamson, 1996:222). Contract law and the limits of court ordering play important roles in TCE in two important ways: first, each generic mode of governance is supported by, and defined by, a distinctive form of contract law; and second, a contract is viewed as a framework which almost never accurately indicates real working relations. Thus, the main contractual action takes place between the parties in the context of 'private ordering' which may be cheaper and more satisfactory, than 'court ordering'. The key practical lesson is that all of the relevant contracting action cannot be concentrated in the *ex ante* incentive alignment but some spills over into *ex post* governance. These issues have been further developed in the principal-agent approach, which unpacks issues of firm-level governance, to be discussed shortly.

In his later work, *The Economic Institutions of Capitalism* (1985), Williamson developed the idea that economising on transaction costs is mainly responsible for the choice of one form of capitalist organisation over another. This hypothesis was then applied to a wide range of phenomena, ranging from vertical integration and labour organisation, to corporate governance and technology transfer, i.e. any issue that could be posed directly or indirectly as a contracting problem. However, Williamson held that TCE does not always operate smoothly or quickly, and that 'economising operates through weak-form selection and works through a private net benefit calculus' (1996:233). Barring these qualifications, TCE maintains that economising is mainly determinative of private sector economic organisation; the relevant criterion for assessment is that of 'remediableness', according to which, the outcome for which no superior alternative can be described and implemented with net gains, is presumed to be efficient.

Finally, TCE subscribes to the proposition that history matters and relies on it to explain the differential strengths and weaknesses of alternative forms of governance. However, it does not hold that *only* history matters, and emphasises that 'intentionality and economising also explains a lot of what is going on out there' (Williamson, 1996:240). As Williamson states conclusively, transaction costs economics contemplates 'success', as taking the institutional environment as given, economic agents purportedly align transactions with governance structures to effect economising outcomes, a proposition he affirms has been successfully demonstrated in empirical terms (1996:5).

Principal-agent theory

Coase's work on the firm has become the basis for rapidly expanding research on 'principal-agent' relations. The contracting hazards that concerned TCE were first identified in the insurance industry, and then observed more generally, wherever contracting problems existed. These had gone unaddressed within neoclassical economic theory, which treated the firm as a 'black box', by remaining silent on how the owners of firms succeed in aligning the objectives of their various members, such as workers, supervisors and managers, with profit maximisation (Laffont and Martimort, 2002). The principal-agent approach attempts to rectify this approach by incorporating 'incentives' as the central focus of its analysis. It looks at the strategies that the two sets of players – principals and agents – will engage in while interacting in order to accomplish a collective effort. It is fundamentally a contracting problem concerning how much of the value that the agent produces should go back to him/her in the form of a payment.

However, the approach is distinctive for its additional assumption of asymmetric information, which means that the agent knows more than the principal about the service in question in a manner that affects the contracting outcomes. When there is asymmetric information, a host of difficulties arise in the process of selection of agents, negotiation of contracts and monitoring of information. These difficulties have been summarised into two main types: *adverse selection*, which means opportunism before the making of the contract between principal and agent; and *moral hazard*, which means opportunism after making of the contract between principal and agent (Lane, 2006; Laffont and Martimort, 2002). Thus, conflicting objectives and decentralised information are the basic ingredients of incentive theory. If the agent had a different objective function but no private information, the principal could propose a contract that perfectly controls the agent and induces the latter's actions to be what he would like to do himself in a world without delegation (Laffont and Martimort, 2002).

While the principal-agent idea is essentially derived from the private sector, there have been efforts to apply it to the public sector. Yet, while it may be easy to identify the principal and the agent in any principal-agent interaction in the private sector, who may these be in the public sector? Attempts have long been made to analyse democratic politics, or the 'input' side of politics as principal-agent interaction, with the electorate as the principal and political parties as agents. The Public Choice approach to democratic politics inherently contains a principal agent conception of politicians 'offering policy packages, against basically private rewards including power, prestige and money' (Lane, 2006:4) The Public Choice approach, pioneered by James Buchanan (1975), focuses on government excesses (which lead to the waste of social resources and individual alienation) and the need to curtail the role of government in economic decision-making. However, it is commented that such 'election contracting' is far too elusive to fall under the principal-agent framework. The notion of an election as a 'contract' is questioned on a number of grounds including the precise nature of parties involved, the content of the contract, and most importantly, its enforceability. Lane (2006) proposes that perhaps the principal-agent model may be more relevant in analysing the 'output' side of politics, where the government (in its post-election phase) needs to 'get the job done'. It may thus be possible to speak of a 'contractual relationship' as the government will pay for the services of agents who will contribute to the achievement of the government's goals.

Besley (2006) observes that there is an established tradition that addresses the issues of incentives in politics. This tradition is encapsulated within approaches to political resource allocation that are concerned to understand how particular assumptions about the structure of political institutions and organisation shape policy choice. The most influential model was that proposed by Downs (1957), where he described politics in the language of competing firms called 'parties', where customers were voters. Besley presents a sophisticated critique of this approach, mainly arguing that since it is concerned with seeking median preferences among the electorate, it is not particularly useful in looking at institutional differences in the policy process (2006:25–27). Further, he states that the Downsian model sees policies, not politicians, as the currency of political competition, whereas in a representative democracy, it is politicians that are elected and charged with making policy. Besley advocates therefore the need to adopt a 'candidate-centred' view of political competition.

Approaches to political resource allocation view politics as mainly a problem of preference aggregation, since the conflicts of interest they address are between different groups of citizens who have divergent policy interests. Besley focuses instead on political-agency models that address conflicts of interest between citizens and government, and elections as mechanisms that can resolve such conflicts. He argues that while elections have been viewed as incentive mechanisms (previous studies have illustrated how the threat of not being re-elected could curtail rent extraction by politicians), not so many have viewed elections as selection mechanisms, where the 'best candidates' are selected. Besley greatly endorses this neglected approach, and further attacks the narrow self-interested view of politicians which is adopted by political economy models. He suggests that a broader conception of motivation needs to be taken into account. In this respect, Besley discusses three other models of motivation in politics: ego-rent, policy preference and fiduciary duty (Besley, 2006:32–34). The first motivation suggests that some politicians are motivated by the trapping of office and the sense of self-esteem that comes when they win. The second suggests that others are motivated by their desire to see something happen and the third indicates some sort of intrinsic motivation, where engagement reflects a sense of duty and care.

Besley makes the case that politicians are heterogeneous in important ways, being a trustworthy politician is a type of politics rather than a consequence of incentives, and the role of elections is to find ways of sorting out such politicians rather than incentivising them. In the principal-agent models that he discusses citizens who have delegated authority to policy-makers experience two main problems: *monitoring*, where there is a need to establish whether the policy-maker has acted opportunistically and to reward/punish behaviour accordingly, and also *selection*, where there is a need to select the most competent policy-makers and/or those whose motivations are most likely to be in tune with public interest.

Besley thus advances his principal argument that there are institutional preconditions to effective government, but finding them requires both an understanding of incentives, as well as the process by which the 'political class' is selected. In this respect, the political agency model becomes an analytical tool, facilitating a greater understanding of how to ensure that democracy gives voters what they want. While this approach widens the use of the principal-agency framework in political analysis, Besley warns that real world democracies are incredibly complex and advises that models need to be highly specific in their ambitions in order to retain their analytical rigour.

A rules-based conception of governance: North

At the 'micro-level', to use Williamson's terminology, the new institutional economics has focused attention on governance as an exercise in assessing the efficacy of alternative modes of organisation. The explanatory role of governance has been to understand why and how different institutional frameworks – of markets, hybrids, hierarchies and bureaus – develop in order to minimise transaction costs. Further, the principal-agent framework, by further focusing on the complexities of contractual arrangements due to asymmetries of information and incentives in the firm and beyond, has offered a useful (albeit contested) analytical tool for contemplating democratic politics and the role of government. At the 'macro-level', NIE conceives of institutions as the rules that reduce uncertainty in human exchange. It is this rules-based conception of institutions that is the new institutional economics' principal contribution to governance, as it is widely understood today.

Like Douglass North, who defined institutions as 'the rules of game in a society, or more formally, the humanly devised constraints that shape human interaction' (1990:3), a number of other theorists have defined institutions from a rules perspective. Ruttan and Hayami define institutions as 'rules of a society or of organisations that facilitate coordination among people by helping them form expectations which each person can reasonably hold in dealing with others' (1984:204). Runge defines institutions as 'public systems of rules that specify certain forms of action as permissible, others as forbidden, and provide for certain penalties and defences, which channel the behaviour of people with respect to each other, providing assurance by setting the rules of the game' (1984b; as cited in Sinha, 1990:14). There have been several others (Thomson, 1981).

In this tradition, institutions have three key characteristics (Nabli and Nugent, 1989:1335). The first is the 'rules and constraints' nature of institutions. Ostrom has defined these rules and constraints as 'prescriptions, commonly known and used by participants, to order repetitive and interdependent relationships' where 'prescriptions refer to which actions are required, prohibited or permitted' (1986:5). It is important, she clarifies, to think of configurations of rules, rather than single rules separately, and it is these sets of rules that are considered as basic characteristics of institutions. The second characteristic of institutions is their ability to govern the relations among individuals and groups. To serve an institutional role, these rules and constraints must be applicable in social relations, whether 'voluntarily' accepted or 'enforced' by an external authority. The third characteristic of institutions is their predictability. Agents should expect these rules and constraints to have some degree of stability, or else they would not have an institutional character (Nabli and Nugent, 1989:1335).

Explaining the emergence of institutions has perhaps posed the biggest conceptual challenge for new institutional theorists. This has been tackled at a number of levels. North, an economic historian, addressed this challenge by trying to explain the widely divergent paths of historical change, a phenomenon he regards as the 'central puzzle of history' (1990:6). The diversity in societal progression around the world is, according to him, even more perplexing in terms of standard neoclassical and international trade theory, which implies that, over time, economies, as they traded goods, services and productive factors, would gradually converge. In his earlier work (North and Thomas, 1973) he offered an essentially efficient explanation, where changes in relative prices create incentives to construct more 'efficient institutions'. In his 1981 work, North abandoned this 'efficiency' view, postulating that institutions are not necessarily, or even usually, created to be socially efficient; rather they, or at least formal rules are created to serve the interests of those with the bargaining power to create new rules. This approach however did not explain why 'political entrepreneurs in stagnant economies did not quickly emulate the policies of the more successful ones' (1990:6). This is the question that he sought to answer in his landmark work titled *Institutions, Institutional Change and Economic Performance*.

North's principal argument is that individuals in a particular society have certain opportunities, which are a product of the specific formal and informal rules or constraints that comprise their institutions. Organisations are created to take advantage of those opportunities, and as the organisations evolve, they alter the institutions. The resultant path of institutional change is shaped by the lock-in that comes from the symbiotic relationship between institutions and the organisations that have evolved as a consequence of the incentive structure provided by those institutions, and the feedback process by which human beings perceive and react to changes in the opportunity set. The complexity of the environment, given the limited processing ability of the actor, explains the subjective perceptions of reality that characterise human understanding.

Within this analytical framework, of institutional constraints as opportunity sets, is contained an explanation for institutional stability and why they typically produce many different margins at which choices are made. Stability derives from the fact that there are a large number of specific constraints that affect a particular choice. Significant changes in this institutional framework involve a host of changes in a variety of constraints, not only legal constraints but norms of behaviour as well. At the same time, North argued, the complex of informal and formal constraints 'make possible continual incremental changes at particular margins' (1990:68). These small changes in both formal rules and informal constraints will gradually alter the institutional framework over time, so that it evolves into a different set of choices than it began with.

North was concerned with the costliness of measurement and enforcement of the institutional constraints, both formal and informal, which are devised to shape human exchange. Transaction costs are the most measurable dimension of the institutional framework that underlies the constraints in exchange. The higher these costs, the more the exchanging parties will invoke informal constraints to shape the exchange, although in the extreme, very high costs would inhibit exchange completely. Further, the more complex the exchanges in time and space, the more complex and costly are the institutions necessary to realise cooperative outcomes. While complex exchange can be realised by creating third-party enforcement via voluntary institutions that lower information costs about the other party, ultimately viable impersonal exchange that would realise the gains from trade, inherent in the technologies of modern interdependent economies, requires institutions that can enforce agreements by the threat of coercion. Such a role can only be provided by the state, but North considers that the development of a state that is able to monitor property rights and enforce contracts effectively is as yet an unsolved puzzle. 'No one at this stage in our knowledge knows how to create such an entity' (North, 1990:59). This has raised the issue of whether 'self-enforcing' constraints are a possibility, a subject tackled by Elinor Ostrom and others in her footsteps. North concluded that the degree to which we are able to assess these costs is directly linked to the progress in measuring the effectiveness of institutions. In his work, he demonstrates not only that institutions are central to economic performance, but also that they are the underlying determinant of the long-run performance of economies, a subject we will return to in the last section.

Even as they sought to clarify relationships between individual rationality and collective action, the principles of NIE engendered in turn a collective choice paradox. It was argued that if institutions were intended to reduce uncertainty in human interaction, then would their creation itself not be subject to a collective choice dilemma, of the sort proposed by Olson (Bates, 1988, 1995)? The new institutionalist economics suggests that should individuals encounter a social dilemma, they would forge new institutions to transcend it, but 'given that the new institution would make all better off, the institution itself constitutes a public good, and would not then, the act of its provision also generate incentives to free ride' (Bates, 1988:44)? He points out that viewed in terms of the incentives faced by individuals, it appears that the demand for institutional solutions does not imply their supply. As such, NIE appears to be ensnared within a basic contradiction.

This is a fundamental dilemma for NIE, which regards cooperation amongst individuals as imperative. That institutions are necessary to reduce uncertainty in human exchange is clear, but how should such institutions be supplied? North proffered a historical explanation, but he too conceded that institutional constraints need to be enforced, in order to be binding, and the state, as a third party enforcer, may not always act as a neutral arbiter. Self-enforced constraints would be an option, but he also questioned how far they would be possible, alluding implicitly to the persistent collective action problem, which has been the subject of more than one theoretical enquiry, from the prisoner's dilemma to the tragedy of the commons.

Ostrom: common-pool resources

Elinor Ostrom's analysis, conducted in the particular context of common-pool resources (CPR) (that embody collective action problems in relation to a highly specific category of public goods), is significant because it addresses the collective dilemma that niggles away at the NIE perspective on governance. Ostrom takes exception to Hardin's (1968, 1982) prescriptions of state centralisation or privatisation, as the only solutions to the collective action problem, for both imply that institutional change must come from 'outside' and be 'imposed' on the individuals concerned (1990:14). She argues that instead of presuming that the individuals sharing a commons are inevitably caught within a trap from which they cannot escape, it needs to be recognised that the 'capacity of individuals to extricate themselves from various types of dilemma situations *varies* from situation to situation' (Ostrom, 1990:14; italics in original). Starting from this premise, Ostrom presents empirical evidence of both 'successful and unsuccessful' attempts by individuals to evolve institutions to achieve 'productive outcomes in situations where the temptations to free ride and shirk are ever present'. In her view, a theoretical explanation based on human choice for self-governed enterprises needs to be developed and accepted. She attempts to do the same in her seminal 1990 book *Governing the Commons: The Evolution of Institutions for Collective Action.*

The 'contractarian dilemma' posed by Bates (1988) refers to the problem of how a group of principals or a community of citizens can organise themselves to solve the problems of institutional supply, commitment and monitoring. Without monitoring, there can be no credible commitment, and without credible commitment, there is no reason to propose new rules. Ostrom writes, 'Dilemmas nested inside dilemmas appear to be able to defeat a set of principals attempting to solve collective-action problems through the design of new institutions to alter the structure of incentives they face' (1990:45). Ostrom observed that most current analyses of CPR problems (and collective action problems more generally) focused on a single level of analysis, called the 'operational level', where it is assumed that the rules of the game and the physical, technological constraints are given and will not change during the time frame of analysis (1990:50). She made the case for an alternative set of assumptions, whereby the analyst must assume both that technology and rules are subject to change over time. Further, the rules affecting operational choice (or the working rules) are made within a set of 'collective choice' rules that are themselves made within a set of 'constitutional-choice' rules. The constitutional-choice rules for a micro-setting are affected by collective choice and constitutional choice rules for larger jurisdictions. In proposing a framework of nested rules that impact and are impacted by one another, Ostrom made the case that self-organising and self-governing individuals trying to cope with problems constantly go back and forth across levels as a key strategy, and any institutional analysis must take these multiple 'arenas' into account. Her framework is useful to appreciate the possibility of institutional change in a far more nuanced way, once it is recognised that changes in the rules used to order action at one level occur within a currently 'fixed' set of rules at a deeper level, and changes in deeper-level rules are usually more difficult and costly to accomplish, thus increasing the stability of mutual expectations among individuals interacting according to a set of rules (1990:52). Importantly, Ostrom recognises that rules are changed less frequently than are the strategies that individuals adopt within the rules.

Using this framework, Ostrom tries to understand why it is that some 'appropriators' of CPRs can supply themselves with rules, gain quasi-voluntary compliance with those rules, and monitor each other's conformance to the rules, while others cannot. She offers an initial explanation for credible commitments and mutual monitoring in which CPR rules conform to a set of 'design principles' (Ostrom, 1990:Ch.3) drawing on assumptions about fallible, norm adopting individuals who pursue contingent strategies in complex and uncertain environments (1990:185). Drawing on a number of case studies, her book includes an in-depth account of the conditions wherein individuals would find it rational to cooperate to devise rules to regulate use and access of the commons they are dependent on. Importantly however, Ostrom warns that 'designing and adopting new institutions to solve CPR problems are difficult tasks, no matter how homogeneous the group, how well informed the members are about the conditions of CPR and how deeply ingrained are the generalised norms of reciprocity' (1990:210). She suggests that not only can overcoming collective action problems 'never be assured', given the strong temptation to act opportunistically that usually exists, but also that if individuals find rules that work relatively well, they may have little motivation to continue the costly process of searching for rules that will work even better. Importantly, she concludes that institutional change is hard to predict, and that it is dependent not only on the variables that characterise a particular CPR situation, but (given the nested rules that exist at different levels) also the type of 'external political regime' under which the CPR is appropriated.

At the 'macro' level therefore, this focus on institutions as the 'rules' of the game and the accompanying attention to how these rules are formulated, has been particularly useful for contemplating the problems of collective decision-making in any setting, anywhere. If collective decision-making is the concern of governance, in its broadest sense, then this concern is at the heart of NIE. The questions raised here reverberate through the rest of the chapters in this book.

The limits to NIE's understanding of governance

NIE originated in economics, with the attempt to radically extend the domain of neoclassical theory. It seeks to provide an economic theory of non-market institutions, which has facilitated the wider applicability of NIE's principles to analyse a wide variety of problems. However, it has been persuasively argued that NIE trots over the terrain of politics, but does not acknowledge it explicitly. In fact, Bates goes as far as to state that the 'new institutionalism is profoundly apolitical' (1995:46). This is indeed a worrying accusation and if it has foundation greatly limits the potential of NIE to inform debates on governance.

Bates's critique captures the principal problem with NIE succinctly. The new institutionalists suggest that people create institutions in an effort to move towards social optimum, the Pareto frontier. However, he views that such a theory is blunt as there is an 'infinite number of non-equivalent points in the Pareto set', and the theory does not make any distinction among these (1995:41). If institutions promote movements towards the Pareto frontier, then such moves also constitute public goods and therefore (as has been pointed out earlier), will be subject to the 'free-riding' problem. Bates contends, apropos Olson (1965) and others, that the supply of public goods, or the creation of institutions in this case, is contingent on the mobilisation of select incentives, such as coercion, or the exploitation of 'size effects', wherein large actors find it privately advantageous to incur the costs of providing public benefits. The first, 'implies the use of political power' and the second, 'implies the mobilisation of large interests', which is also connected with political power. Bates makes the case that the very institutions that support the attainment of efficient outcomes (by reducing transactions costs), not only create but also rest within unequal structures of power. Property rights, contract law, the power to regulate the production and exchange of commodities, all economic institutions that reduce the uncertainty in exchange, are created by the state in settings such as the legislature or the court room, where some actors are clearly more powerful than others. The types of institutions that are created thus depend on the structure of politics, explaining which requires political, not economic analysis (Bates, 1995:46).

The core emphasis in NIE is on choices, not on constraints, and thus, what is omitted from the accounts of NIE is that institutions are often imposed, not chosen, and that being backed by the power of the state, institutions provide the means whereby some individuals can and do benefit more than others. Although prominent theorists like North recognise that institutions are not created to be socially efficient and that at least, the formal rules are created to serve the interests of those with the bargaining power, politics and the state find no explicit treatment within the main works of new institutionalist economics. Other new institutionalists, prominently Williamson, have been less concerned with the issue of power, which is dismissed as a rather 'diffuse' concept (1996:238). This is problematic especially when it is considered that the core proposition of NIE – the creation of institutions – comprises fundamentally political elements. Thus, Bates reiterates that to fulfil its own agenda, NIE must move into the study of politics. It must 'take into account the allocation of political power in society and the impact of the political system on the structure and performance of economic institutions' (1995:44).

Omissions of the state in new institutionalist analysis have led to theoretical dilemmas of a second sort as well: how does the state figure in explanations for locally-initiated, community-level attempts at the formation of self-governing institutions? Theorists like Elinor Ostrom explored alternatives to 'externally-imposed' solutions of collective action, delineating systematically the theoretic conditions that could explain how certain collectivities could devise their own self-governing institutions when other collectivities could not. Her analysis represented a progression over that of communitarian theorists like Michael Taylor, who explored the conditions under which social order can be maintained in 'anarchy', i.e. without a state. Taylor (1982) ascribed three key characteristics to collectivities for them to qualify as 'community', which would then create conditions where individuals would find it rational to cooperate. First, commonality of beliefs and values that are shared, articulated and systematised; second, direct interpersonal relations that are unmediated by external agencies such as representatives or bureaucrats, or for that matter any institutions that belong to the state; and third, reciprocity, a term used to cover a range of arrangements, relations and exchanges, including mutual aid. These conditions, in effect, wished away the problem of collective action by creating ideal, utopian visions about community. Ostrom's approach was more realistic and pragmatic because she explicitly recognised the existence of nested rules at different levels, and acknowledged the importance of the external political regime on the 'operational rules' at the level of the community. Taylor, in his later work, modified his position somewhat by introducing the notion of 'political entre-preneurs' to justify state action where conditions of community, though existent, are weak. This explained the role of the state in situ-ations of revolutionary peasant collective action, such as the French, Chinese and Russian occurrences (Taylor, 1988, 1989). Taylor gen-eralised that in such cases, political entrepreneurs can assist in organ-ising collective action by facilitating conditional cooperation. This view in fact led to a benign view of the state, which facilitates col-lective action by prescribing conditions whereby communities are able to develop institutions endogenously.

Ostrom too has been attacked by those who consider that much like Taylor, she does not go beyond the 'benign' state form. Subir Sinha, in a detailed critique, argued the following, 'Posed as an alternative to statist and market based solutions to the "tragedy framework", Ostrom's formulation hides two paradoxes regarding the role of the state. Local institutional innovation seems impossible until resource users and the state are involved in one or both of two sorts of relation-ships, either of autonomy or recognised independence' (Sinha, 1990: Conclusion:7). In his own work, Sinha critiqued theorists of endo-genous institutional change, for 'being pre-occupied with collective action, they have neglected to read from the same examples the poten-tially adversarial relations between state actors and rural resource users' (1990:33). The enabling role of the state cannot be taken for granted, as communitarian theorists like Taylor do, and that the state is not a singular, neutral entity that must be recognised.

This issue has assumed critical importance particularly in studies of the governance of natural resources. In this field in particular, new institutionalist economics has been criticised for constituting a 'pre-dictive and generalising theory of the economic and collective insti-utions for collective action' (Mosse, 2003:274). A number of empirical studies have illustrated how the lack of proper emphasis on the state has yielded misleading interpretations of the capacities of local com-munities and their capacities to devise institutions 'endogenously'. These studies emphasise that the state and community are mutually constitu-tive concepts, and all too often, state power is asserted precisely through 'community control'. Further, critics hold that NIE analysis that projects all communities as similarly capable of self-sufficient cooperative behaviour, is based on examples of 'successful, long enduring arrangements of cooperative and sustainable resource use' to generalise conditions which may not hold in all cases (Sinha, 1990:34). Admittedly Ostrom cannot be held guilty of producing a generalising theory, for she argues that the capacities of individuals to cope with collective action dilemmas varies from one situation to another and it would therefore be wrong to simply assume that no self-organised collective action was ever possible (1990:14). However, extended applications of her analysis may be responsible for transposing an analytical framework into a generalising theory.

Conclusions

The new institutional economics has focused theoretical attention on the role of institutions in society. In addition, it contemplates tricky questions regarding the emergence and formation of institutions, which make it particularly relevant for policy-makers who are concerned with governance. As indicated by Williamson's useful distinction between the two levels of institutional analysis that NIE includes, governance is conceptualised both at the macro-level, as the larger institutional environment that prevails, and the micro-level, as the specific mechanisms of governance. At both these levels, NIE's proponents specifically consider the nature of institutional change and the extent to which it may be possible to deliberately reform or create 'new institutions'. For those interested in institutional reform for the sake of improving governance, which seems to be the principal concern today in fields ranging from the environment, to development, to the corporate sector, new institutionalist analysis performs an extremely pertinent role.

A useful way of differentiating between the nature of institutional change at the macro- and micro-levels is with respect to intentionality (Williamson, 1996:5). Broadly speaking, institutional change at the macro-level is explained by 'path dependence', which purports that although specific short-run institutional paths are unforeseeable, the overall direction of institutional change in the long run is both more predictable and harder to reverse. Thus, the immense difficulties of changing the institutional environment in order to promote economising outcomes in the aggregate helps explain North's conclusion that 'economic history is overwhelmingly a story of economies that failed'

(1990:98). At the micro-level however, Williamson (1996) argues that attempts to align the intentional actions of agents to desired outcomes has been more successful. Let us consider the larger implications of these views in turn.

North considers two important questions underlying social, political and economic change: first, what determines the divergent patterns of evolution of societies, polities or economies over time, and second, how do we account for the survival of economies with persistently poor performance over long periods of time (1990:92). His analysis rejects the market-driven natural selection explanation of long-run development. It stresses, by contrast, the limited information available to different groups and the diverse mental modelling of available information within different ideologies and cultures, which in turn generate their own institutional arrangements, including both organisations and social practices. He elaborates that in a world in which there are no increasing returns to institutions and markets are competitive, institutions do not matter. But with increasing returns, institutions matter. Further, North describes how the interdependent web of an institutional matrix produces massive increasing returns. As long as the consequent markets are competitive or even roughly approximate the zero transaction costs model, the long-run path is an efficient one. Given reasonably non-controversial assumptions about preferences, neither divergent paths nor persistently poor performance would prevail. But if the markets are incomplete, the information feedback is fragmentary at best, and transaction costs are significant, then the subjective models of actors modified both by very imperfect feedback and by ideology will shape the path. Then, not only can both divergent paths and persistently poor performance prevail, the historically derived perceptions of the actors shape the choice that they make. In a dynamic world, characterised by institutional increasing returns, the imperfect and fumbling efforts of the actors reflect the difficulties of deciphering a complex environment with the available mental constructs – ideas, theories and ideologies (North, 1990:95).

North's work triggered off other related works on path dependency, with the basic idea that the legacy of the past conditions our future. The key theoretical insight to emerge from the path dependency literature is that increasing returns experienced by the involved actors, keeps them along the same path; a vocal advocate of this notion, Pierson has shown how institutional arrangements in politics are particularly hard to change (2004, 2000a, 2000b, 2000c). He argues that unlike in the world of economics, any corrective measures are less likely to operate. The prospects for efficiency gains through learning and adaptation are limited because politics is a murky business where the judgement of success and failure lacks any universal measuring rod. Moreover, complexity makes learning problematic because it is difficult to discern which option is superior. Further, short-time horizons count against a radical shift in path as gains tend to be achieved in the long run and the costs are mostly felt in the short run. Finally, the widespread dominance of change-resistant institutions tend to lock in a *status-quo* bias. Pierson points out that there are two broad reasons why political institutions are designed to be change resistant: first, in many cases, designers seek to constrain themselves and secondly, more importantly, those who design institutions and policies may wish to bind their successors. This lack of continuous control has implications both for how institutions are designed and for the prospect of changing institutions once they are created.

The strand of new institutionalist economics that focuses on the macro-level institutional environment is thus relatively pessimistic about the possibility of intentional, designed institutional change. However, there are other strands within NIE that are more optimistic about institutional design. The principal-agent approach is a case in point. As discussed earlier, this approach uses contracting hazards to understand more generally how asymmetries of incentives amongst agents and principals impact the realisation of a collective outcome (such as profit). Thus, the principal-agent approach attempts to remedy certain aspects of neoclassical economic theory, which remained silent on how the owners of firms succeed in aligning the objectives of their various members, such as workers, supervisors and managers, with profit maximisation (Laffont and Martimort, 2002). Yet the approach is rooted within a rational choice account of political action, which suggests that political agents will act according to the incentives and constraints that are provided to them. More recent work in principal-agent theory suggests that principals can get the outcomes they want if they pay careful attention to design and its impact on discretion (Epstein and O'Halloran, 2002).

Ostrom's analysis, rooted firmly within the new institutionalist analysis, also illuminates the possibilities (albeit complex) of institutional design. Ostrom took exception to the prevailing belief that solutions to collective action problems amongst a group of agents could only be externally initiated, either through state centralisation and privatisation. Her analysis, rooted in empirical evidence, illustrates the conditions in which individuals would find it rational to cooperate to devise self-governing institutions. She provides a set of design principles, which if observed, would facilitate the process of designing and adopting new institutions. However, she warns that this is no easy task, and concludes that institutional change is hard to predict (1990:210). Nevertheless, Ostrom, views institutional design as a distinct method of bringing about institutional change; in which rational individuals are potentially free to choose options subject to knowledge of rewards and sanctions, as established within rules or adopted norms.

What NIE tells us is that any attempt to design social institutions occurs within the backdrop of a set of past practices, which brings with it its own peculiar constraints and possibilities. This observation, which links the macro and micro perspectives of NIE on institutional change, is perhaps the most important message that this field holds for policy-makers today. The dynamic for change comes from aligning incentives with norms and oversight in order to encourage actors to modify their behaviour in the desired direction. What is also vital is that the actors understand and accept the governance arrangements they are being asked to adopt and that they believe that others share that understanding. Predictability and credible commitment is what intentionally rational actors demand because then the tricky business of cooperation becomes more possible.

4
Governance and International Relations

This chapter examines the literature from International Relations (IR) in terms of its treatment of governance. There is an enormous variety of literature that takes a range of different theoretical and epistemological positions but shares in common a sense that globalisation is the driving force behind the growing interest in governance. It is the destabilising effects of globalisation that has created the governance response that is observed. The chapter opens with a review of the range of broad approaches to governance in the literature, all of which challenge the idea, previously dominant in IR and strongly associated with a realist position, that it is the battling and contesting interests of nation states that provide the only powerful dynamic of international politics.

Governance has become a central concern of the IR discipline. The emerging processes of globalisation in particular, have thrown up new issues regarding government, politics, inter-state relations and the global order. Most commentators on global governance agree on the primacy of globalisation as the essential context for analysis (Douglas, 1999; Lake, 1999; Haas, 1999; Payne, 2005; Prakash and Hart, 1999; Sandholtz, 1999; Wilkinson, 2002). The 'transnational' and indeed 'global' character of contemporary issues makes analysis difficult within the 'realist' framework that has dominated the discipline thus far. The world of IR is about more than the zero-sum contests of nation-states. It involves a range of other actors – international organisations, non-governmental bodies (NGOs), public-private agencies, and indeed, at the broadest level, civil society. The governance turn opens up the possibility of governing without government, or at least a recognition that nation states operate in a complex institutional environment in which their capacity for action is checked and balanced by power that is not held solely in the hands of other nation-states alone. For the IR literature the focus on governance, particularly 'global' governance, reflects many of the conceptual and methodological concerns of the discipline. Yet, there are significant differences of approach on the character of governance, its explanatory dynamics and its normative options. The aim of this chapter is to explore some of the richness of that literature.

The chapter has four main sections. First we explore some of the key literature that defines the scope and reach of the governance turn in the IR literature. We confirm that governance is strongly connected to globalisation and that these processes create a complex dynamic with often contradictory pressure for change. Second we examine some of the competing schools' understanding of the underlying dynamics of global governance, from the work of rational choice institutionalists, to insights from those that take a more constructivist position. A third section looks at the understanding of power relationships embedded in governance within the IR literature by exploring the standing of state power in an era of global governance, the fairness of the global architecture of governance and the hegemony of neoliberalism in practical, if not academic, debates. The fourth section offers some broader reflections on key debates in the literature. The conceptual and methodological divisions in approach are evident, but we argue that together, different perspectives provide insights into what is a developing arena of global governance. On a more normative tack the key debates reflect concerns about whether the emerging system of global governance is capable of displaying some semblance of order and subjecting itself to democratic direction in some form.

A governance turn?

Conceptualisations of governance, and global governance, are striking in their sheer breadth and have been criticised in IR, as in other fields, for being 'loose' and 'vague' (Payne, 2005; Smouts, 1998). In the early 1990s, James Rosenau offered the earliest definition of governance in the field of IR. In his classic work *Governance without Government* (co-edited with Ernest-Otto Czempiel), Rosenau defined governance as 'a set of regulation mechanisms in a sphere of activity, which function effectively even though they are not endowed with formal authority' (1992:5). He distinguished governance from government in that 'it refers to activities backed by shared goals that may or may not derive from legal and formally prescribed responsibilities and that do not necessarily rely on police powers to overcome defiance and attain compliance' (1992:4). Rosenau's early definition of governance came under fire for excluding nothing. However, his critics were unable to provide convincing definitions of governance either. Lawrence S. Finklestein suggested that 'Global governance is governing, without sovereign authority, relationships that transcend national frontiers' (Finklestein, 1995; as cited in Smouts, 1998:82). Smouts comments that this definition is hardly more focused and succinct than that offered by Rosenau but she and other critics in the end argue that the governance turn in the IR literature has brought new issues into focus.

The governance literature in IR carries a number of important messages. The first is that globalisation begets governance processes of considerable complexity and ambiguity. The second is that beyond nation-states there is a whole array of actors and institutions involved in global governance. The third is that nation-states have had to change their behaviour in the light of global governance.

Rosenau's definition of governance, although broad, did tie the concept to the whole global order (Payne, 2005). This was a significant advance over previous attempts to understand government at the global level, principally rationalist studies of regime formation, inspired by the work of Robert Keohane (1984). These studies had concluded that states could learn to cooperate in non-zero-sum ways, if they formed intergovernmental institutions, or regimes, in particular policy areas. By taking the idea of governance beyond states, Rosenau had set the ground for creative understandings of the global order within the IR discipline. Rosenau's image of the global world is one where different creative forces stand in tension with one another. He is critical of the limits of IR theorising because of its narrow focus on the behaviour of states and argues instead for a focus on 'politics on a global scale' (Rosenau, 2000:171). The dynamics of that politics is driven by processes of change and considerable complexity. Ambiguity and even contradiction appears to be a central feature of the processes of global politics in the shadow of governance. The most noticeable of these dialectic processes according to Rosenau (2000:177) is 'the simultaneity of dynamics promoting integration, centralization and globalization on the one hand, and those generating disintegration, decentralization, and localization on the other hand'. Pressures lead at the same time to the search for global solutions to global problems and at the same time a greater recognition of the specific character and qualities of citizens in different parts of the globe that demand specific and tailored responses. The ambiguity of the environmentalist slogan 'think global, act local' is a reflection of a wider set of tensions in the way societies are being challenged that Rosenau (2000:177) refers to as 'fragmegration' to capture that processes of fragmentation and integration can be observed at the same time.

For IR theorists the idea of governance has mainly centred on its 'global' dimension. Yet, the discipline's realist orthodoxy 'remains wedded to an understanding of world politics that perceives states as the most significant actors, and attributes little to the role of international organisations or non-state actors' (Wilkinson, 2002:1). Rorden Wilkinson remarks that although there is much to be learnt about global governance through developments in international organisation, the former has at least two distinctive aspects. The first is a recognition that it comprises an 'array of actors', not only those 'visible aspects of world political-economic authority' like the UN, WTO, IMF and the World Bank (WB), but also quasi-formal intergovernmental gatherings such as the Group of 7 (G7) and the World Economic Forum (WEF); combinations of state and non-state actors such as the ILO; mercenary groups like Sandine International; non-governmental organisations like WWF and Oxfam; transnational religious bodies, political movements, financial markets and others. The second distinguishing feature is 'the way in which varieties of actors are increasingly combining to manage – and in many cases, micro-manage – a growing range of political, economic and social affairs' (Wilkinson, 2002:2). In these respects, the global governance 'approach' has identified some of the ways in which IR appear increasingly to be conducted outside the realist model.

Murphy (2000) takes a strong line when it comes to the alphabet soup of organisations that now populate the world of global governance. He argues that some have gained power and some have lost, and that overall there is no evidence of a transfer of power from nation states to international organisations. But what we have seen is the growth of 'global-level "private" authorities that regulate both states, and much of transnational economic and social life' (Murphy, 2000:794). These agencies include private bond-rating agencies and global institutions for reinsurance, accounting, and high-level consulting. These organisations frame what it is that both public and private actors can do. There are also global and regional cartels in industries as diverse as mining, electrical products, computer software and internet suppliers. Organisations such as Microsoft and Google are able to muster as much power and certainly more organisational resources and wealth than many nation states according to this line of argument. Further, suggests Murphy, there is the hegemonic power of economists who establish and maintain a dominant wisdom about the way that economies should be run. These private power blocs are joined by an array of regulators that oversee international markets and trading. These regulators are often pushed to impose 'global' standards so that all producers face the same social, environmental and labour add-ons as those that come from the more developed and regulated economies. On the more social side the pressure to do something globally is also encouraged by a range of non-governmental organisations that have done a lot over recent years to promote particular causes and interests.

Geoffrey Underhill (2000) emphasises the need to conceptualise how states are embedded in increasingly transnational social structures and how key socio-economic constituencies of non-state actors are integrated into the institutional processes of states within the International Political Economy (IPE) approach. Further, his argument is based on the premise that 'IPE is not an offshoot of traditional International Relations, but as rooted in the broad tradition of political economy which emerged in the European enlightenment' (Underhill, 2000:807). He underscores the contingent and dynamic relationship between political authority and markets as the key issue concerning political economy. Both the liberal and realist positions (the first privileges the market as the organising principle of the world political economy and the second advocates that politics, centred around states, will dominate economic processes) appear limited in his analysis. Instead, Underhill adopts an historical approach to highlight how the growing interdependence amongst nations since the 1960s rested on interlocking relationships between the economic and political domains, an aspect unduly disregarded within IR. The distinctiveness of IPE as a discipline from IR derives from the recognition of such interdependence. IPE therefore has a crucial role in analysing global economic transformations with their concomitant implications for global governance.

Strange (1995, 1996) leads a more explicit charge in recognising the way that globalisation has changed the context for states so fundamentally that they have had to change their behaviour and character. Although in the past nation-states competed over territory and the resources to be found in them now they compete over trade and share of the global economic market. Strange (1995:60) argues that as 'a direct consequence of this largely economic competition, the nature of states and their behavior has changed, I mean that industrial policy and trade policy are becoming more important than defence and foreign policy. States are obliged by structural change to seek commercial allies rather than military ones. Some of these allies will be other states, as in regional economic associations. Others will be foreign-owned firms. States are not powerless or entirely ineffective in the context of this competition. But there is a developing consensus, according to Strange (1995:65) that:

> the state is coming to share authority in economy and society with other entities. These include, in my interpretation, not only trans-national companies (TNCs), including banks, accounting and law firms, and international institutions like the International Monetary Fund (IMF) or Inmarsat, but also non-governmental organizations like Amnesty International or the Olympic sports organization and transnational professional associations of doctors, economists, and scientists. Within the state the authority of central government is, perforce, increasingly shared with local and regional authorities. The proposition, in short, is that state authority has leaked away, upwards, sideways, and downwards.

As a consequence 'tacit premises about the state as the most important unit of analysis, in that much of Western social science, is obsolescent, if not yet quite out-of-date' (Strange, 1995:61).

The demand has emerged for a new form of governance in the light of the idea the state has 'hallowed out' or is in some form of power deficit. Marie-Claude Smouts (1998:86), notwithstanding her scept-icism about the general and loose way in which governance literature has developed, argues that its most valuable insight is the way it brings into focus the way that nation states and other actors are having to learn 'new techniques for managing joint affairs'. This insight is seen as having been borrowed from the early studies in governance from public policy that focused on networks, partnership and forms of coor-dination that did not rely on the use of authority and hierarchy. Global politics has patterns of governance that resemble those in operation in local and national settings. Smouts (1998) values a 'governance approach' that seeks to give social visibility to actors who are often ignored within the literature of realism and neorealism, she is critical of the ways in which the governance discourse 'disregards the fight to the death, the phenomenon of outright domination and the problems that arise from the ungovernability of whole sections of international society' (Smouts, 1998:88). Focus on partnership and joint working should not lead ana-lysts to neglect the harder-edged aspects of global governance.

A further correction to a naïve adoption of governance understanding is presented by Drezner (2007). He argues that despite globalisation, states

– particularly the great powers of the United States and the European Union – still dominate international regulatory regimes so much so that the goals and policies of these regimes are driven by the domestic interests of the great powers. Moreover the positive engagement of these 'major powers' is central to the successful operation of a global regulatory regime. If they agree then a strong form of regulation emerges and if they are divided then at best only a weak form of regulatory governance can emerge. In short global regulation is driven by powerful regional blocs such as the United States or Europe. When the 'great powers' agree you can get harmonised standards and where they do not, you get sham standards. Governance is driven by power and not the search for a consensus among all state and non-state players. Moreover when discussing state power in relation to global governance it is essential to remember that some states are considerably more powerful than others.

The institutions and structures of global governance

Global governance is now the central focus of work in IR and the related sub-discipline of IPE. But there are different explanations of how the institutions of global governance came about and how global governance is structured. The principal dialogue in this respect has been between the institutionalists and the constructivists. An institutionalist perspective in this reading views human behaviour as rational or consequence driven. Rational behaviour means that individuals assess the costs and benefits prior to action. The central assertion of new institutionalism is that institutions affect behaviour by altering the incentives facing actors. Importantly, institutions are viewed as human artefacts that can be established, strengthened, weakened or abolished (Prakash and Hart, 1999:27). Constructivists, in contrast, take the view that it is the meaning that actors give to action that also explains that action and a dominant challenge for the analyst is to understand the different perspectives and interpretations that are at play in exchanges between actors.

David Lake (1999) deploys a new institutionalist perspective to equate governance with contracting. 'It is the design, construction and maintenance of mechanisms to enforce agreed upon behaviours that lies at the heart of contracting, as a process, and governance, as both an analytic concept and the set of mechanisms actually employed' (Lake, 1999:33). In Lake's understanding therefore, organising collective action involves two analytically distinct processes: bargaining and contracting. Bargaining divides the available costs and benefits between actors, while contracting enforces the bargains that have been reached. The crux of governance, for Lake, lies in contracting. Further, since central to contracting is the right to residual control, hierarchies emerge whenever this residual control is lodged in only one party to a contract (Prakash and Hart, 1999:25).

This conception of governance has at least three implications for our understanding of IR. First, governance is not equivalent to government or formal institutions. Second, governance is a variable. Anarchy, which vests residual rights in states, is but one form of international governance; hierarchy is a second form and there are mixed types in between. The location of governance structures on the anarchical-hierarchical continuum is a function of three variables: scale economies, expected costs of opportunism and governance or agency costs. However, any cooperative endeavour can be undermined by the fear of opportunistic behaviour; that the other actor will manipulate the contract to its advantage. The cost of opportunistic behaviour varies with the relation-specificity of assets. Though hierarchies are expected to mitigate the costs of opportunism, they suffer from governance costs due to principle-agent conflicts (agency costs). Hence, the location of any governance structure on the hierarchy-anarchy continuum reflects the efficient trade-off between governance costs on the one hand, and the potential gains from cooperation and lowering costs of opportunism on the other. Finally, global governance is not limited to contracts between states. Other actors like NGOs and MNCs play an important role as well (Lake, 1999:36–43).

Finally, Lake suggests that globalisation processes have been facilitated by specific kinds of governance structures of early industrialisers, particularly Britain and the United States. These *laissez-faire* economies were characterised by large numbers of small private actors with non-specific assets and the liberal order vested substantial residual rights in them. The domestic governance structures of the early industrialising states first created spheres of private activity and then, by virtue of their hegemony, helped generalise these spheres to the international arena. Lake considers these private actors to be the prime movers of globalisation, integrating markets and societies, breaking the constraints of space and time, and erasing local variations. He then puts forward his principal counterfactual position: There are powerful vested interests that gain from this governance structure, and in turn globalisation. While globalisation might appear to require new governance structures, there are important sources of inertia that thwart efforts to construct greater hierarchy at the global level. Somewhat paradoxically therefore, were more hierarchical forms of supranational governance to emerge, such structures would undermine anarchy, the main condition facilitating this process. He concludes, 'Far from being mutually reinforcing, globalisation and global governance may well stand opposed to one another' (Lake, 1999:48).

Michael McGinnis (1999) also employs a new institutionalist perspective to reach slightly different conclusions. His basic premise is that any conceptualisation of governance needs to be broken down into its constituent service components. Corresponding to the three basic human needs of wealth, physical security, and emotional attachment, he identifies three realms of collective action: economic-productive, coercive-protective and social-communal. The fourth realm – political-governance – provides services for coordinating the other three realms. His important insight is that no single realm can solve its collective action dilemmas by itself. In the Hobbesian conception of a state, all four realms are concentrated within a single organisational structure, the Leviathan. This is also a basic premise of the Westphalian system. By challenging this monopolisation, McGinnis considers that globalisation processes force changes in existing governance structures.

McGinnis also identifies two elements of the costs of maintaining a governance organisation: start up costs in establishing new organisations and the governance costs to which Lake alludes in his writing. According to McGinnis however, for any governance system to survive in the long run, it must build legitimacy. This is often done by redistributing some of the gains of collective action from winners to losers. Globalisation processes, with their emphasis on quick changes in production technologies and increased exposure to foreign trade, will create many losers in the domestic economy. As a result, institutionalised mechanisms for redistribution are required to maintain legitimacy. The existing institutions of governance, particularly the state, may be better placed to provide such redistributive services than any new ones. He feels that even though such extant institutions may not minimise governance costs, they may be better placed for providing redistributive services due to their lower start-up costs. As a result, such institutions are well placed to survive the onslaught of the processes of globalisation (Prakash and Hart, 1999:27).

In contrast to the new institutionalist perspective on globalisation and global governance, in which agents are 'ontologically superior' to structures, is the constructivist perspective where individuals and structures have equal ontological status. Wayne Sandholtz (1999) is critical of the new institutionalists for taking as given the social and institutional foundations of 'interests' and 'utility'. Constructivists assert that actors have interests or goals only in the context of social relations that produce shared meanings and values. Thus, for Sandholtz, institutions are much more than bargaining forums where utility-maximizing states with autonomous preferences construct arrangements for minimising transaction costs. He goes on to offer a rule-based conception of governance and international institutions, whereby rule structures or institutions are a fundamental and pervasive feature of IR. Rules provide the context in which actors conceive of their interests and delineate ranges of justifiable action in pursuit of their interests. Sandholtz considers governance to be the process by which rules are generated. Governance, thus defined, can include both formal organisations that authoritatively establish and enforce rules, as well as patterned social interactions that produce shared rules without the formal structures of government (Sandholtz, 1999:80–90).

Sandholtz elaborates how globalisation promotes the development of transnational society and consequently, the elaboration of transnational rules, public and private, formal and informal. Rules that emerge in response to globalisation will be elaborations of, or modelled after, existing rules. As rule structures become increasingly articulated, they begin to sustain normative discourses that define and redefine the meaning of the rules, and thus the bounds of warranted behaviour. As rule systems become more elaborate, they start to resemble legal systems, with an accompanying tendency towards formalisation. Thus, if globalisation continues, some international rule systems will become increasingly codified and will gradually develop specific organisations for managing rules and resolving disputes. In Sandholtz's analysis, contrary to that of Lake, globalisation and global governance are not antithetical to one another.

Peter Haas (1999) also pursues a constructivist methodology to explain the evolution of the international governance system. It consists of deductively identifying the possible consequences of ideas on practice, specifying a credible mechanism linking new ideas to changes in practices, combined with a process tracing to determine if the hypothesised change occurred through the proposed mechanisms. He directs his analysis to a particular issue area of international governance: the evolution of multi-lateral environmental governance. Haas argues that the institutionalisation of a new ecological perspective embodying norms, rules and strategies was articulated by ecological epistemic communities and disseminated through formal governance institutions.

Epistemic communities are 'networks of professionals who share common normative and causal beliefs, accept common truth tests, and are engaged in a common policy enterprise' (1999:28). In the absence of epistemic communities, governance in IR is primarily state centred. However, in environmental governance, there is a powerful global epistemic community that holds governments accountable to new standards of environmental behaviour. Consequently, a relatively stable set of expectations has been established that is becoming more comprehensive over time.

Constructivists and new institutionalists therefore remain poised at very different ends of the debate on global governance: while constructivists have been effective at problematising extant institutions, they have not posed a theory of why certain alternatives are chosen or constructed as new institutionalists have attempted to do. Their respective emphases on structure and agency (individuals) have differed accordingly, with constructivists emphasising the contingent relationships between rule structures (interpreted as institutions) and the individual agency; and new institutionalists privileging the individual agency in the formation of institutions.

Although there is disagreement on the origins of global governance, there is greater consensus on its evolutionary and changing character. Wilkinson comments, 'It is premature to speak of the existence of a complete and fully coherent system of global governance. Global governance is better understood as emerging' (2002:2–3). Further, as outlined earlier, the explanatory focus of the discipline is devoted to capturing its evolutionary nature. While new institutionalists attempt to understand why actors choose certain institutional paths not others, constructivists endeavour to analyse the structural factors that influence the actions of actors.

Understanding of power relationships

There are three main issues concerning power relationships in governance within the IR literature: first, the standing of state power in the context of globalisation and global governance; second, the fairness of the global architecture of governance; and third, the hegemony of Anglo-American ideology, principally neoliberalism, over globalisation. We will discuss these in turn.

State power through global governance

The hegemony of neoliberalism bears a critical impact on perceptions of the role of the state in the era of globalisation and global governance.

Indeed, the relationship between globalisation and the state has been the subject of fierce debate (Evans, 1997; Mann, 1997; Strange, 1996). As we saw earlier, Strange (1996, 1995) offers an account that suggests that state power has become dispersed but not diminished entirely. The state has 'hallowed out' or developed a deficit in its capacities but as other writers are quick to point out the state remains an influential actor in global governance.

Michael Mann (1997) puts forth four theses on what supposedly undermines the nation state: first, capitalism, now global, transnational, postindustrial, informational, consumerist, neoliberal and restructured, is undermining the nation-state; second, new global limits, especially environmental and population threats, producing perhaps a 'risk' society, have become too broad and menacing to be handled by the nation-state alone; third, identity politics and new social movements, using new technology, have increased the salience of diverse local and transnational identities at the expense of both national identities and those broad class identities which were previously handled by the nation-state alone; and fourth, post-nuclearism which undermines state sovereignty and 'hard geopolitics' since mass mobilisation warfare that underpinned much of modern state expansion is now irrational (Mann, 1997:473–474). Peter Evans (1966a, 1966b) observes how developments such as the pre-eminence of TNCs, a radically globalised financial system and contingency of strategic alliances with those who control global production for access to capital and technology certainly contribute to the perceived evaporation of state authority.

In their respective works however, Mann and Evans convincingly argue that the state continues not only to be relevant, but central, to the processes of globalisation and global governance. Mann (1997) counters each of the four theses on the declining influence of state institutions, and demonstrates that state institutions, both domestic and geopolitical still have causal efficacy because they do provide the necessary conditions for social existence, especially the regulation of those aspects of social life that are distinctively 'territorially centred'. He also directs attention to the variations between states, which fundamentally shape how unevenly globalisation unfolds in different parts of the world. Mann concludes emphatically, 'We must beware of the more enthusiastic of the globalists and transnationalists. With little sense of history they exaggerate the former strength of nation states, with little sense of global variety, they exaggerate their current decline and with little sense of their plurality, they downplay international relations' (1997:494).

Evans (1997) uses the case of East Asia to demonstrate the possibility of a positive connection between 'high stateness' and success in a globalising economy. Moreover, he points out that private transnational actors, however pre-eminent, need competent, capable states in order to achieve their goals and preserve their returns. Evans astutely observes, 'While globalisation does make it harder for states to exercise economic initiative, it also increases both the potential returns from effective state action and the costs of incompetence'. This emphasis is reflected in the theoretical development of new institutional economics (NIE), which advances over neoclassical economics, in its explicit consideration of imperfect market situations and emphasis on the pervasive importance of non-market institutional frameworks. Evans concludes that in the light of historical evidence that the state continues to play a dominant role in globalisation and global governance therefore, the 'currently pervasive belief that the institutional centrality of the state is incompatible with globalisation must be explained in terms of the ideological face of the current global order'. This viewpoint has ample support within the literature. Political scientists Martha Finnemore and John Ruggie for instance, recognise that despite the real diffusion of power above and below the state, powerful states remain the most significant sites of consolidated power over people and territory in the contemporary world (Murphy, 2000).

Despite the apparent hegemony of the neoliberal ideology that downplays the centrality of the state in global governance, there is growing support for the notion that governance involves positive sum relationships between the state and other non-state actors, both from the market and civil society (Evans, 1997). The definitional framework for global governance offered by Wilkinson (2002) and others explicitly mentions the myriad novel ways in which 'varieties of actors' are increasingly combining to manage a growing range of political, economic and social affairs. This approach is not without precedent – Robert Keohane's paradigmatic work (1984) advanced thinking on how states could form intergovernmental regimes in order to pursue non-zero sum games – and the global governance literature has further attempted to free itself from the dominant realist orthodoxy of the IR discipline.

However, this positive sum view of power within the global governance literature has come under scathing attack. Ian Douglas (1999) adopts a Foucauldian view of power to present an acutely critical analysis of global governance. In particular, he examines the official discourse of the Commission on Global Governance, which constitutes a seemingly timeless and benign view of governance as human evolution. 'The development of global governance is a part of the evolution of human efforts to organise life on the planet, and that process will always be going on. Our work is no more than a transit stop on that journey' (Commission on Global Governance, 1995:xvi). Douglas draws from Karl Popper's earlier warning against the tyranny of any political discourse that claims to be riding a tide of inevitability to argue that the Commission's discourse conceals the real intervention of power that continues to transform people's lives. He objects to the masking of what he calls a 'disciplinary governance' not only as positive, but also predestined (Douglas, 1999:134).

Douglas's key propositions are as follows. He contests a view of the state as 'defective' and 'hollowing out' as currently dominant within discussions of globalisation and global governance (refer to Strange, 1996; Cerny, 1996). He adopts instead key insights offered by Foucault's historical studies. In essence, Foucault described the simultaneous 'spatialisation' and 'deterritorialisation' of political government throughout the course of modernity. In the first instance, government widens its reach, intervening in an ever greater number of spaces, and on the other hand, government becomes integral, diffused at the level of the social body as a whole. Douglas also cites Paul Virilio (1995), whose work is a more focused description of the 19th and 20th century of moving, and its correspondence with political technology and the genealogy of governance. For Virilio then, as for Foucault, the aims of modern political technology are clear; to make mobile the citizenry within the parameters of order, reason and tranquillity.

Following this approach, Douglas goes on to rethink globalisation as governance. He argues that the contemporary dissolution of the face of government (institutional fragmentation, dispersion of state authority, diminishing policy autonomy and so on) says nothing of the longer history of diffusion that lies at the heart of modern rational order. He demonstrates how the disappearance of the state has run parallel with the ascendance of new modalities of governance based on the positive constitution of individuals themselves. He suggests therefore 'that the birth of bio-power at the level of subjectivity is the rightful precursor of the globalisation of the state' (Douglas, 1999:152). Conceiving 'governance' as 'diffusion' and 'diffusion' as 'civic security', Douglas argues that 'globalisation actually extends, rather than fragments, state ordered power'. He clarifies that this form of 'government' cannot be reduced instrumentally to the actions of institutions. The notion of power thus, as Foucault reflects, 'is greatly impoverished if posed solely in terms of legislation, or the constitution, or the state, or the state apparatus. Power is much more complicated, much more dense and diffuse than a set of laws of a state apparatus. One cannot understand the development of the productive forces of capitalism, nor even conceive of their technological development, if the apparatuses of power are not taken into consideration' (Foucault, 1996:235). In thinking of globalisation *as* governance, Douglas concludes that a 'simple distinction between diffusion (anarchy) and centralisation (authority)' as drawn by commentators like Susan Strange and Phillip Cerny, 'simply misreads the history of the modern state and the genealogy of modern power' (1999:153).

What can be concluded is that state power has not gone away although decision-making capacity may be more widely dispersed than before. Perhaps even more crucially some states are more equal than others in the context of governance and a new global order. Developing a framework offered by Cox (1981) Payne (2007) suggests that a mix of constraints and opportunities are created for states by three factors: their material resources and capacities, their ability to provide dominate ideas and ways of understanding and their privileged position or otherwise in a range of international institutions. On the last point the next section develops the argument further but Payne's key argument is that international organisations and the dominance of systems such as the now regular G7/8 summits lead to some countries having more influence than others. The result is a complex pattern of structured inequalities. Some countries enjoy advantages along all three dimensions. 'What is apparent is that ideational and institutional power is being used by a number of leading countries...to entrench still further the dominance they enjoy' (Payne, 2007:7).

Fairness of the global architecture of governance

What Paul Cammack has recently dubbed a 'global architecture of governance' reflects the uneven power relationships that underpin the globalisation process as a whole (Cammack, 2002). The neoliberal ideological consensus described below cloaks the functioning of the most powerful of public institutions: the IMF, WB and the WTO being the foremost among these. The dominant discourse of global governance is deeply grounded within liberal institutionalism, a theory that rests on the fundamental premise of neutral and fair public institutions (Payne, 2005). There is however, profound scepticism regarding the ability of the institutions of global governance to manage globalisation in favour of the growing numbers of the world's poor. Craig Murphy comments,

'Global governance is likely to remain inefficient, incapable of shifting resources from the world's wealthy to the world's poor, pro-market and relatively insensitive to the concerns of labour and the rural poor' (2000:789). He argues that the IMF, WB and WTO have through their promotion of unregulated economic globalisation contributed to the growing numbers of the world's poor. The point about how private transnational interests gain from the existing governance structures and resist more stringent regulation has been made variously (Cammack, 2002; Lake, 1999; Murphy, 2000).

Paul Cammack (2002) has turned a critical lens to the functioning of the WB, and to its recently launched 'Comprehensive Development Framework' (CDF) in particular. Contrary to the discourse of inclusive ownership central to the CDF, Cammack argues that the CDF is a vehicle for global governance managed and coordinated by the Bank. He demonstrates that the CDF is absolutely rigid in the set of macroeconomic disciplines it imposes. It is presented as a vehicle for incorporating social and structural policies to country governments, so that they reinforce and extend macroeconomic discipline, while subordinating them to the imperatives of capitalist accumulation. Rather than the emergence of a meaningful process of reform, Cammack sees in the CDF the 'consolidation of a finely tuned, multifaceted system of governance that extends from the corridors of the WB down to the nooks and crannies of local life' (Wilkinson, 2002:6). His vision of developmental governance is of a system coordinated by the WB that is intimate in its intrusion and acutely hierarchical in structure.

There are at the same time, important voices of dissent that see a radical and progressive change in the decision-making structures of the global economy. Randall Germain (2002) examining the reform of the (much maligned) international financial architecture regards that a 'significant turn' has been made in the understanding of what constitutes good governance in global finance. It consists in inclusive decision-making structures which provide mechanisms not only for the creation of international standards and processes, but which also allow a certain flexibility in how those standards are interpreted so that emerging market economies can work towards them without being unduly penalised. This means most importantly, recognising that different balances between public responsibility and private gain that will need to be struck across economies with different needs and development trajectories. It also consists in a decision-making structure, which can begin to address the distributional distortions consequent upon the core-periphery divide within the global financial system.

The hegemony of neoliberalism

The processes of globalisation, which serve as the essential context for global governance, are underpinned by the hegemony of the Anglo-American ideology, principally neoliberalism (Cox, 1981, 1983, 1996). Robert Cox's seminal contribution to IR and IPE was to expose the ideological face of governance. He writes, 'There is a transnational process of consensus formation among the official caretakers of the global economy. This process generates consensual guidelines, underpinned by an ideology of globalisation, that are transmitted into the policy-making channels of national governments and big corporations. Part of this consensus formation takes place through unofficial forums like the Trilateral Commission, the Bilderberg Conferences, or the more esoteric Mont Pelerin Society. Part of it goes on through official bodies like the OECD, the Bank for International Settlements, the IMF and the G7. These shape the discourse within which policies are defined, the terms and concepts that circumscribe what can be thought and done' (Cox, 1996:301). Payne wholeheartedly endorses Cox's analysis, 'It is no revelation to say that the leading discourse to have been shaped in this way over the past two decades has been neoliberalism...It embraces within its orbit not only a series of practical stances towards markets, taxes, investments and the like, but also more tangible matters like attitudes, values and styles, including those pertaining to modes of governing' (Payne, 2005).

Payne (2005) makes a helpful distinction that could be applied to the governance literature in IR and beyond between 'projects of governance' and 'theories of governance'. The latter are the dominant focus of this book and reflect largely academic attempts to understand and explain emerging new forms of governance. The latter refer to conscious attempts to proselytise particular ways to organise social and economic relations. The key proselytising literatures deal with respectively public management, good governance and global governance and the first two of these are dealt with in Chapters 2 and 5 respectively. Earlier in this chapter reference was made in critical terms to the Commission on Global Governance (1995). Payne's view on the Commission is considerably more positive than that taken by our Foucauldian-inspired author Douglass (1999). Payne's position is that the Commission is to be congratulated because it sought to explicitly challenge a neoliberal agenda and suggest that public, private and civic actors, working together, could tackle global issues of concern. According to the Commission on Global Governance:

> Governance is the sum of the many ways individuals and institutions, public and private, manage their common affairs. It is a continuing process through which conflicting or diverse interests can be accommodated and cooperative action may be taken. It includes formal institutions and regimes empowered to enforce compliance, as well as informal arrangements that people and institutions either have agreed to or perceive to be in their interest....At the global level, governance has been viewed primarily as intergovernmental relationships, but it must now be understood as also involving non-governmental organizations, citizens' movements, multinational corporations and the global market. Interacting with these are global mass media of dramatically enlarged influence (Commission on Global Governance, 1995:2–3; cited in Payne, 2005:60).

Payne argues that the Commission's aim was to reject the neoliberal view that there is nothing to be done in the face of the dynamic market forces of globalisation and to argue instead that through concerted action by state, civil society and business issues such as the imbalance of trade between North and South could be addressed. As Payne notes, although many (broadly social democratic) reform proposals of the Commission generally fell by the wayside, the Commission is not alone is trying to challenge neoliberal assumptions about the direction of global governance.

Main themes for debate: global democracy or anarchy?

The emergence of global governance encouraged a number of debates that are often left unresolved. In addition we examine some of the connecting underlying elements of normative debate attached to the governance turn in IR.

Conceptual debates unresolved

The principal methodological issue for contention is simply whether there is anything to be gained by the IR discipline from the 'progression' of concepts, from multi-lateralism to transnationalism to global governance. Despite a vigorous defence of the global governance concept by its proponents, scepticism regarding its analytical properties continues. But this chapter takes the side of the optimists who see that the governance debate, although it has its confusions and limitations, has offered IR a way into analysis that is valuable and original. The governance turn, as in other disciplines, has been an opportunity for a rich range of interventions from a range of epistemological positions, leading to competing interpretations that all in very different ways, make a contribution, at least as far as Murphy (2000:996) is concerned, given his argument that 'different schools ...seem to have different parts of the overall puzzle as to why we have what we have'. Although perhaps he also laments perhaps no one has yet found a way of putting the different insights together in an effective way.

There are three principal conceptual themes for debate around governance that traverse the IR discipline. The first concerns the role of the state in global governance. There is little concurrence on the extent to which the state continues to be explanatorily useful as a unit of analysis in global governance. This issue is tied in with vehement disagreements regarding the ideological biases of global governance. Does it spell the end of the state or rather a way of western neoliberal values coming to dominate globally?

The second has to do with the causal relationships between globalisation and global governance. While the majority of IR theorists consider globalisation to be the essential context for the evolution of global governance, there are dissenting voices that regard global governance and globalisation as sharing antithetical relations. Still it is difficult to consider the governance turn within IR without recognising how the discourse of globalisation has at a minimum opened the way to different schools of thought about global governance.

The third relates to the potential of global governance to alter the 'northern bias' of global power relations. Amidst widespread cynicism in the unfairness of the global architecture of governance, there is also a sizeable constituency of theorists who believe in the increasingly radical and progressive interpretations of global governance. But here we are straying into more normative territory.

Normative debates: world order and democracy

There is a strong normative dimension in the governance literature in IR. Typically as in other spheres of governance debate analysts are interested in not only how the world works but whether in some respects it could be made to work 'better'. There are several debates within the literature but two of the most dominant focus on the issues of the nature of world order and the potential to 'democratise' global governance.

Given the fluidity and ambiguities of global governance in the context of globalisation some express a fear that has long been at the heart of IR literature, namely that there is a lack of order or even anarchic flavour to the dynamics of governing. Strange (1995:66) captures this sense of fear about a world that is beyond control:

> (W)here is that authority to come from, if we agree that the centrifugal process of diffusion of authority away from the state is unlikely to be reversed. The diffusion is no problem in itself. It only becomes a problem if, in the process of dispersion of power, there are tasks that someone should do and no one, no institution nor association, does. Functionalists, old and new, put faith in the professionals, in technocrats and bureaucrats who they believed might be more attentive to the public interest, less swayed by personal interest. The experience of bureaucracies in international organizations, and notably in the European Commission in Brussels, hardly sustains their faith. But could better systems of accountability and probity be devised?

It would seem unwise to expect there to be an orderliness in world affairs. It is an arena where the observer must expect a degree of turbulence and occasionally chaos but it is possible to see a number of ways forward.

Some take a route that suggests a degree of utopian thinking. George Monbiot (2003) in *The Age of Consent: A Manifesto for a New World Order*, argues for a democratically elected world government, with in-built privileges and access for the world's poorest countries. He argues for four main changes to global governance. These include: a democratically elected world parliament; a democratically-controlled United Nations General Assembly to replace the unelected UN Security Council; an 'International Clearing Union' which would automatically discharge trade deficits and prevent the accumulation of debt; and a fair trade organisation which would regulate world trade in a way that protects the economies of poorer countries. What is far from clear in this discussion is how such a set of changes could be brought about.

As David Held (2004) points out problem-solving at the global level is beset with a range of difficulties. First the existing institutions of global governance are fragmented, have mandates that frequently compete. For example the goals of the WB in terms of health and social policies are not the same as those as the World Health Organization or The United Nations' organisation UNESCO or the International Labour Organization. The G7 group of advance industrial economies might be clear about its economic and social aims but they are often very different from those of the G77, the coalition of southern developing states. A second problem is that global institutions often lack a capacity to act. The result too often is an 'inability to mount collective problem-solving solutions faced with disagreement over means, objectives, costs and so no' (Held, 2004:95) A third major difficulty is the accountability deficit surrounding the institutions and the scale of power imbalances between nation-states and then between states and non-state organisations. The reform agenda would have to grapple with each of these challenges. Global governance needs to be structured in order to encourage more effective and coordinated international organisations. It needs to develop the capacity to act more effectively and globally and it should be driven the principle of inclusivity; to give all stakeholders a locked-in part in decision-making processes. For Held (2004:100), a commitment to inclusiveness and subsidiarity means that 'those whose life expectancy and life chances are significantly affected by social forces and processes ought to have a stake in the determination of the conditions and regulation of these, either directly or indirectly through political representatives'.

As Murphy (2000) comments, the best arguments for reforming global governance may be those derived from a moral or ethical standpoint but the world governance that we have remains premised on not directly challenging state sovereignty and a piecemeal approach to crises and challenges. As a result, calls for a 'pro-poor', democratic world government are unlikely to be heeded, and instead global policies are likely to remain pro-market and relatively disinterested in the concerns of the world's poor. Reform strategies need to be guided by a sober realism. Payne (2007) offers just such a framework for broadening global governance that avoids utopian dreams of world government. First he suggests that the G7/8 format should be expanded to include at a minimum China, India, Brazil and South Africa. Second this broader group should be part of reframing of membership of the UN Security Council, with the EU representative also present. Third the voting powers and procedures of the IMF and the WB will need to be reformed and made more balanced. Finally the processes of the WTO will need to be based on a stronger spirit of consensus decision-making.

It is plain that these measures are difficult to achieve because these will only partly address the challenge of constructing democratic governance at the global level. If the domestic scholarship of political scientists leads them to doubt, the democratic credentials of emerging governance arrangements would appear that IR researchers are even more sceptical of the capacity to marry governance and democracy.

5
Governance in Development Studies

Since the 1990s, the idea of 'governance' has come to occupy the centre stage in thinking about development. This occurrence closely mirrors the evolution of a dominantly pro-market perspective in mainstream development policy to one that recognises the significance of the state and the nature of politics more generally in impacting on development processes and outcomes. Governance is the term, indeed the overarching category, which is predominantly used by international development agencies to encapsulate these recent concerns. However, the more popular and seemingly consensual the use of the term became amongst policy-makers, the more contentious and critical were the responses it generated amongst scholars. As a result, the literature on governance within the Development Studies discipline is sharply polarised. This polarisation reflects the contested nature of the discipline itself. Development Studies has been described as an 'unusual enterprise' (Corbridge, 2007:179) for it appears to be committed at the same time to the principle of 'difference', in treating the 'Third World' as different from the West, and that of 'similarity', in development's mission to make the peoples and processes of the developing world more like that of the developed world. For a number of reasons which we will explore in this chapter, the governance agenda encapsulates both these dimensions. While on the one hand, it has accompanied the growing realisation that universalistic free-market policies cannot succeed in the countries of Asia, Africa and South America unless due consideration is given to their particular governance structures and processes (the principle of difference), on the other hand, western governments and aid agencies have formulated a very clear articulation of what they regard as 'good governance' on the basis of western experiences and contexts (the principle of similarity). In this sense, debates around governance mirror the larger concerns of the discipline of development studies.

The concept of governance has allowed for the intellectual advancement of development studies in offering explanatory frameworks for understanding the contradictions and crises generated by the free-market paradigms of the 1980s. What was special about the governance idea was the ease with which it allowed even mainstream development organisations to see eye-to-eye with critics on the causes of these contradictions and crises. This chapter explores what precisely allows governance to perform this function, where other concepts might not have succeeded, and the implications of this seeming acceptability. Equally, the concept of governance has elicited a new wave of critical responses that aim to understand the fundamentally unequal nature of relationships between and within the developed and developing parts of the world. This chapter also aims to show why these critiques are so relevant to the continuation of the core debates in development studies. For narrative ease, the chapter is organised in three sections. Section one discusses briefly the evolution of the concept and the key conditions that led to its rise. It focuses on the central definitional framework for governance in development studies, that of 'good governance'. It also demonstrates how there are different shades to this good governance idea depending on the principles and concerns of the sponsoring organisation. Section two unpacks the apparent consensus around governance and discusses the major areas of debate around it. Section three focuses especially on how the concept of governance has been used to further an incisive understanding of the very unequal relationships of power that define the concerns of development, and of development studies.

Context and meaning

Major epistemological developments

In 1989, the World Bank (WB) published a report titled 'Sub-Saharan Africa: From Crisis to Sustainable Growth', which declared that Africa was witnessing a 'crisis of governance' (World Bank, 1989:60). This observation came at the end of nearly a decade of structural adjustment, which had been the basis of a new wave of policy-oriented loans by the WB, International Monetary Fund (IMF), and other western donors to several developing countries (Lancaster, 1993; Williams and Young, 1994). Structural Adjustment Programmes or SAPs reflected the predominant neoclassical position that extolled the virtues of the free market and upheld that the 'state's economic role should be confined to assuring the proper functioning of markets as the operative mechanism of resource allocation' (Sklar and Whitaker, 1991:341). However, the experiences of SAPs in the 1980s in Africa, and elsewhere too, decisively showed that adjustment was a political matter, with major impacts of the production and distribution of resources (Leftwich, 1994; Haggard and Kaufman, 1989). What also became clear during this time was 'that the ability to plan and implement adjustment was largely a consequence of both *political* commitment, capacity and skill, as well as *bureaucratic* competence, independence and probity' (Healey and Robinson, 1992; cited in Leftwich, 1994:370). As World Bank President Barber Conable put it, 'If we are to achieve development, we must aim for growth that cannot be easily reversed through the political process of imperfect governance' (Conable, 1992; cited in Doornboos 2001:98). The crisis of governance then, as described by the WB, referred to a crisis in areas that were not officially within its domain. The Bank is constrained by its Articles of Agreement, which expressly forbid taking non-economic considerations into account in its operations (Articles III 5b, IV 10 and V 5c in Williams and Young, 1994:84). It is with no coincidence then, that it is frequently said that 'the international community, especially the WB and IMF, has taken refuge in the concept of governance or institutions when referring to things political' (Hyden, *et al.*, 2004:12; others like Doornboos, 2001; Gibbon, 1993; Leftwich, 1994; Lockwood, 2005; Martinussen, 1998a; and Williams and Young, 1994; have voiced similar views).

While the concern for sustained economic growth continued to provide the principal impetus for the thrust on governance, a number of attendant factors are significant to consider. Leftwich (1994) regards the collapse of communist regimes in Eastern Europe to be important in shaping the emergence of western interest in governance. In his view, the 'new international circumstances' after 1990 meant that the 'west' could attach explicit political and institutional conditions to aid without fear of 'losing its third world allies or clients to communism' (Leftwich, 1994:369). Moreover, the collapse of communist regimes discredited those political systems as 'bureaucratically sclerotic', 'non-democratic' and 'inefficient', while upholding elements of western political systems (in the USA and Western Europe) such as political liberalisation and administrative decentralisation (World Bank, 1991; as cited in Leftwich, 1994:369). This association of western liberal democracy with governance has continued to be an abiding one within mainstream discourse.

Historically too, the 1980s witnessed pro-democracy movements in Latin America, the Philippines and Eastern Europe, stimulating similar movements elsewhere (Huntington, 1991; as cited in Leftwich, 1994). In Africa for example, between 1989 and 1992, a combination of internal and external pressures put a whole host of countries on the path of democratisation, though not without resistance from incumbent regimes (Leftwich, 1994). These events proved to be seminal in legitimising the west's preference for liberal democratic systems, as opposed to communism, and laid the ground for the active pursuit of democratisation to promote governance. Others have commented that a distinction needs to be made between the Bretton Woods institutions (WB and IMF) and the US Government, as 'promoting democracy abroad is not a new policy for the United States' (Lancaster, 1993:12). She views such emphasis in Washington as a 'practical response to a variety of domestic political imperatives.... such as finding a rationale for a $15 billion a year foreign aid programme' (Lancaster, 1993:13). Still others like Barya (1993) and Gills and Rocamora (1992) regard the concern for democracy as a clear manifestation of the 'onward march of global capitalism, which had been delayed by the bipolar world' (as cited in Leftwich, 1994:370). Indeed, the motives for the pursuit of democratisation through governance are amongst the most contested within the Development Studies literature. This is perhaps because they, more than anything else, reveal the fallacy of the 'apolitical' stance adopted by the international donor community under the cover of governance, while dealing with matters that are explicitly political.

These issues are clearly reflected by the progression of events in the adoption of the governance idea by the international donor community, with the WB in the lead (see Uvin, 1993; as cited in Doornboos, 2001:98 for more information). In 1991, the WB convened its Annual Development Economics Conference with the express purpose of discussing its future agenda, which in principle comprised nothing less than a 'reform of politics in aid-dependent countries' (Summers and Shah, 1997; as cited in Doornboos, 2001:98). Amidst considerable uncertainty regarding the extent to which the governance idea could be cast in political terms, the notion of 'good' governance emerged as a necessary instrument enabling the launch of a new generation of political conditionalities. The use of the 'good governance' theme to drive political and institutional reforms of a particular sort through aid, marked a watershed in the character of international development. It has been closely related to strategies of institutional globalisation, and 'provides a handle for the formulation of political conditionalities by external actors, which previously did not dispose of "politically oriented" instruments for intervention and direction' (Doornboos,

2000:63). This sort of intervention simultaneously marked a break from previous ideas as 'national sovereignty' and 'non-interference in internal affairs', for long held in high esteem in international politics (Doornboos, 2001). There is also the view that political conditionalities have long accompanied aid provision with decisions on country aid allocations being influenced by strategic, diplomatic and ideological considerations. However, Doornboos maintains that 'the new strategy of externally led political reform should not be confused with earlier examples of external political pressures to demand a particular policy position' because the 'posing of demands on theoretically sovereign states regarding the manner in which they should organise their institutional apparatus, policy implementing procedures and indeed their political systems, goes a step further' (2000: 66). In practice, the rise of good governance further facilitated the extension of conditionalities around aid programmes. These were both economic (such as keeping inflation below 7% per annum, or removing subsidies on fertilisers) as well as political (notably moving to a multi-party system and promoting freedom of press) in nature.

Although the WB has for several years stuck to a strictly non-political projection of governance, it has also accepted the role of secretariat for various donor consortia stipulating the political as well as economic conditionalities that had to be met. This has given it the extremely strategic position, of formulating, guiding and monitoring political conditionalities, without actually compromising its stated non-political mandate (Doornboos, 2001; Gibbon, 1993; Martinussen, 1998a). However, further evidence of non-compliance and partial reforms that conditionalities engendered in recipient countries led to the view that conditional aid was an ineffective instrument of policy change, and that recipient governments needed to 'own' their reforms themselves (Killick, 1998). This led to the argument that conditionality ought to be abandoned altogether, and 'selectivity' should be adopted as a guiding principle in lending, with donors 'selectively giving aid to countries that already owned reforms that donors liked' (Lockwood, 2005:54). The shift from conditionality to selectivity was staunchly advocated by the WB in its 1998 report titled *Assessing Aid*, nicknamed the Dollar Report after its principal author (other WB publications endorsing this shift include Collier and Dollar (1999) and Devarajan *et al.* (2001). This report argued that 'good' performers are better able to absorb and utilise aid and therefore selectivity in aid disbursement is rationalised as the most 'cost-effective' and 'results-oriented' strategy for donors. This view was quickly endorsed by large parts of the donor community, and is practised (albeit to differing degrees) by the WB, the US and Dutch governments and the UK. Lockwood significantly observes that 'while many donors have embraced selectivity, they have *not* actually abandoned conditionality, but rather practise combinations of both' (2005:54). Yet, the idea that 'good policy environments' mattered for aid to nurture reform has unmistakably influenced donor thinking in recent years. More and more donors have relied on the concept of good governance to guide their 'selective' aid allocations, but not without difficulty, a theme to which we return in section two.

'Good' governance

The rise of the governance agenda served a very particular purpose for donors like the WB. It allowed them to move away from a narrow focus on the market, an approach which had proved to be disastrous through the 1980s, and engage more broadly with other types of institutions as well. As discussed earlier, this is most visibly manifested in the launch of broader conditionalities to do with political and institutional reforms. In this context, the 1997 publication of the WB's World Development Report (WDR) *The State in a Changing World* signals an important epistemological landmark in the making of a new and very powerful development discourse, i.e., the re-entry of the state into international development. It argued that states must become 'credible partners' in a country's development, and wherein they lack the capacity to do so, such capacity can be reinvigorated. Precisely in this definition, the Bank has carved a space for itself and other donors to get involved in the broader internal affairs of recipient countries. This issue of state capacity has been interpreted by and large in terms of institutional capacity, and 'good governance' broadly associated with the forging of various types of 'desirable' institutional reforms. In one swift stroke, therefore the emphasis on good governance appeared to acquit the WB and other development organisations from accusations of the parochialism of the free-market idea.

The rise of good governance has been understood as marking a departure from the theoretical principles of the New Political Economy (NPE) that dominated in the 1980s, with their rather negative views of the state as 'predatory' and corrupt and correspondingly laudatory views of the market as efficient and conducive to individual freedom (see Colclough and Manor, 1991; Nonneman, 1996). In fact, the current emphasis on governance reflects an astute recognition of the limitations of NPE which assumes that transactions between economic actors are relatively costless, and an endorsement of the New Institutional Economics (NIE) which explicitly sought to explain how and why institutions were necessary in order reduce these transaction costs that arose from the essential uncertainty characterising all human transactions. Governance policies of the 1990s all focus on the centrality of institutions. Doornboos (2000) comments that governance in this respect, is the latest in a whole series of concepts that have been proposed to understand the institutional dimensions of state-society relations and guide international development interventions (precursor concepts include capacity-building, institution-building, institutional development, institutional reform etc.). Governance is undoubtedly the most flamboyant of all these concepts, for it allows donors to address matters broader than the government, to include various types of institutions from the official state apparatus to market institutions, to institutions from the civil society or voluntary sector, and all without explicitly talking about politics.

Nearly every active international development organisation in the world today sports its own definition of good governance. These definitions are described as being 'policy-oriented', but a further distinction has been made on administrative-managerial and more limited understanding of governance, as associated with the WB and a more political understanding of the same as associated with western governments. He clarifies that while the latter involves a concern for sound administration, it also includes an insistence on competitive democratic politics. Yet, while this divide may have been conspicuous in the early 1990s, it has increasingly narrowed over the years for two reasons. Firstly, as discussed earlier, the WB itself has taken an explicit interest in the state and its functioning, particularly in participatory decision-making and democratically elected regimes (apropos its 1997 report *The State in a Changing World*) despite retaining an overall apolitical stance (Martinussen, 1998a). This is also the result of increasing pressures from Western bilateral donors to address aspects of governance concerning the 'form' of political regime and not limit itself merely to the capacity of governments to design, formulate and implement policies and discharge functions (Hyden *et al.*, 2004:15). Secondly, the loaded political overtones of the Bank's emphasis on the administrative and managerial aspects of governance have been better exposed, with the recognition that good governance is a 'function of state character and capacity which is in turn a function of politics'. This has led to increasing acceptance of the political character of 'good governance', as exemplified by the growing practice of using democratisation as an explicit conditionality of aid (Barya, 1993; and Healey and Robinson, 1992; cited in Doornboos, 2000).

What is also interesting is that the various definitions of good governance are similar in many respects, but there are also a few critical points of difference especially in the way particular principles are emphasised and prioritised. The WB's position on governance was first outlined fully in a definitive statement in a report titled *Governance and Development* in 1992, where it defined good governance as 'synonymous with sound development management' (World Bank, 1992:1). This policy document focuses on four main areas of public administration in general and public sector management in particular, which it considers to be within its mandate:

a) *Accountability* – which in essence means holding officials accountable for their actions.
b) *A legal framework for development* – which means a structure of rules and laws that provide clarity, predictability and stability for the private sector, which are impartially and fairly applied to all, and which provide the basis for conflict resolution through an independent judicial system.
c) *Information* – by which is meant that information about economic conditions, budgets, markets and government intentions is reliable and accessible to all, crucial for private sector operations.
d) *Transparency* – which is basically a call for open government, to enhance accountability, limit corruption and stimulate consultative processes between government and private interests over policy documents (Leftwich 1994: 372).

Following this definition, a number of other international organisations and donor agencies came up with supporting definitions that closely resembled the World Bank's emphasis to the extent that some or all of these principles were always included. However, they were not all identical. It is instructive to consider a few of the following. The IMF sees itself as an established advocate having and focuses on three key areas of governance, which are related to its role of maintaining surveillance over macroeconomic management: the transparency of government accounts, the effectiveness of public resource management, and the stability and transparency of the economic and regulatory environment for private sector activity (IMF, 1997). To the Asian Development Bank (ADB), good governance is likewise seen as integral to its strategy to reduce poverty and ensure the efficient management of resources in public finances. This includes challenges of a constitutional nature that establish rules of political conduct, creative interventions to change rules and structures, and the nature of interactions and types of relationships between states, citizens and other actors. The ADB has identified four critical objectives of governance to guide its work: accountability, participation, predictability and transparency. It concentrates its activities in a further eight areas of 'good governance' practices, and these include anti-corruption, corporate regulatory frameworks, legal and justice reform, participation of the civil society in public decision-making, pro-poor service delivery, public administration, public financial management and sub-national/local governance.

The World Bank, IMF and ADB's definitions concentrate on the quality of government in providing efficient services and creating a stable environment for the working of the private sector. Of the three, ADB is the only organisation that specifically mentions participation as a core governance objective as well as an area of governance practice, but here too, the weight of the emphasis (as evident from the majority of its governance practices) is not on participation. We see a fairly different picture when we examine the definitions of good governance of three other organisations: the Swedish International Development Agency (SIDA), Canadian International Development Agency (CIDA) and the Office of the United Nations High Commissioner for Human Rights (OHCHR). Each of these organisations specifically relates its conceptualisations of good governance to democratisation more broadly and to human rights in particular. For SIDA, good governance is a subset of democratic governance, and is linked to issues concerning democracy, human rights, popular participation and the principles of the rule of law (SIDA, 2007). As for CIDA, good governance is described as the effective, honest and accountable exercise of power by governments. It is closely linked to human rights and democratisation on the basis that all three have common underlying values, which include respect for human rights, justice, equity, participation and accountability (CIDA, 1996). This latter set of concerns is most unequivocally articulated by the OHCHR which endorses a rights-based approach to governance. Its underlying principles mirror those listed by CIDA, though more explicit mention is made of non-discrimination, attention to vulnerability, empowerment and the forging of links to international human rights instruments (United Nations, 2002)

The Department for International Development (DFID) has considerably advanced thinking on governance with its 2001 Target Strategy Paper called 'Making Government Work for Poor People'. DFID has zeroed down on seven key 'governance capabilities' that it believes that states need to develop, in partnership with the private sector and civil society, in order to meet previously defined International Development Targets (IDTs). The International Development Targets broadly classified into three categories – economic well-being, social and human development and environmental sustainability and regeneration – have been agreed by the entire UN membership, following a series of summit meetings held by the UN and its specialised agencies over the past ten years or so.

These governance capabilities contain a fair mix of emphasis on issues related to the quality of government and administration and the provision of a sound macroeconomic environment (as associated with the WB, IMF and ADB's definitions) as well as with broader issues to do with democratisation and rights-based development. These key capabilities are listed as follows: a) operate political systems which provide opportunities for all the people, including the poor and disadvantaged, to influence government policy and practice; b) provide macroeconomic stability and facilitate private sector investment and trade so as to promote the growth necessary to reduce poverty; c) implement pro-poor policy and raise, allocate and account for public resources accordingly; d) guarantee the equitable and universal provision of effective basic services; e) ensure personal safety and security with access to justice for all; f) manage national security arrangements accountably and to resolve differences between communities before they develop into violent conflicts; and g) develop honest and accountable government that can combat corruption (DFID, 2001).

In subsequent years, and unlike many other donors, DFID has moved away from the 'good governance' agenda by focusing instead on the idea that each country has its own particular agents, institutions and structures that drive change, and these need to be understood and addressed. This notion lies at the heart of what it describes as the 'Drivers of Change' (DOC), an analytical framework developed internally within DFID to enable it to 'interact with the politics of development' (Warrener, 2004:1). In practice, the DOC approach has led to the commissioning of broad-based country-specific political analyses by DFID country offices, with commissioned inputs from external consultants, to inform the development of their country assistance plans (DOC Team, DFID 2006). Twenty two such studies have been undertaken so far, and there are attempts to conduct DOC studies in particular sectors, as for example social protection in Zambia. However, while the DOC approach is conceptually savvy and has been welcomed by DFID staff in many countries for its recognition of 'political obstacles' (Warrener, 2004:5), it is unclear whether its sophisticated approach to governance will translate into practicable lending strategies given the presence of various constraints faced by donors. These include the presence of limited resources, need to produce clear outcomes and seek wider public legitimacy (Chhotray and Hulme, 2008 for a comprehensive treatment).

A few other donors have tried to share DFID's brave conceptual attempt to locate ideas about governance in the empirical realities of particular countries. Notable endeavours include SIDA's 'power analysis' and a multi-donor initiative within the Development Assistance Committee (DAC) to understand better the political and institutional contexts shaping the incentives of key actors. All these attempts reveal that donors are increasingly aware of the 'very unsettling questions about the "good governance" agenda', and of how little is actually known about the 'key causal linkages – between institutions and growth, growth and corruption, democracy and poverty reduction – and about which reforms to prioritise in different country circumstances' (Unsworth, 2005:9). The work of scholars like Goldsmith (2003, cited in Unsworth, 2005) and Chang (2002) have been particularly influential in this respect. They take a historical approach to question the 'governance first' model of economic development by demonstrating that this was never the case in developed countries where institutions arose incrementally, in response to particular circumstances and crises.

While these initiatives are encouraging, they do not detract from the fact that the good governance agenda in development remains largely identified with the valorisation of predominantly western concepts and principles. Leftwich writes how this conception of governance is 'unexceptional, it re-identifies precisely the principles of administration that have long been argued as being of benefit to developing countries...these are impeccably Weberian in spirit' (Leftwich, 1994:372). Equally, it is hard to miss the very large range of objectives (from anticorruption to human rights) encompassed within the concept of governance, lending it a mysterious quality. And with larger numbers of donors embracing selectivity in lending, 'good governance', whatever it may be understood to be, is now assumed to be present to begin with, and 'bad governance', posed as the opposite of the 'good', will remain so unless the recipient country is keen enough for aid to revise its governance structures first (Doornbos, 2001; Martinussen, 1998b). This in fact is the stated philosophy of the US Millennium Challenge Account, the Bush administration's flagship big-budget scheme recently launched in 2002 at Monterrey. The key point remains that there is a

striking lack of clarity about the various aspects of its meaning (Doornboos, 2000; Williams, 1996). Indeed, it could be said that the lack of
specificity of the governance idea has allowed it to be like a flexible
carrier, which can be used to convey varying combinations of messages, while appearing to be coherent and objective. This 'elasticity' of
meaning, as Doornboos (2000) calls it, has been the precise strength of
the concept for donors and policy-makers. Others like Goran Hyden
(1992) have argued that this elasticity or flexibility is what stands governance apart from other concepts and underpins its conceptual strength.
Hyden remarked that the advantage of the governance concept was
that 'it does not prejudge the locus of actual decision-making, which
could be within the state, within an international organisation or within
some other structural context' (1992:6). Doornboos agrees that in this
regard, the governance concept 'facilitates new analytical pursuits into
the exercise of political power, unhindered by formal boundaries, and
may fit discourse analysis, embedded structuralism and mainstream
thinking alike' (2001:96). Little wonder then, that governance has
been richly assimilated within development parlance, both by its proponents and its adversaries.

Consensus or not? Major tensions within 'good' governance

The impressive show of support for good governance by a vast array of
international development organisations and western governments
might lend the impression of consensus. There is hardly any doubt
that the concept of good governance has been extremely influential
and pervasive for all the reasons discussed so far. But at the same time,
it is equally true that no matter how coherent development discourse
appears to be around good governance, there are major tensions that
continue to splinter support for it. Each of these tensions arises from
the very political nature of the concerns that constitute governance
(indeed, problems arising from the exclusion of these concerns were
what had led to the focus on governance to begin with). The first
relates to the question of method; how is governance, so defined, to be
implemented by donors, and in what ways governance criteria can
facilitate effective aid policy that meets its objectives. The second
relates to the specific governance concern with democratisation, and
whether it is at all feasible to link donor attempts at creating good governance with the constitution of democratic political systems. There
are disagreements both on whether it is at all right for donors to intervene in the constitution of democracy as well as what might be the

best way of doing so. The third major area of debate and reflection involves the implications of popular governance related policies for the role of the state.

Governance and aid

The frustrating experience of implementing economic conditionalities through structural adjustment in the 1980s led to the emphasis on political conditionalities through an emphasis on good governance in the 1990s. But there was no reason to expect that implementing political conditionalities should have been any easier, and very soon, it became evident that implementation was anything but easy. There were a number of problems encountered by the WB and other donors in this regard. One, these conditionalities were complex, comprising a multitude of policy objectives, and there was no way to determine the extent to which it would be possible to monitor compliance. Structural adjustment loans, which constituted economic conditionalities, could have as many as 100 different policy instruments that require complex and disparate policy change and involved conditions that that could not be achieved in a short period of time. There was no way of checking hard-pressed developing countries pledging commitment to undertake structural adjustment even when they had absolutely no intention of doing so. Two, local reception of policy conditionalities, whether economic or political, was intrinsically tied up with local political processes and implementation frequently predicated upon bargaining with local political elites (see Harrison's (1999) fascinating piece on conditionality and adjustment in Mozambique). Donors increasingly realised that political conditionalities only introduced new and unpredictable elements into the policy process and created very difficult situations for donors and recipients alike (Doornboos, 2001). Donors were at risk of 'getting further enmeshed in the internal policy processes of recipient countries than they thought they had bargained for' (Doornboos, 2001:102; Harrison, 1999). This was to be cumbersome and difficult, and would lead to a strategic reorientation of donor policy, which has gradually shifted since, from conditionality to 'selectivity'. As discussed earlier, this was expected to save the donors from having to monitor attempts at 'ameliorating' policy processes towards 'good governance'.

However, the move to selectivity brought with it its own set of problems, as donors still needed to conceptualise what they regarded as desirable policy environments towards which aid could be selectively directed. Countries which did not possess such environments, but needed aid, would have to change and move towards this ideal. The US Millennium Challenge Account (MCA) takes this principle to its logical extreme. MCA is a new foreign aid programme announced by the Bush administration in 2002 designed to provide substantial new foreign assistance to low-income countries that are 'ruling justly, investing in their people and encouraging economic freedom'.[1] Only countries that have successfully demonstrated, largely through quantifiable scores that they meet all 16 indicators that have been devised to satisfy these three criteria will be eligible to receive aid. These indicators were supplied by organisations like the WB, Freedom House and Heritage Foundation. MCA reflects a philosophy that has been clearly articulated by conservative think-tanks like the Heritage Foundation that the failure of US overseas development assistance is not due to lack of funding but because past governments had misdirected aid to governments with bad policy environments, or in fact bad governance. MCA claims to be results-oriented and very tightly monitored, but in fact, 'the choice and construction of particular performance indicators; their monitoring and measurement by neoliberal American and American-dominated institutions...problems with data accuracy and reliability' (Mawdsley, in press) have all been vehemently criticised. Former World Bank economist William Easterly (2006) points out how in June 2005 the MCA had reached agreements with two countries: Honduras and Madagascar. Yet, in 2004, Honduras' government was ranked by the World Bank as among the worst third in the world for corruption, while Madagascar was in the middle. MCA's claims to neutral selectivity are also suspect on account of the inclusion of countries like Colombia, Egypt, Jordan, Turkey and Russia in the pool of countries that are eligible to compete for MCA funding, as this implies that decisions to award MCA funds will be determined by political and strategic rather than the stated criteria. All this illustrates the difficulties for external agencies to reach consensus on which countries are better governed. In short, MCA's experience suggests that the move to selectivity shows that donors continue to impose their ideas of what it means to be well governed on recipient countries, and with limited degrees of success (see Chhotray and Hulme, 2007 for details).

Despite all the problems encountered during implementation, MCA remains in operation and its proponents are optimistic that many of

---

[1]For details of the President's speech, see http://www.whitehouse.gov/news/releases/2002/03/20020314-7.html

the 'kinks associated with slow start-up' will be ironed out (Herrling and Rose, 2007:1). Its reliance on universalistic governance criteria has in fact facilitated the adoption of concrete, actionable strategies. These may well engender more problems than they solve, and yet they continue as they are compatible with the general framework of aid-giving and affirm dominant neoliberal economic values. In stark contrast, DFID's Drivers of Change which attempts to formulate a more nuanced view of governance has faltered to translate itself into practical strategies (Chhotray and Hulme, 2007). There is also no concrete evidence on the precise ways in which DOC studies have impacted decisions regarding DFID's aid decisions. Nevertheless, DFID appears to be taking its DOC initiatives seriously and has commissioned further work to refine its analytical tools (see Leftwich, 2006).

The debate on the role of governance in giving aid reiterates the tension between difference and similarity that we introduced at the beginning of this chapter. There remains a very strong belief, especially amongst donors and international development organisations that it is 'possible in principle to search for universally valid criteria of proper management and policy making' (Doornboos, 2000:72). Geoffrey Hawthorn's insightful observation – that the notion of good governance is formulated in terms of 'optimal paths to optimal outcomes', a supposition which he rejects as simply untrue in politics (1993:24) – is still not the favoured view.

Governance and democratisation

The concept of good governance has historically shared a strong association not just with western models of government and administration, but more fundamentally with western liberal democratic politics. The pro-democracy movements witnessed in parts of Latin America, Africa and East Europe in the late 1980s and early 1990s led to an association between multi-party democracy, western-style, and good governance. The subsequent use of good governance based on political conditionality to forge similar or identical democratic politics in countries around the world has been criticised as highly suspicious. The promotion of democracy abroad is not a new policy for the United States, and while the Bretton Woods institutions may have shied away from discussing democratisation as a specific governance concern in the early 1990s, the Bank, reflecting the concerns of a number of western donors, was much more willing to do so by the end of the decade (following WDR, 1997). More recently, the UN and other bilateral donors (CIDA and SIDA for instance) relate good governance explicitly with a broader concern for democratisation.

However, more than one critical observer has put forward the proposition that the new political conditionalities (of the 1990s) had nothing to do with the desire for democracy, and that a positive correlation between the two has yet to be demonstrated (Barya, 1993; Cranenburgh, 1998; Doornboos, 2000; Healey and Robinson, 1992; Lancaster, 1993). To begin with, in the past Cold War era, western countries frequently supported dictatorial regimes, as in Zaire, Liberia and Uganda, under the label of 'bulwarks against communism' (Barya, 1993:16). Barya forcefully argues that the new political conditionalities use a 'populist ideology of democracy' to create a new economic and military world order following the collapse of state socialism and the end of the Cold War (1993:16).

Moreover, western donors largely interpret democratisation as multi-party politics, and there is wide scepticism whether this is either adequate or even appropriate to the needs of the host countries. The majority of debates in this context have been played out in Africa. The skilful manner in which authoritarian regimes in Kenya and Ethiopia transformed themselves into dominant parties within façade type multi-party systems showed that multi-partyism without concomitant social and ideological pluralism would ensure only a farcical democracy (Doornboos, 2001). Cranenburgh comments, 'It is highly questionable whether current reforms centring around multi-party elections will lead to significant changes in the manner in which policies are formulated' (1998:78). His concern is that political parties, multiple as they may be, may still lack the capacity to present a coherent policy programme, failing both to provide credible political opposition as well as allowing a dangerously large amount of autonomy to the dominant party. For Cranenburgh, the appropriate response for the donor community would be to formulate a 'strategy to increase the capacity of democratising elites' (1998:78). He even considers that such activities are better pursued by bilateral donors than by a 'financial institution' as the World Bank.

Others are less sanguine in their analysis. There is a fundamental questioning of whether democratisation, as understood by the international donor community, is the appropriate path ahead for Africa, and the developing world more generally. Countries like Uganda have 'struggled to get recognition for an alternative to multi-partyism, arguing that multi-partyism as it had evolved in the western experience did not necessarily constitute the sole route to democratic political processes, or to "good governance" for that matter' (Mugaju and Oloka-Onyango, 2000; cited in Doornboos, 2001:101). Hawthorn comments, 'It is perfectly possible that neither the government of a state nor the majority of that state's citizens believes that the benefits of social cooperation are in fact best served by a competitive multi-party system. And it is perfectly possible that they could be right in that belief' (1993:26).

Experiences in parts of Africa (Congo) and East Asia (South Korea) have illustrated how competitive electoral politics has posed a tangible risk to security and prosperity; both in Kinshasha (with the civil war between 1960–65) and Seoul (with the factional disputes within the leading party and the subsequent coup in 1960), security and the authority of the state to provide it were at a premium. While it may be true that 'external threats' to nation-states are no longer as serious in the 1990s, and therefore 'governments predicated on "national security" were no longer defensible', internal disorder or the threat of such disorder is still widespread (Hawthorn, 1993:27). The relationship between order and the success of democracy is now well theorised. Przeworski concludes, 'Democracy is about rules, not outcomes, and competing parties will only accept defeat if they can be sure that the rules will stay in place and give them a chance for victory in the future' (1991:1040). This observation supplements Schumpeter's earlier proposition that 'such rules will only be accepted if there is widespread agreement on the general shape and direction of society' (Schumpeter, 1950; cited in Hawthorn, 1993:27).

In this context, dissonances between donors, African governments and the African people regarding the meaning of democracy and how it must be achieved emerge as a highly pertinent, yet inadequately explored, concern. Donors project their interest in democratisation as necessary 'to ensure that repressed popular energies and misappropriated aid monies are both released for development' (Barya, 1993:18), but this is not necessarily the perception of African governments or African people for that matter. African governments and other official African institutions like the United Nations Economic Commission for Africa (UNECA) can be divided into two broad groups in this regard: those who favour democracy but argue that it must not be imposed and its definition must be left to the African people (some African leaders like President Museveni of Uganda, the Organisation for African Unity and UNECA fall into this group) and those who are opposed outright to democracy although they pay lip service to the concept (such as the ruling regimes in Zambia, Kenya and Mali who have been forced to accept the multi-party definition of democracy by a combination of the political conditionalities for aid as well as internal resistance).

Attempts to capture the 'popular' view of democratisation mainly convey the need to go beyond a narrow interpretation of democracy as political pluralism, and focus on 'its social and ideological dimensions' making it as comprehensive as possible for the whole of civil society (Mamdani, 1992; cited in Barya, 1993:20). Mamdani comments further that although opposition movements and 'new breed' middle class leaders are forced to acknowledge the need for pluralism and autonomous organisations of civil society, it remains uncertain whether they too would tolerate the 'militancy and autonomy' of these organisations if voted into power. The social and ideological foundations of democracy remain a low priority for donors as much as African leaders, old and new.

Support for the idea that democratisation need not follow a western liberal democratic model has come more recently through an influential study conducted in 16 countries. Goran Hyden, Julius Court and Kenneth Mease (2004) have drawn on a new set of data on governance to provide a complementary perspective on democratisation and the relationship between politics and development. The authors adopt a rule-based rather than a result-oriented definition of governance. They define governance to 'refer to the formation and stewardship of the formal and informal rules that regulate the public realm, the arena in which state as well as economic and societal actors interact to make decisions' (Hyden *et al.*, 2004:16). They further clarify that governance deals with the 'constitutive' side of how a political system operates rather than its distributive or allocative aspects that are 'more directly a function of polity' (Hyden *et al.*, 2004:16). They identify six 'institutional arenas' to understand and investigate the functional dimensions of governance: civil society, political society, government, bureaucracy, economic society and the judicial system (for further details refer to Hyden *et al.*, (2004:22–28).

The results of their empirical research lead the authors to conclude that 'development stagnation and obstacles to democratisation stem from a failure to undertake the necessary steps to establishing a system of rules that legitimate political choices and political behaviour' (Hyden *et al.*, 2004:193). They thus arrive at a rather different causal relationship to that prescribed within conventional donor thinking: that the elements of 'good governance' (centring on the formal and informal rules that regulate the public realm) provide opportunities for democratisation and development, and not the other way around, where a western liberal form of democracy is advocated as the path to 'good governance', which in turn is vaguely defined. They clarify that 'in this respect, getting politics right means a set of normative and institutional changes that transcend the liberal democratic model' (Hyden *et al.*,

2004:194). Their study includes examples of countries like China, Thailand and Jordan, where development has been driven by an emphasis on rules that are not identical to those associated with liberal democracy.

Governance and the state

The rise of good governance in international development is usually associated with marking a clear break with the dominant neoliberal paradigm of the 1980s. The emphasis on institutions of all kind, and not just market institutions, that it brought in its wake was seen as representative of the 'post-Washington' consensus (see Stiglitz, 1998). WDR 1997 *The State in a Changing World* supposedly contained a more 'balanced approach between the state-managed and market-managed models' (Martinussen, 1998a). But to what extent *did* the good governance agenda reverse the neoliberal state minimalism that had led to its rise in the first place? This is a deeply significant question as the development orthodoxy relies heavily on good governance to claim that it has moved beyond state minimalism.

Moore (1999) makes a powerful case that the neoliberal message is quite clearly evident in the WB's 1997 report. The two 'jobs' listed by the WDR for all states are firstly, to get the 'fundamentals' right – these include the law, macroeconomic stability, investment in basic services and protection of the environment, and secondly, to take advantage of the opportunities represented by the private and voluntary sectors and not attempt to be the 'sole provider'. Moore argues that the focus of this message is plain, and the WB desires states to intervene to establish property rights, to maintain law and order and to preserve macroeconomic stability but not to be the principal provider of health, education and social welfare. The overall refrain in the report, that states should not take on tasks that do not match their 'capabilities', reflects the basic neoliberal distrust of the state. These accusations are resounding and numerous: good governance is hence viewed as the 'political counterpart of economic neoliberalism' (Archer, 1994; cited in Orlandini, 2003:18), the extension of structural adjustment to the political systems of developing countries (Guilhot, 2000; cited in Orlandini, 2003:18), the promotion of a neoliberalism on a national and global scale (Moore, 1999) and the 'World Bank/IMF consortium's last refuge' (George and Sabelli, 1996; cited in Moore, 1996:138).

The concern that has followed these accusations is that despite the theoretical departure to new institutionalism and the policy focus on increasing institutional capacity, actual governance policies may paradoxically be doing 'more to reduce, rather than strengthen Third

World governments' capacity for policy making and implementation' (Doornboos, 2000:72). Such policies include for example, externally induced creation of autonomous institutions for improved management that may undermine local government capacity or diversion of aid flows to NGOs that may weaken the government departments charged with responsibility to the areas concerned. This is not uncommon given key governance strategies of decentralisation and the increased involvement of civil society. Moreover, demands for compliance with contradictory instructions from different donors have been known to result in confusion and distortion, in addition to overburdening qualified manpower which is frequently in short supply (Doornboos, 2000; Wuyts, 1996). These processes have been referred to as 'squeezing' or 'splitting' the state (Mackintosh, 1992) and seriously undermine key governance objectives. Moreover, the continued pervasiveness of neoliberalism offers 'limited clues by way of policy on how to respond to the problems of de-institutionalisation' that typically plague governance in developing countries (Bangura, 1994; cited in Doornboos, 2000:72).

In the same vein, the Bank has been criticised for subscribing to a narrowly economic perspective which prevents it from considering seriously the developmental state model that inspired the focus on governance (Martinussen, 1998a). The successes of state intervention in development in several East Asian countries were also associated with other dynamics such as the close nexus between the bureaucracy and major business groups. Such aspects were never seriously regarded, even though they revealed critical aspects of the wider institutional settings in which government bureaucracies in these countries operate. WDR 1997 contains a few references to culture, history, informal rules and norms (1997:157), but aspects of 'social embeddedness', as those referred to above, must be taken much more into consideration in order to understand why governments behave so differently from one another (Martinussen, 1998a).

Finally, it is alleged that proponents of the good governance idea do not adequately explore the meaning and implications of the 'developmental state', despite the significance of East Asian developmental states to the whole emphasis on governance. Leftwich (1994) in particular, notes that current models of good governance and the developmental state are in conflict. This is because WB-led ideas of good governance are projected in depoliticised terms, with little recognition that governance is in fact very much a function of state form, capacity and political practice (Leftwich, 1994). He reiterates that the 'remarkable' achievements of the East Asian states that have inspired the recent emphasis on governance have 'not been the kind of depoliticised governance now being urged on in developing societies'. Drawing from the work of other authors like Chalmers Johnson (1982) and Robert Wade (1990), Leftwich (1994) makes the case that growth in East Asian societies has been masterminded by 'developmental states', that possessed the requisite autonomy to shape and pursue nationally-determined development objectives. He also argues that developmental states could be both democratic and non-democratic, a point which contradicts the ostensible consensus regarding the significance of democratisation for development by the proponents of good governance. Obsession with the liberal democratic state thus leads to a patent disregard for the varying social and cultural contexts that differently structure state-society relationships.

Governance and power

The critical element within development studies is underpinned by a view of governance as a western construct that attempts to mask the power relationships between the developed and developing world. The WB-led donor agenda of 'good governance' is regarded as a fundamentally 'transformative' project that is presented as a depoliticised and neutral endeavour. The following extract from a 1994 World Bank document reveals its grand plans for governance: 'Good governance is epitomised by predictable, open and enlightened policy making (that is a transparent process); a bureaucracy imbued with a professional ethos; an executive arm of government accountable for its actions; a strong civil society participating in public affairs; and all behaving under rule of law' (1994:vii). According to Williams and Young, such transformation is attempted at three levels: 'at the institutional level with the creation of a "neutral" state; at the social level with the creation of a "liberal public sphere" or "civil society"; and at the personal level with the creation of a liberal "self" and "modern patterns of behaviour"' (1994:99). Thus, at each of these three levels, the authors contend that the World Bank constructs governance, in part at least, from liberal theory, and in the process, it reproduces some important ambiguities and tensions that exist within it. It is perhaps instructive to consider these attempts in turn.

The first level, i.e., creation of a "neutral" state stems from the recurrent theme of separating technical from political issues within the Bank's formal discourse. We have already discussed how the Bank's interest in governance signals a formal departure from its stated apolitical stand, and yet, the Bank has continued to retain its posture while engaging with blatantly political matters. At a conceptual level, the very idea of a neutral basis of the Bank's engagement with recipient countries stands to challenge, and indeed unsustainable within liberal theory itself. The main point of criticism is 'even if neutrality is taken as a guiding principle rather than a foundational one, it generates neutralist conclusions only with respect to those who already accept liberal principles' (Williams and Young, 1994:94). It follows therefore, that the principles of 'good' governance promoted by the Bank stem from a prior conception of the good; the good for which the World Bank stands for is a market economy and "neutral" state which ensures the proper functioning of that economy by means of the enforcement of property rights and contractual obligations.

The second level, i.e., creation of a 'liberal public sphere' or 'civil society' is among the most innovative of the Bank's recent positions with respect to governance and development. Indeed, there is a widespread consensus around the need for enlightened participation by civil society in public decision-making. Traditionally, such a civil society was seen as a sphere of interactions free of state interference and characterised by pluralism and tolerance and much of the governance literature heeds the historically familiar liberal imperative of tolerance. The Bank does not want to be seen as prescribing any particular political system, and its official documents resonate with directives to its recipient countries to 'devise institutions which are consonant with its social values' (World Bank, 1992). However, on closer inspection, it emerges that that not all forms of the indigenous are acceptable to the Bank and its allies, and indeed only those that are compatible with modernisation are to be encouraged (Landell-Mills, 1992). Although the Bank and other donors now rely on a rosy discourse of 'partnership' and 'ownership' by the recipient country, the actual experiences of their dealings reveal ample contradictions. Mercer (2003) reports on how donors and international NGOs in Tanzania 'cherry-picked' a handful of elite NGOs to conduct their professional interactions, while excluding the large majority of NGOs. Moreover, the Bank's vision of the civil society is an explicitly western one, and there is no space for 'family and ethnic ties' or other 'affective and community groups'. Civil society, as referred to within good governance agendas, includes 'contractual, non-community, non-affective groups, such as professional associations, chambers of commerce and industry, trade unions and NGOs' (Williams and Young, 1994:96). Social transformation along these lines is explicitly suggested by the Bank's favoured academic experts as Goran Hyden (1983). Williams and Young (1994) argue that the Bank's selective tolerance can be better understood by an examination of the underlying liberal assumptions. The liberal idea of a pluralistic civil society stems from the fundamental liberal premise of the utter sanctity of individual freedom. However, seminal liberal thinkers like J.S. Mill base their position on a highly problematic distinction between those who are and are not autonomous (such as those residing in 'uncivilised' nations), sanctioning breaches of liberty of the latter (Williams and Young, 1994). Liberal ideas of individual freedom are accompanied by highly loaded notions of moral progress that mask their apparent universality.

Attempts at transformation at the third level relate to the individual itself and the liberal conception of the 'free self' lies at the heart of good governance. This is particularly evident in the emphasis on democratisation. Within liberal theory, the 'characteristics of the individual agent, and especially in relation to economic life, have been assumed to be universal underneath the superficial variety of culturally conditioned behaviour' (Williams and Young, 1994:97; Douglass and Bara, 1990). Such conceptions of universal economic behaviour have been extended to the political and social realms as illustrated by the NPE approach to politics that continues to be influential within the Bank and other donors. Western legal and bureaucratic organisations and the market economy, that form the cardinal elements of the Bank-led discourse of good governance, are 'premised upon the individual who has no other "public" ties than the contractual ones he chooses for himself' (Williams and Young, 1994:98).

While the good governance agenda allows the Bank and other international institutions to pursue such fundamentally transformative projects, little or no emphasis is placed on reorienting the external constraints to good governance as experienced by developing countries. The gradual progression of the political conditionality approach from 'conditionality' to 'selectivity' has shifted the burden of responsibility for achieving good governance from donors to host countries, but without any commensurate shift in power over conceptualising its meaning. To conclude, it is precisely the understanding of power relationships in governance that defines the divide between mainstream development agencies and critical interpreters of development. As we have tried to summarise here, there is a sharp divide in the literature between those who advocate good governance and those who question it. To its proponents, good governance is a benign and universally applicable notion, worthy of pursuit, but to its opponents, it is yet another instrument of power that the developed minority continues to wield over the vast developing regions of the world.

6
Governance in Socio-Legal Studies

Socio-legal studies evolved out of a tradition of empirical research conducted by anthropologists and sociologists that questioned the relationships between laws, as understood within the legal discipline, and wider social processes. The law is widely regarded, represented and taught as a 'conscious "attempt" by society to be rational and fair, orderly and just, and a bulwark against anarchy' (Moore, 1978:2). At the heart of this ideology are three key propositions: one, the law epitomises man-made, intentional action and constitutes the means by which a rational and considered attempt to direct society can be undertaken; two, social behaviour that departs from the law is 'deviant' from that which is widely accepted as legal and correct; and three, the state and its legal institutions are central to the process of law-making and enforcement, and thus, stand at the core of all social discipline. These propositions underpin traditional legal approaches to governance and are closely related to hierarchical modes of governing that political scientists have long written about.

Socio-legal studies challenge each of these propositions stemming from a fundamentally different starting point: that law and the social context in which it operates must be studied together. In fact, it has been argued that 'it is the society that controls the law and not the reverse' (Cochrane, 1971; as cited in Moore, 1978:55). Leading on from this premise is the understanding that social behaviour cannot be intentionally controlled and directed, as behaviour has underlying causes that are not within the conscious control of actors. These studies are equally sceptical of the compliance/deviation framework implicit within the legal discipline, on the grounds that it obscures the more complex and colourful elements of social life into pre-ordained categories. Further, research in this tradition has demonstrated both that the state is not the only source of the legitimacy and sanction that laws are required to possess and that the whole question of legal legitimacy is not a straightforward one (Benda-Beckmann and Benda-Beckmann, 1991; Benda-Beckmann, *et al.*, 2005).

In as much as studies in the socio-legal tradition offer a sociological rooting or conceptualisation to law, they also contain a more nuanced and wholesome perspective for undertaking socio-cultural analyses. As one author put it, they are essentially concerned with all the ways in which 'conscious efforts are made to build and/or reproduce durable social and symbolic orders' of which law is only one product (Moore, 1978:6). They emphasise that legal facts are not empirical facts, and that the social significance of the law, as conventionally understood, was 'mostly assumed, rather than empirically researched' (Spiertz, 2000:177). At their broadest, these studies are about the governance of social behaviour, of which the formal law as ratified by the state is one amongst several elements. Viewed in this way, socio-legal studies attempt to understand the forms of 'regulation' outside formal law that perform the same function as law (Merry, 1988). This focal point of inquiry allows the socio-legal tradition to make a unique offering to the wider debate on governance. Understanding this contribution is the principal objective of this chapter.

There are four sections to this chapter and in each of these the attempt will be to contrast perspectives originating from the socio-legal approach or discipline (more loosely put) with those arising from traditional legal approaches. In a sense this is inevitable for the socio-legal approach is a dissident discipline and its very content is derived from criticising classical legal perspectives to law and society. Section one maps out the intellectual domain of the socio-legal approach by abstracting three principal questions frequently raised within its extensive literature: 'what is the law; where is the law; and is there any chronology to the emergence of the law'. It is mostly with respect to these three questions that the socio-legal approach varies from the traditional legal approach. Section two focuses on the intellectual conflict between the socio-legal orientation to governance and the notion of governance as implicit within the mainstream 'good governance agenda' with its strong normative emphasis on the 'rule of law'. Section three discusses the tricky relationship between law and the exercise of power, drawing in particular from Foucauldian perspectives on the subtle use of law and other strategies of regulation that aid the construction of individual identity through a design of permissible behaviours and thoughts and constitute our 'modern experience of power' (Rose, 1996). Section four finally considers the specific analytical tools that the socio-legal approach makes available for wider governance analysis.

Intellectual domain of socio-legal inquiry

What is the law?

Destabilising a deductive view of the law as an institution central to social order is the defining characteristic of the socio-legal inquiry. Instead, socio-legal studies have attempted to develop a more sophisticated view of the relationships between law and social behaviour. Such studies consistently reject 'legal centralism', an ideology that the state and the system of lawyers, courts and prisons is the only form of social ordering (Griffiths, 1986). Instead, drawing from a tradition of legal anthropology, a notion of 'legal pluralism', that acknowledges the coexistence of multiple legal systems pertaining to the same domain of social life, has gathered strength (Griffiths, 1986; Merry, 1988; Spiertz, 2000). Within this perspective, 'lawyers' law should be seen as forming only one part of a multiplicity of institutional arrangements and normative repertoires of society' and 'other officially non-legal institutions and normative lexicons generated and maintained in social life' should be included in any conceptual framework of socio-legal analysis (Spiertz, 2000:179). A key development in the shift from legal centralism to legal pluralism concerned the conceptualisation of the role of the individual in relation to the law. From being perceived as a passive subject whose behaviour could be shaped and reshaped by a set of coherent laws, the individual is positioned at the intersection of different legal systems and normative repertoires and is both constrained and enabled by these (Spiertz, 2000) (later in the chapter, we discuss the rather different Foucauldian characterisation of the individual in relation to the law).

Legal pluralism has its roots in the early 20th century studies conducted by anthropologists in the colonised societies of Asia, Africa and the Pacific. These researchers realised not only that colonised peoples had both indigenous and European laws, but also that the introduction of European colonial law had created a plurality of legal orders while considerably overlooking the complexity of previous legal orders (Merry, 1988). Such analysis, which focused on the intersection between indigenous and European law but was not restricted to it, has been referred to as the 'classical legal pluralism' (Merry, 1988:872). More recently, since the 1970s, scholars have been interested in applying the concept of legal pluralism to non-colonised societies, especially the advanced industrialised countries of Europe and the United States. Their inquiry, known as the 'new legal pluralism', suggests that plural normative orders are found not in post-colonial societies alone, but in virtually all societies. Merry (1988) comments that non-state normative orders are harder to discern in societies without colonial pasts, and it is for this reason that apart from notable exceptions like Ehlrich's concept of the 'living law' (1913) and Macauley's work on 'private ordering (1963), these were largely ignored until the mid-1970s.

There is thus a move away from questions solely of the effect of law on society and *vice versa*, towards those aimed at conceptualising a more complex and interactive relationship between 'official and unofficial' forms of social ordering (Merry, 1988). The new legal pluralism views plural normative orders as participating within the same social field. Griffiths (1986) has further distinguished between the 'juristic view' of legal pluralism as a particular problem of dual legal systems resulting from the imposition of European law on colonies and the 'social science' view of legal pluralism as an empirical state of affairs in society. However, with the shift to the new legal pluralism, scholars increasingly agree that legal pluralism does not describe a type of society, but is a 'condition to be found to a greater or lesser extent in most societies' (Merry, 1988:879).

Legal pluralism posits the existence of multiple legal spheres but more importantly, is concerned with developing hypotheses regarding their mutual relationships. Historically thus, there has been a shift in the way the relationship between state and non-state law has been described (Merry, 1988:879–881). The major stages of this process can be summarised as follows. During the 1960s and early 1970s, keeping in line with the general trend of examining the 'impact' of law on society, several studies demonstrated the power of state law to reshape the social order (Massell, 1968; Diamond, 1973). These suggested the dominance of this form of law over other normative orders. Law appeared to be a 'tool for modernisation in third world countries' and for creating social justice in the first world (Merry, 1988:879). During the 1970s, a more cautious and limited view emerged, and a number of studies showed limits to the capacity of law to transform social life (Burman and Harrell-Bond, 1979). Accompanying increasing evidence that imposed law did not necessarily act as an instrument of social change, was detailed research on the constant creation of customary law, a process in which subordinate groups were neither passive nor powerless (Moore, 1978; Merry, 1988).

In this respect, Moore's notion of the 'semi-autonomous social field' was a significant attempt to explain why the power of legislation to change behaviour is limited. She explained this was because laws or other attempts to direct change essentially tinkered with 'ongoing social fields' that have 'areas of relatively autonomous activity and self-regulation' (Moore 1978:7, 58). Moore viewed the semi-autonomous social field as a way of defining a research problem. Such a conceptual-isation allowed anthropologists to study 'social fields' in terms of their 'semi-autonomy', precisely because these could generate rules, customs and symbols internally, but were at the same time vulnerable to rules, decisions and other forces emanating from the larger world. Moore argued that a close examination of semi-autonomous social fields strongly suggests that the various processes that make internally gen-erated rules effective are often also the 'immediate forces that dictate the mode of compliance or non-compliance to state-made legal rules' (1978:58). Her approach laid down the ground for a more nuanced understanding of the dialectics of acquiescence and resistance in rela-tion to the law.

Reflecting the new legal pluralism, research in the 1980s has increas-ingly focused on the mutually constitutive relationship between state law and other normative orders. This dialectic has been further enriched by the development of a number of related conceptualisations. One such view interprets the law as a symbolic and ideological system (see *Law and Society Review* special issue on 'Law and Ideology' 1988, Volume 22, No. 5). Another studies the law as a 'system of meanings' and a 'cultural code for interpreting the world' (Geertz, 1983). A third regards that legal pluralism is the key concept in a 'post modern view of law' (de Sousa Santos, 1987). Here, the author uses the metaphor of a map to discuss the law, and suggests that the law is a 'system of signs' that both represents as well as distorts reality through various tech-niques, of scale, symbolisation and projection. Each of these views, in essence, reflects a greater recognition of the 'interconnectedness between social orders' (Merry, 1988:880).

The mutually constitutive relationship between state law and other normative orders has also been described as 'integral plurality' (Fitz-patrick, 1984), and such integral pluralism has been further understood as a 'dialectic of power and counter-power' (Merry, 1988). Indeed, research through the 1980s has persuasively demonstrated both the way 'state law penetrates and restructures other normative orders through sym-bols and through direct coercion, and at the same time, the way non-state normative orders resist and circumvent penetration or even capture and use the symbolic capital of the state law (Merry, 1988:881). Galanter's (1981) research showed how state law can constitute a 'bargaining' tool even when not in use. Benda-Beckmann (1981) illustrated the remarkable use of plural legal and normative orders as a valuable resource by local disputants, a phenomenon she captured slickly as 'forum-shopping'. The author describes how disputants 'shop for forums for their problems and forums compete for their disputes, which they use for their own political ends (Benda-Beckmann, 1981:117). The theory of integral plurality, it is argued, provides space for individual actions even for the relatively powerless (Henry, 1985). Viewed from this perspective, it is possible to acquire a finely textured understanding of the domination of and resistance to state law. Yet, as Merry (1988) rightly points out, this is a difficult area of research; while attention to legal pluralism examines limits to the ideological power of state law (areas where it fails to penetrate, is co-opted and/or subverted), it may obscure an analysis of how the law in its ideological role constructs 'modes of thinking and implicit understandings' as a key component of its power.

Even as socio-legal theorists have sought to dismantle a hegemonic conception of state law as a coherent institution that successfully governs social behaviour, research and writing on legal pluralism has evoked some introspection amongst scholars as to what can rightfully be considered as the law. Merry, a keen observer of legal pluralism, writes, 'Where do we stop speaking of law and start describing social life?' (1988:878). She puts forth the view that once legal centralism has been done away with, calling all forms of social ordering that are not state law blunts the analysis. Moore similarly questions whether the 'enforceable and binding rules of all durable, organised social units should be considered "laws" or should the term be confined to the binding rules enforced by the government or the state?' (1978:17).

This issue has sparked a lively debate within the discipline. Pospisil (1971) has argued that every society has a multiplicity of 'legal systems and legal levels', which range from family to the state, and that law as a 'category' of social phenomena exists in all of them. Moore regards (1978) that such a framework is more useful in analyses of 'simpler' societies, but while understanding more complex societies, there is an advantage in preserving the conventional distinction between rules potentially enforceable by the government from those enforceable by other organisations. She adds that 'law is a category of our own culture' and thus the conventional criterion does not apply while understanding societies that are without government and thus have a fundamentally different social structure. Instead, Moore proposes the idea of 'reglementation' as an inclusive idea that encompasses governmental law as well as non-governmental sites of rule-making and enforcement

(1978:17–18). The sociology of reglementation recognises that rules are made within organisations other than the state, both in societies without government and in societies having an overarching state organisation. She explains that pre-state or non-state societies have political units that can be mobilised to exert physical force to enforce widely accepted norms, and thus perform the same conceptual role as the government does with respect to law enforcement in more centralised systems. With the idea of reglementation in place, Moore suggests the term 'law' can be strictly reserved to refer to rules that are enforceable by the government.

Further, theorists have also considered the merits of different criteria as the basis for distinguishing 'legal' norms from others, if purely for analytical purposes. State enforcement is most closely associated with the legitimate use of force, and thus force is proposed as a useful criterion. Moore (1978) points that an emphasis on the capacity of this force should not disregard other agencies and modes of inducing compliance. Following on, Moore also argues that similarly effectiveness cannot be a criterion for distinguishing 'legal' norms from others as both sets may be effective, and clearly 'neither effective sanctions nor the capacity to generate binding rules are the monopoly of the state' (1978:79).

Where is the law?

Studies in the socio-legal tradition are vitally interested in the sociological nature of the official law, but even more importantly, are concerned with the nature and dynamics of other rules, norms and regulations that perform the same function attributed to the law, i.e., governing social behaviour. They reveal that the governance of social behaviour is mediated by plural normative repertoires that are integrally and inextricably a part of social life. In this approach, what also emerges is a new positioning of the individual, which is quite different from that within the conventional legal discipline. The individual is not perceived as passive and his behaviour is not understood in terms of compliance versus deviation alone. Instead, the analytical focus is centred on the individual who stands at the intersection of many different legal domains (or spheres) (Spiertz, 2000). This viewpoint allows both for finely grained analyses of domination and resistance in relation to the law, and also for a greater insight into the use of law as a resource by those perceived as powerless.

In the spirit of keeping the analytical focus on the individual alive, socio-legal studies have also approached the question of the law from a spatial perspective. By asking the question 'where is the law' and 'where does it exist', they point our attention to the fact that it is not enough to assume that the law exists, and individuals' knowledge of the law impacts greatly on its use and socialisation. The social existence of legal phenomena is always 'geographically specific' and the 'law is unevenly distributed in most societies' (Benda-Beckmann and Benda-Beckmann, 1991). As such, descriptive generalisations about legal phenomena remain unspecified unless tied down to a particular locality. The authors reason that not only can the spatial distribution of the law be a relevant factor in the explanation of socio-politico-economic relationships, but also that the uneven spatial distribution of the law is in itself a subject worthy of investigation.

It has been viewed that while spatial referents to the law abound (Galanter 1981, 1983; Moore 1978) these perspectives need to be enriched by considering the spatial dimension in which the 'metaphorical rooms, fields, places are actually located' (Benda-Beckmann and Benda-Beckmann, 1991:120). Studies using spatial metaphors have tried to distance themselves from the boundaries defined by state law, and have discovered other relevant points of exclusion and inclusion and thus, of 'external' or 'internal' law (such as Moore's concept of semi-autonomous social fields). However, in social interaction, normative boundaries are dynamic and prone to reinterpretation, and this change can impact on particular spatial references to which law is 'external' or 'internal' to a particular community.[2] Attention to space needs to be made not in a banal 'purely geographic' sense, but to space as 'socially constituted by reference to material and social constituents' that is irreducible to either of these elements (Sayer, 1985; and Thrift, 1985; cited in Benda-Beckmann and Benda-Beckmann, 1991:120). Space as defined in legal norms is not the same as the space upon which it is projected; only too often, the constructions of legal spaces into which law-makers project their own law or that of others are not the only ones, and not necessarily the most important ones (de Sousa

---

[2]Drawing on their fieldwork in Indonesian villages, Benda-Beckmann and Benda-Beckmann (1991) explain how a state cooperative and state law may be spatially located within a village, but in terms of the *adat* (religious law) social and political definitions of the village, it may be external or internal, depending on village level interpretations. The local *adat* normative and institutional complex of a village, on the other hand, is usually considered external to the inhabitants of neighbouring villages, even though in a general sense, they are all part of the regional *adat* community.

Santos, 1987). This is most conspicuously reflected in the conceptualisation of state law along the lines of territory and hierarchy of its personnel and institutions. Thus, the state is both higher than the local and also external to it. This reflects the tendency to mistake an 'abstract construct' to be a 'concrete phenomenon' (Benda-Beckmann and Benda-Beckmann, 1991).

Moreover, to say that a law exists in a particular place, say village, must at the very least mean that people have some knowledge of it. They must be aware, to some extent, of the legal rules, principles and institutions in place and use it in their decisions. This knowledge should be reflected particularly at the interactive level, in the formulation of new rules or in tackling situations of collective uncertainty or interpersonal conflicts. Thus, 'knowledge can be regarded as the minimal existence of law and mere knowledge can become important in social life, when people orient their behaviour by it, in the sense of it being a calculus or other orientation point for their behaviour' (Benda-Beckmann and Benda-Beckmann, 1991:124). Others have commented on how knowledge even of distant law allows people to act 'in the shadow of the law' (Mnookin and Kornhauser, 1979; as cited in Benda-Beckmann and Benda-Beckmann, 1991:124). However, the authors emphasise that how significant this knowledge is for the reorientation of social behaviour, whether by way of conformity, manipulation or resistance is an empirical question and cannot be generalised.

Apropos legal pluralism, just as there are many laws, there are also many different 'knowledges' of the law (Wickmann, 1990; as cited in Benda-Beckmann and Benda-Beckmann, 1991:125). Individuals usually acquire fragmentary knowledge of various sets of laws. It follows that the means of communication through which such knowledge is acquired vary. Citing their empirical research in Indonesian villages, Benda-Beckmann and Benda-Beckmann (1991) distinguish between the 'general socialisation processes' of village meetings and public transactions that disseminated knowledge of 'traditional laws' and the more sporadic interface that villagers had with itinerant state officials and other outsiders that were the source of knowledge of state law. Thus, peoples' knowledge of different sets of laws inevitably goes through a process of interpretation and mediation by a range of actors and situations. This attention to the plural and particular meanings that laws hold for individuals reinforces the central quest of the socio-legal tradition, which is to dismantle conceptualisations of state law as a hegemonic tool for social control.

Is there any chronology to the emergence of the law?

Legal scholars have a definitive view of how the law, as we know it, came about. In fact, this view constitutes a core aspect of the larger conceptualisation of the law as a rational attempt by society to counter anarchy and create order. A dichotomy between 'law' and 'custom' is central to this understanding. To put it simply, scholars of historical jurisprudence treated custom as the 'precursor of law', as its evolutionary source (Moore, 1978:13). Early work in classical legal pluralism has also referred to a distinction between law and custom. Diamond described these 'dichotomous' relations in the following manner: 'Custom – spontaneous, traditional, personal, commonly known, corporate, relatively unchanging – is the modality of society; law is the instrument of civilisation, of political society sanctioned by organised force, presumably above society at large, and buttressing a new set of social interests' (1973:322–323). His own view was to reject the notion that 'custom is a form of primitive law that will gradually develop into state law', and he argued instead that 'the advance of law contradicts and extinguishes custom' (Merry, 1988:875).

Indeed, 'the vision of simpler societies dominated by integrated traditions of ancient origin gave scholars to differentiate with exaggerated sharpness between the customs of such "early" societies and the statutes of self-conscious modern states' (Moore, 1978:14). In legal studies, 'customary law' was conceptualised as 'an intuitive law based on traditionally supportive consensus' (Podgorecki, 1991:66). It was believed that the law 'does function differently on various levels of technical and civilisational change' and 'underdeveloped' societies are characterised by the prevalence of intuitive law (Podgorecki, 1991:156). A contrast was thus drawn between 'tradition and culture' that shape the law of 'primitive societies' and 'intellect and intention' that shape the law of 'modern societies' (Moore, 1978). The corollary to this premise was that modern legal systems are logical systems, whose basic character can be reduced to a few basic postulates. Of course, as discussed in the previous chapter, much of the socio-legal inquiry has been devoted to revealing the fallacy of this belief. From a sociological point of view, the 'piecemeal historical process' by which legal systems are constructed and that ostensibly rational actions do not have 'fully controllable aggregate effects' together prevent the 'full systematic rationalisation of any legal system' (Moore, 1978).

The prevalence of custom has been attributed both to colonised as well as early European peoples (Moore, 1978). It has been accorded a distinct political significance in both settings. In the colonies, as works in classical legal pluralism revealed, the 'laws of indigenous populations' were of major importance to the governing powers as colonial administrators 'could not possibly hope to revamp completely the indigenous legal/political system, and for that matter did not aspire to do so' (Moore, 1978:15). Thus, in a sense, recognition of custom and the 'customary law' was of a parallel legal order that lay alongside the European law, precisely what Griffiths (1986) referred to as the 'juristic' view of legal pluralism. European ideas about customary law however date from an earlier period than the colonial expansion in the 19th century. From the Roman Empire to medieval times and afterwards too, successive governments and the church were concerned, especially for administrative purposes such as the centralisation and standardisation of control, with the range of 'ethnic communities and regions' in Europe and the variety of their local laws (Moore, 1978). Interestingly, in both these settings, local customary law and the law of the overarching polity were distinguished by the type and level of political unit within which the rule was regarded as legitimate. Moore explains how '"laws" in these settings were the rules of the dominant and geographically widest regime, "custom" its term for binding practices of localised subordinate peoples' (1978:15).

This duality between law and custom has been criticised severely by a range of scholars, particularly those researching the question of custom in Africa (Besteman, 1994; Mamdani, 1996; Peters, 2004; to name a few). These studies have demonstrated that the notion of an unchanging custom was a myth of the colonial era, while customary law itself was a product of the colonial encounter. They showed how the formation of customary law, especially with regard to communal land tenure, served to promote both state and private European interests in African colonies. Interestingly, Africans also ended up defending colonial constructions as one of the few ways to unsuccessfully try to fend off further land appropriations, and somehow, the terminology of customary law and communal land was furthered by Africans themselves. Moreover, the practice of customary law often resulted in a form of 'decentralised despotism' in which so-called traditional leaders benefited at the cost of those in their charge, while also preserving the official impression that custom was 'static' as an expedient cover for their actual practices (Peters, 2004). These observations reveal the nature of custom as an ongoing and dynamic process, imbricated within the formal law and not rigidly distinct from it.

It is clear thus that the socio-legal tradition rejects an evolutionary perspective from custom to law. A more acceptable way of understanding the differences between societies and the nature of laws that govern social behaviour was put forward by Moore (1978). She sought to differentiate societies in terms of degrees of complexity. So 'the more complex the society, the more the layers of rule-systems; the more adjacent they are, and the more numerous and diverse the separate "jurisdictions" or autonomous fields; the more intricate the questions of domination/autonomy, hierarchy/equivalence, proliferation/reduction, amalgamation/division, replication/diversification in the relations within and amongst the constitutive units and levels' (Moore, 1978:28). She perceptively remarks that the more complex a society, the greater appearance there will be of rational control, but the more areas of discretion and 'semi-autonomous' activity there will be in the 'sub-parts' of the society, both formal and informal (1978:30). This approach serves as a worthy reminder of the central message of the socio-legal tradition: that social life has plural normative repertoires that mediate behaviour, rational control is the discourse rather than reality, and as rules represent behaviour rather than dictate conduct (see Mosse, 2003 and 2006), any attempt to understand what really is going on must penetrate layers of 'formalism' and 'self-representation'.

The socio-legal response to 'good governance'

This overwhelmingly empirical orientation of the socio-legal approach to governance is at odds with the normative tone of the World Bank-led 'good governance' agenda. This agenda has been the subject of stringent criticisms within the development studies literature, but it has a special significance in the socio-legal tradition as well. It has been argued that a particular notion of the 'legal' is at the core of the discourse of good governance and central to its epistemological evolution, and that this notion is a 'normative fairyland' which disregards the social realities it is presumed to regulate (Benda-Beckmann, 1994). So for example, 'good governance' outcomes are all too frequently associated with legal prescriptions that are enshrined in law or management policy which may be drastically different from the 'informal rules' governing access to resources or services. The law as conceptualised within the good governance agenda, we consider, has received relatively little analytical attention beyond the acceptance of the 'rule of law' as an essential pre-requisite.[3] This obsession on the 'rule of law' has detracted

---

[3]This section relies predominantly on a seminal article by Franz von Benda-Benda-Beckmann published in *The International Journal of Knowledge Transfer and Utilisation*, 1994.

from the 'rules-in-use' that not only illustrate peoples' capabilities but also the ways in which they may subvert or ignore the prescriptions of formal institutions.

Good governance concerns an 'optimal division between government, market and civil society' for which legal and administrative changes are necessary (Benda-Beckmann, 1994:56). It was essentially a legal constraint on the World Bank in its Articles of Agreement that forbade the Bank from taking non-economic (or political) considerations (see Section 10, article IV). Benda-Beckmann points out that this was a discussion regarding the legal meaning of the concepts 'economy' and 'political' and of the relationship between the two. However, increasing evidence in the late 1980s that structural adjustment was essentially a political phenomenon, the rise of pro-democracy movements in parts of Latin America and Eastern Europe and the growing interest in democratisation of western powers together revealed the need to formulate a new stated relationship between the economic and the political. It is no coincidence thus that the Bank (functioning within this legal constraint), and the rest of the western community in tow, increasingly resorted to the notion of governance while referring to political issues (Leftwich, 1994 and Lockwood, 2005; among others). This paved the way for novel interpretations of the so-called 'non-economic' no-go area, as the Bank tried to bring in various other issues (notably the environment) into its fold of attention. Its World Development Report, 1991, was an important epistemological landmark that made the following unprecedented statement: 'The proper economic role of government is larger than merely standing in for markets if they fail to work well. In defining and protecting property rights, providing effective legal, judicial and regulatory systems, improving the efficiency of the civil service, and probably the environment, the state forms the very core of development. Political and civil liberties are not, contrary to a once popular view, inconsistent with economic growth' (World Bank, 1991:4).

With this development, political and legal-administrative factors are no longer regarded as 'external' to the economy, but as internal to it. 'Law rises as a phoenix from the ashes of economists' forgetfulness' and it is acknowledged that the spheres of economy and good governance are articulated and bound together by law (Benda-Beckmann, 1994:57). It is through law that the reconfigured public and private domains derive their 'legitimate structure', and these rules and principles are summarised as the 'rule of law' which have become the 'guidelines' for legislative, administrative and judicial activities (for further information on the 'rule of law' visit the Carnegie Endowment for International Peace at http://www.carnegieendowment.org/programs/global/index.cfm?fa=proj&id=101&proj=zdrl). The 'rule of law' in general and the safeguarding of clear property rights in particular, are deemed as essential for the optimal functioning of the free and competitive market, in order to promote economic development.

Within this analytical framework of the relationships between good governance and the economy, purely normative considerations prevail. These relationships are described as how they ought to be, and not how they actually are. Benda-Beckmann also notes that economic, political and legal factors are not accorded an equal significance within the discourse of good governance, and that in fact, politics and law are subjected to economics (1994:58). The 'rule of law' is not a goal unto itself, but 'is only relevant to the extent that it establishes a set of preconditions for development' (World Bank, 1992; as cited in Benda-Beckmann, 1994:58). This asymmetry in discursive emphasis, explains Benda-Beckmann, is only to be expected as if all elements of good governance has been taken into account systematically, then the Bank would violate the legal constraints that bind it. This reinforces the wider observation that 'governance' has been used as a shroud under which the Bank can engage with political issues without changing its constitutional charter. The Bank 'is neither concerned with establishing new scientific insights about the relationship between economy and governance, nor with the establishment of rigid rules for a new policy; rather, it is concerned with creating a wider berth for pragmatic manoeuvring within the legally constrained sphere of its activities' (Benda-Beckmann, 1994:58).

From the socio-legal perspective, while it is 'promising' that more attention is finally being given to the law, the 'assumptions underlying such attention are disquieting in their simplicity and normative orientation' (Benda-Beckmann, 1994:61). Legal frameworks are not a precise depiction of the social behaviour they seek to regulate. They may however serve as representations of behaviour and also as valuable resources structuring socio-political interaction. In fact, as we discussed earlier, the law is only one element of a number of norms, rules and regulations that overlap over each other. Governance, within the socio-legal tradition, is an overarching concept to describe the complex and multifaceted social processes – official and unofficial, intended and unintended, visible and invisible – that together mediate social behaviour and conduct. Governance, within the 'good governance' agenda is an instrumental idea, referring to the ideal political-administrative and crucially legal conditions that must prevail for free-market-led economic growth and development to occur. In the former, there is an incontrovertible acceptance that social behaviour cannot be rationally and consciously directed, changed or engineered, and to this extent, governance is not a goal to be pursued but rather a description of social reality. In the latter, the ambitious pursuit of 'good governance' agendas by western governments and donors in the developing parts of world confirms this quest as its most distinguishing characteristic. It is quite evident that the two conceptualisations stand far apart.

Law and power

The issue of power occupies an important part within the socio-legal explanation regarding the nature of the law. Following on from the previous discussion, four important points may be summarised here. One, socio-legal studies oppose the hegemonic conceptualisation of the law as a coherent institution endowed with the power to direct and change social behaviour. On the other hand, they examine limits both to the ideological and actual power of the state and thus the law, as an instrument of state power. Two, socio-legal studies are critical of the way in which 'law is usually subsumed under the categories of culture, governance/politics, ideology or economics' within analyses, on the grounds that these categories are not mutually exclusive and it is therefore problematic to include law within any of them (Benda-Beckmann, *et al.*, 2005:2). Moreover, it is argued that reducing the legal dimension to the economic or political (as the good governance discourse does) would 'negate' the important legitimising function of law in social, economic and political organisations. It would also disregard the fact that the law (both official and unofficial) is a 'powerful form of cultural expression' that operates as a potential force of socio-economic and political power, constraining and enabling social practices with both intended as well as unintended outcomes. Third, the concept of legitimacy itself is widened beyond the state, both in the sense that the state's law may derive greater or lesser legitimacy depending on social conditions (see Moore's concept of the semi-autonomous social field (1978)), but also that multiple norms, rules and regulations may be both legitimate and effective without necessarily drawing on state sanction. Interestingly as well, socio-legal studies explore how state law and non-state normative orders penetrate one another symbolically, drawing from one another, to (successfully or not) further their own legitimacy. Four, an important shift implicit in the treatment of power within the socio-legal tradition concerns the positioning of the individual. Instead of treating the individual as a passive recipient of the law, which is imposed by the state from above, these studies focus their analytical attention on how the individual stands at the crossroads of different normative repertoires, and often uses this plurality as a resource.

Foucault's key propositions on 'governance', power and the law

A significant contribution to socio-legal studies comes from within the Foucauldian tradition of analysis. Foucault's approach to governance, power and particularly the law is relevant to socio-legal thinking primarily because it departs from the 'traditional' framework of analysis for governance. Such a framework is orientated towards the formulation and maintenance of laws, regulations and rules by a state apparatus that develops its means in accordance with this 'internal end' (Beresford, 2003:87). Foucault and his followers on the other hand direct attention to the 'strategic and tactical moves, micro-power techniques and the various movements of power below the radar of sovereignty and the law' (Foucault, 1991:95), thus rejecting a notion of cohesive state power exerted through the execution of the law, within which individuals are merely passive spectators. Thus, Foucault's form of governance synchronises means in accordance with an 'external end', the perfection and intensification of the processes which it directs through 'the instrument of multiform tactics' rather than uniform, universalistic laws (Foucault, 1991:95).

In this framework of analysis, the state for all its omnipotence, does not occupy the whole field of actual power relations. Moreover, it is visualised not as 'a single entity that has power' (Ferguson, 1990), but as a set of institutions, i.e., political leadership, bureaucracy, legislative bodies, police, planning apparatus, that act as the most important points of references for all power relations. Foucault considered the state to be the principle 'referent' of all power relations (1982), which operated on the basis of other already existing power relations. The view that the state does not extend its sway throughout society by extending its control apparatus, and that we need to think in terms of the 'governmentalisation of the state' for the exercise of political rule follows. Thus, unlike the traditional approach to governance, where the phenomenon of power is dependent on the state apparatus (and its traditional political systems such as law and prohibition), in Foucault's analysis, power exists in social relations, and the population is a participant in the government's attempt to control the social environment (Beresford, 2003). His clear intent to distinguish sovereignty from government followed from this viewpoint. While sovereignty was a concept centred on the divine power of the king and conveyed a hierarchical relationship between the state and the individual, government required that 'we cut off the king's head' and pay attention to the ways in which we direct conduct through the systems of the body of society (Foucault, 1980:121).

Foucault was therefore fundamentally interested in the rationality of government or 'governmentality', as he termed it. Governmentality constitutes the common ground of all the modern forms of the arts of government or 'political rationalities', to the extent that they construe the tasks of rulers in terms of a 'calculated supervision and max-imisation of the forces of society' (Rose, 1990:5). As an array of tech-nologies of government, governmentality is to be analysed in terms of the 'strategies, techniques and procedures' in use by various authorities 'to enact programmes of government in relation to the materials and forces to hand and the resistances and oppositions anticipated or encountered' (Rose, 1996:42). Following from his notion of govern-ment as the 'conduct of conduct' (Foucault, 1988a; as cited in Burchell, 1996:19), Foucault correspondingly understood power less as a con-frontation between adversaries and more as a question of government. He theorised that power is and can only be exercised over 'free sub-jects', as a mutual relationship between two elements within a 'field of possibilities' in which the behaviour of 'active subjects' is able to inscribe itself.

In this context, Foucault was particularly interested in the 'making' of individuals, in the 'specific techniques of power that regards indi-viduals both as objects as well as the instruments of its exercise' (Dreyfus and Rabinow, 1982:156). He described the evolution of disciplinary techniques since the 18th century, and emphasised that discipline was 'a technique not an institution' that did precisely this (Foucault, 1977; as cited in Dreyfus and Rabinow, 1982:153). His work illustrated how prisons, hospitals and so on were the only clearly articulated expres-sion of more generalised practices of disciplining both individuals and populations. His analyses of objectification concerned the processes by which an authority effects changes on 'mute and docile bodies' (Dreyfus and Rabinow, 1982). However, the modern subject is not mute and 'must talk', and Foucault was fascinated by developments in medicine, education, social reform and religion through which the individual gradually became an 'object of knowledge, both to himself and to others, an object who tells the truth about himself in order to know himself and to be known, an object who learns to effect changes on himself' (Dreyfus and Rabinow, 1982:174). He saw the confession, and especially confession about one's sexuality, as a central component in the expanding technologies for the discipline and control of bodies, populations and society itself. Foucault labelled these particular techniques as 'techniques of the self', which complemented the 'technologies of discipline'. His goal has consistently been to 'isolate' the interconnections between power and knowledge, to show how all the objects of study within the banner of the 'legitimate social sciences' have in fact been inextricably wound up with the 'micro-practices' of power. For Foucault, power *is* knowledge and he examined man as a simultaneous subject and object of knowledge (Gordon, 1980:34). And yet, we are reminded that Foucault's overarching objective was not to develop a general theory of power, but in fact to 'create a history of the different modes by which, in our culture, human beings are made subjects' (Foucault, 1982:208). It is to this issue that we now turn.

The individual as subject: strategies of self-regulation

Within the Foucauldian tradition of analysis, there has been a lot of interest in understanding the particular and subtle role of the individual in sustaining a system of governance through her own subjectivity. This analytical focus complements the attention accorded to understanding the micro-practices and techniques of power 'beyond' and 'beneath' the formal state and its law. Freedom as associated with modern, liberal societies is regarded neither as 'ideological fiction' nor as an 'essential feature of existence' within them. It is understood fundamentally and necessarily as a 'formula of rule' (Barry, *et al.*, 1996:8). It was variously argued that the freedom on which the liberal strategies of government depend is no 'natural property' of political subjects (Rose, 1996:61). The key lesson learnt was that governing society has come to require governing individual subjectivity. Liberalism, it was argued, is thus not about governing less, but governing more cautiously (Barry, *et al.*, 1996). This realisation stemmed from the acknowledgement of a new reality, the idea of society as such, with its 'own laws and mechanisms of disturbance' that the government had to deal with. This was the moment of the emergence of a 'domain of society', and of liberalism not as the absence of government, but the invention of practical and intellectual techniques that could distinguish civil society as a distinct entity, 'distinct from political intervention and yet potentially alignable with political aspirations' (Barry, *et al.*, 1996:9; also for three propositions on liberal rule when viewed from a governmentality perspective see Rose, 1996:39–40).

Early liberalism has also been understood in terms of how market freedom could be reconciled with the unlimited exercise of political sovereignty, a formulation that contained an implicit critique of the previous 'police state' (Burchell, 1996). *Laissez faire* is viewed both as 'a limitation of the exercise of political sovereignty *vis-à-vis* the government of commercial exchanges and a positive justification of market freedom on the grounds that the State will benefit more...by governing less' (Burchell, 1996:22). For more modern versions of liberalism, referred to as neoliberalism or economic liberalism, the problem still is a question of a critical reason pertaining to the limits of government in relation to the market. There is a difference between the two with respect to the construction of individual rationalities. So for early liberalism, to govern properly involved linking the principle of rationalising government activity to the rationality of the free conduct of the governed individuals themselves, but for neoliberalism, the rationality for limiting government activity had to be determined by reference to artificially contrived forms of the 'free, entrepreneurial and competitive conduct of economic-rational individuals' (Burchell, 1996:23–24). The common point however, is that neither case deals with a simple exercise of domination over individuals as beings with certain clear aptitudes or capabilities, and in both cases, the principle of government requires the proper use of liberty, either 'natural' (as with early liberalism) or as an 'artefact' (as with neoliberalism).

Investing further the 'strategies of self-regulation' that make up our modern experience of power involves asking the question of how did the 'obligations of political authorities come to extend to the health, happiness and well-being of the population and those families and individuals who comprised it?' (Rose, 1996:38). Liberalism, as a mentality of rule, abandons the fantasy of a totally administered society and accepts that rulers cannot exercise their 'totalising sway' over national space. On the other hand, rulers are confronted with subjects equipped with rights and interests that they cannot govern by the exercise of sovereign for lack of requisite knowledge. This conundrum requires the reformulation of the instruments of rule in reference to the domains of 'market, civil society and citizenship' aiming at the benefit of the entire nation (Rose, 1996:44). As a result, two apparently 'illiberal' techniques: the disciplines of the body and the bio-politics of the population, have become key constituents of liberal mentalities of rule, since liberal rule vitally depends on the 'production and government of a polity of free citizens' (Foucault, 1977; as cited in Rose, 1996:44). Four key features of liberalism from the perspective of government have been identified: a new relation between government and knowledge, as liberal strategies tie government to the positive knowledge of human conduct developed within the social and human sciences; a novel specification of the subjects of rule as active agents in their own government; an intrinsic relationship to the authority of expertise, where experts demanded that economic, familial and social arrangements are governed according to their own programmes; and finally, a continual questioning of the activity of rule (Rose, 1990; 1996:44–47).

By early 19th century, increasing evidence of economic problems and social fragmentation led to the denouncement of the liberal project as a failed one. There was the need to reformulate relationships between the political field and the management of economic and social affairs, and 'welfare' became accepted as the way forward (Rose, 1996). Within newly recoded political, economic and social relationships, the authority of experts in the individual and collective lives of individuals was to be accorded a new role. The state was to be responsible for generating an array of technologies of government that 'would "social-ise" individual citizenship and economic freedom in the name of collective security' (Rose, 1996:48). As is well known, the proposed government interventions in the realm of the market were easily the most controversial aspects of this phase. A part of the new technologies of rule were social insurance and social work, the first being 'inclusive' and 'solidaristic' and the second 'individualising' (O'Malley, 1992; 1996). The 'welfarist' mentality of government saw a reconceptualisation of the political subject as citizen, 'with rights to social protection and social education in return for duties of social obligation and social responsibility' (Rose, 1996:49).

This phase did not last long, and soon, an array of different social and economic reasons highlighted by the Left and the Right weakened the case for social government (for a succinct summary see Rose, 1996:50–52). In response, neoconservative political regimes in Britain and the United States launched a number of different schemes to address the problems of welfare, relating to social costs, the power of professional lobbies and so on. They did not have a unified coherent rationality to begin with, and only gradually came to be assembled as such, into a cogent mentality of government known as 'neoliberalism'. Although neoliberalism managed to revive the sceptical liberal vigilance over political government, it did not abandon the 'will to govern'; indeed, it 'maintains the view that failure of government to achieve its objectives is to be overcome by inventing new strategies of government that will succeed' (Rose, 1996:53).

Neoliberal governmentality witnessed three important shifts. First, there was a new relationship between authority and expertise. Unlike welfare, where expert conceptions of health, economic activity and so on were inscribed into the political machinery of government into enclosures where their authority could not be challenged, neoliberal mentalities of rule have a certain 'formal' character, and the 'powers accorded to the positive knowledges of human conduct are to be transferred to the calculative regimes of accounting and management'. While these new techniques may have had a 'lower epistemological profile' than the positive knowledges, they brought with them an unprecedented flexibility and reach of government across space. Second, there was a 'new pluralisation' of political technologies that aimed to 'autonomise' individuals across the political spectrum, in contrast to the former welfare strategy of the individual as a social citizen. Third, there was a new specification of the subject of government. There was an enhanced emphasis on the powers of the individual as a customer, and a conceptualisation of 'active' individuals seeking to maximise the quality of their lives through conscious acts of choice (see Rose, 1996:54–56; for more details of these shifts). This last shift is the most significant as it ushers in a new regime of the actively responsible self, comprising individuals who 'fulfil their national obligations not through the relations of dependency and obligation to one another, but through seeking to fulfil themselves within a variety of micro-domains or "communities"' (Rose, 1996:57). This ethnical *a priori* of the active individual in an active society is perhaps the most 'generalisable' of these new governmentalities (Rose, 1990, 1996).

This notion of active citizenship has manifested itself in a number of spheres, and two such cases will be discussed here for illustration. The first is the concern with the management of the 'productive self' that was to proceed both through the 'rise of a new international and self-consciously progressive politics of the workplace' and the shaping of a picture of the employee as a 'self-actualising ego whose personal strivings could be articulated into the organisation of the enterprise' (Rose, 1990:103). Rose described how a new 'psycho-technology of work' accompanies and allies itself with the new 'psycho-technology of subjectivity', where work itself could become the privileged space for the satisfaction of human needs (1990:117). The second sphere is to do with crime, correction and individual responsibility. Neoliberalism's concern with rational, responsible and free individuals lead it to vigorously reject detention and correction as methods to address crime (O'Malley, 1992, 1996). Crime is increasingly understood not as a matter of 'personal and social pathologies in need of correction, but as a set of risks, more or less inevitable in some degree, but predictable and manageable in aggregate terms' (O'Malley, 1996:190). Thus, prevention and risk-spreading (as through insurance) by rational individuals who are able to exercise their choice in the matter becomes more important than correctional techniques like detention. This approach has identified the rise of 'acturial' or 'insurantial' techniques of power, as increasing in importance compared with disciplinary techniques. It is argued that acturialism as a social technology invites lower resistance to social technology as it is seen to provide 'security' by managing various types of risk, a seeming 'technical' concern in targeted categories, rather than a 'political or moral concern' with faults or causes.

Actuarialism must be regarded as a technology geared in different ways to specific kinds of political programmes. Indeed, since the 1980s, we have witnessed the partial transformation of 'socialised actuarialism' (as part of the welfare state) into privatised actuarialism or 'prudentialism' as an outcome of political interventions that have promoted the interplay of market forces (O'Malley, 1996:199). The welfare model of dependence on the state and its professionals is modified to one that is consistent with a nation of free-enterprising individuals. In this way, risk management is articulated within an individualising liberal or neoliberal political programme where the discursive construct of a rational and active citizen responsible for his own choices assumes priority.

Analytical tools for governance

The socio-legal tradition is a dissident one. It goes against a state-centric, top-down view of governance, with the law as a key tool for the enforcement of social order, as ingrained within traditional political science and legal analyses. To this end, there is a unified understanding of the idea of governance within the socio-legal tradition. Scholars agree that the official state law is only one amongst plural normative repertoires in society that govern social conduct. This is captured in the move away from legal 'centralism' to legal 'pluralism' to acknowledge the plurality of 'laws', official and unofficial, visible and invisible, that impact upon social ordering and behaviour. Governance thus, as suggested earlier, is more a description of social reality than an objective aim to be pursued. This is the source of its intellectual conflict with the World Bank-led 'good governance' agenda that presumes the existence of a set of ideal legal-political-administrative conditions for optimal economic performance. Indeed, socio-legal studies reject normative approaches to governance and are firmly empirical in character. Given this orientation, they offer unique 'analytical tools' or perspectives for comprehending governance arrangements, processes and outcomes in a range of settings.

Principally, the socio-legal school diverts attention away from formal laws, rules and regulations as the site in which analysis ought to be located. It takes the individual, positioned at the 'intersection' of many different legal domains or spheres, as the focal point for investigation. In this approach, it becomes possible to view how different individuals are constrained by laws but also enabled by it to further their own interests. There is a growing literature on the use of plural laws as resources available to individuals, captured both through ideas like 'forum-shopping' (Benda-Beckmann, 1981) and 'integral plurality' or the mutually constitutive relationships between state law and other normative orders (Fitzpatrick, 1984). Such an approach allows for a very different view of powerlessness than the one implicit within the 'law as an instrument of rule' paradigm, as even relatively subordinate individuals may be able to negotiate plural legal resources to their advantage. A key analytical tool that emerges is to understand individuals' knowledge of laws, as at the minimum, to say that the law exists must mean that individuals are aware of it and use it in their interactions, conflict resolutions, rule formulations and other such activities that constitute the nitty-gritty of governance. The socio-legal approach thus promotes both a 'bottom-up' and 'outward' view of governance.

Second, it similarly offers a useful perspective with which to view individual behaviour, not necessarily as deviant from or compliant to a coherent set of formal laws, but as more subtly mediated by a range of laws and norms, which are official and unofficial. Within the Foucauldian tradition moreover, individual conduct is viewed as a subtle rationality of government, where individuals play an active part in their own government. The conceptualisation of the individual as an active citizen, responsible for instance for the satisfaction of his own needs through work and his own safety through the individualised management of risk, is central to the sustenance of liberal governance. Viewed in this way, individual behaviour is not a passive response to governance imposed from above, but rather comprised of the actions of 'active subjects' who are fundamentally 'free', and thus active participants in the exercise of power.

The third key perspective concerns the role of intentionality as a key constituent of governance. Most socio-legal studies are dismissive of a view of the law as a coherent instrument through which social behaviour can be intentionally controlled. Instead, the understanding that social behaviour has many underlying causes, which are often not within the conscious control of individuals, runs through the heart of the socio-legal tradition. As such, the whole question of 'effective' governance arrangements is not posed as a significant one within a large section of this literature. The issue of effectiveness is harder to resolve within the Foucauldian tradition, since Foucault reinforced the simultaneity of different techniques of power (disciplinary techniques as well as techniques of government) thus refraining from any hierarchical ordering in terms of efficiency or effectiveness. Later scholars like Pat O'Malley have argued against this proposition, maintaining that 'actuarial' techniques (risk management) are more efficient than disciplinary ones as they invite lower social resistance, appearing more 'technical' than 'political' and less 'exclusionary' than the latter (1996:195). Further, the 'claim' to efficiency (or effectiveness, more broadly regarded) is viewed as a characteristic of power rather than being a 'universal proposition'. This suggests that within a Foucauldian perspective, the most effective governance is that in which individuals are most willing to be actively involved in their self-regulation.

7
Corporate Governance

The debate in the literature on corporate governance seeks to examine the form that the governance of corporations takes and whose interests are protected or promoted by different structures and processes of governance. The literature offers not only theories that are descriptive or explanatory but also has a strong normative element in that it seeks to provide advice on what is the most appropriate or effective forms of governance. Shleifer and Vishny (1997:737) note that 'the subject of corporate governance is of enormous practical importance'. What is sought is a direct relationship between theory and practice in the field of corporate governance. The difficulty of connecting theory to practice is a key theme in governance debates and the corporate governance literature gives us a chance to explore the topic. According to John Maynard Keynes: 'the ideas of economists and political philosophers, both when they are right and when they are wrong, are more powerful than is commonly understood. Indeed the world is ruled by little else. Practical men, who believe themselves to be quite exempt from any intellectual influences, are usually the slaves of some defunct economist' (Keynes 1933/1950:383). This chapter suggests that Keynes observation may be particularly true when it comes to the issue of corporate governance – the governing of firms and companies in modern economies.

Given these concerns about the dominant literature this chapter starts with a plea to break from too narrow an understanding of corporate governance. A classic narrow definition of corporate governance refers to 'the ways suppliers of finance to corporations assure themselves of getting return on their investment' (Shleifer and Vishny, 1997:736). As Daily *et al.* (2003:371) point out there have been 'many decades of governance research, in which researchers have focused primarily on the control of executive self interest and the protection of shareholder interests in settings where organizational ownership and control are separated. The overwhelming emphasis in governance research has been on the efficacy of the various mechanisms available to protect shareholders from the self-interested whims of executives'. However, corporate governance is increasingly concerned with the role of stakeholders, and its impact on the collective welfare of society. Hence the OECD (1998, 1999) views the role of corporate governance as twofold. Firstly, it covers the manner in which shareholders; managers, employees, creditors, customers, and other stakeholders interact with one another in shaping corporate strategies. Secondly, it relates to public policy, and an adequate legal regulatory framework, which are essential for the development of good systems of governance. Defined as such, corporate governance is viewed as a key element in improving the microeconomic efficiency of a firm, affecting the functioning of capital markets and influencing resource allocation.

Daily *et al.* (2003:371) provide the widest and most attractive definition for our purposes referring to 'governance as the determination of the broad uses to which organizational resources will be deployed and the resolution of conflicts among the myriad participants in organizations'. This definition encourages the reader to take account of narrow economistic understandings of corporate governance and move into a broader conceptualisation of the field of study. Given the multi-disciplinary aspirations of this book, this is an appropriate direction of travel; plus we will argue one that delivers more insights into how modern firms do, and perhaps should, operate in today's global economy. The corporate governance literature, in short, has not been sufficiently interdisciplinary and as a result lacks depth and range in the focus of its study.

The structure of the chapter is straightforward. First, we examine the dominant economistic paradigms as applied to the issue of corporate governance, drawing on and developing some of the literature reviewed in Chapter 3. Second, we ask if these paradigms have stimulated programmes of reform that have led to clear and effective improvement in the efficiency of firms and the value obtained by shareholders. Third we examine a wider set of non-economics literatures that offer insights and new areas for exploration that are not sufficiently recognised within the mainstream literature. Finally, we explore the nature of corporate governance from a historical comparative and perspective.

Economistic theories of corporate governance

As noted in Chapter 3 the focus on institutions marks a key breakthrough for the governance literature in economics because of the discipline's overwhelming focus on market relationships between actors rather than organisations, rules and cultures that make up the world of institutions. The neoclassical school tended to view the firm as a production function or 'black box', transforming inputs into outputs, with little interest in the internal functioning of firms. This view stemmed from the classical view of the owner-run firm where productivity automatically created reward. The market laws of supply and demand this school assumed would determine the way that firms behaved. In their seminal study on the separation of ownership and control following the 1929 Wall Street Crash, Berle and Means (1932), proposed that the evolution of the modern corporation was such that it produced a condition where the interests of owners and managers diverged. The scale and size of modern firms presented an empirical challenge to the assumptions of the classical school.

The breaking of traditional property relations meant that persons other than those who controlled wealth could now shape industry and individual corporations and was underpinned by two main developments: the factory system and the modern corporation. The factory system, which formed the basis of the industrial revolution, was responsible for bringing large numbers of workers under a single management. The advent of the modern corporation placed the wealth of many individuals under the same central control. The growth of large-scale corporations created new relationships, responsibilities and opportunities for the various corporate stakeholders. The separation of ownership and control provides management with a degree of discretion to pursue non-profit maximising expenditure. The emergence of managerial and behavioural schools of thought cast further doubt on the classical assumption of profit maximisation as they suggested that firms appeared not to aim at equating marginal cost and marginal revenue, but instead focused on such issues as sales, firm growth and their own utility. Others such as Alchian (1961) dismissed the notion of profit maximisation in the face of incomplete information and uncertainty.

Recognition of the potential distorting impact of the large-scale corporation provides the starting point for the dominant traditions in corporate governance literature. The starting point of the corporate governance literature from an economics perspective rests on the Coasian idea that the firm exists as a nexus of market-based contracts. The separation of ownership and control implied that there exists a cost to writing these contracts. There is a principal-agent relationship to be resolved and that the transaction costs involved in resolving these issues cannot be specified in the contract. Hart (1995:681) expresses the core perception of the problem:

> Because of the separation of ownership and control, and the lack of monitoring, there is a danger that the managers of a public company will pursue their own goals at the expense of those of shareholders (we suppose that the latter are interested only in profit or net market value). Among other things, managers may overpay themselves and give themselves extravagant perks; they may carry out unprofitable, but power-enhancing investments; they may seek to entrench themselves. In addition, managers may have goals that are more benign but that are still inconsistent with value maximisation. They may be reluctant to lay off workers that are no longer productive. Or they may believe that they are the best people to run the company when in fact they are not.

Corporate governance from this perspective reflects the challenge to make shareholders the boss again in the context of competing interests and uncertainty. As Hart (1995:678) puts it:

> Corporate governance issues arise in an organisation whenever two conditions are present. First there is an agency problem, or conflict of interest, involving members of the organisation – these might be owners, managers, workers or consumers. Second, transaction costs are such that this agency problem cannot be dealt with through a contract.

Lack of certainty means that a contract cannot be easily specified. so more complex governance arrangements will arise to explain how firms with separate ownership and control can come as close to small-scale enterprise beloved by classical theory. The dominant theories that drive economistic corporate governance thinking come under two headings: principal-agency theory and transaction cost theory. We have dealt with them already to some degree in Chapter 3 so the aim here is to explore their implications for corporate governance.

Agency theory

Agency theory examines the relationship between two parties, a principal and an agent, where the agent makes decisions on behalf of the principal. In the context of the separation of ownership and control, agency theory is used to represent the relationship between owners and management. One of the consequences of the separation of ownership and control is that owners as 'principal' must delegate a degree of control to management as 'agents'. Under the 'zero-cost' neoclassical framework, the owners could instruct the management to maximise profits, as there is no disagreement on the objectives of the firm. Agency theory departs from the neoclassical assumption that the agent's costs and decisions are fully observable. Instead, it agues that owners as risk bearers are primarily concerned with profit maximisation and enhancing shareholder value. Managers on the other hand neither incur costs nor benefit to any large degree from their actions. Managers may have other interests such as salaries, non-monetary benefits, job protection, market share, and particular projects.

Fama and Jensen (1983) argue that an important aspect of an organisation's survival is its ability to control the agency problem. It is unlikely however, that the principal can ensure that the agent behaves in the principal's interest at zero cost. Moreover, it is not possible to write an optimal contract between principal and agent, as this would require contracting for all future eventualities. Hart (1995) sees the three principal costs associated with this as: contracting for all the different eventualities, negotiating costs, and the costs of writing contracts in such a way that they can be enforced by a third party. Given the existence of incomplete contracts, agency costs will be incurred in observing and monitoring organisational behaviour. Jensen and Meckling (1976:308) define agency costs as the sum of the costs of monitoring expenditures by the principal, bonding expenditures by the agent, and the residual loss. Monitoring costs refer to those incurred by the principal's attempts to reduce the agent's on-the-job consumption. Bonding costs represent the costs incurred if the agent takes it upon himself to be monitored. The residual loss refers to the reduction in welfare experienced by the principal due to the divergence between the agent's decisions and those decisions that would maximise the welfare of the principal.

The classic way of resolving the principal-agent dilemma given the difficulty and costs involved in direct monitoring is for the principal to use two broad tactics. The first technique available is for the principal to rely on outcome-based incentives. Effort and process cannot be monitored effectively but there is a greater chance that outcomes can be more effectively checked. Second, the principal can expend time and effort on selection; on choosing or developing agents that share in some way the principal's goals. Incentives and selection are the key levers but neither is without problems. Outcome incentives rest on surrogate measures and agents may be tempted to put their effort towards boosting those surrogate measures rather than the unobservable productive activity that the principal was hoping to stimulate in the agents. Further selection is not an easy process and there is always the possibility that the principal may be deceived or simply lack sufficient knowledge about the agent in order to guarantee their behaviour. Recognition of these factors leads to a third primary result from principal-agent theory – namely that all settlements between principal and agent involve an efficiency trade-off. In short, the theory suggests there that are always likely to be persistent failings and limits in the construction of governance mechanisms and element of constant reflexivity about the way that work would be advisable.

Transaction costs theories

While principal-agent theory is ultimately a normative exercise about how the principal can achieve her interests, transaction costs theories (TCT) as noted in Chapter 3 are more driven by a desire to understand the role of institutions in economic exchanges. Actors are assumed to be boundedly rational but opportunistic and faced with problems of uncertainly. A firm could ask a supplier to provide a key component or element to its product but how can it guarantee that the supplier will deliver what is required, when asked. Coming to an agreement with another has transaction costs. There are search and information costs, bargaining costs, monitoring and enforcement costs in any agreement and costs involved in, for example, protecting trade secrets (cf. Karagiannis, 2007:7). While principal-agent theory concentrates on what bargain to strike, TCT theories warn that even when the bargain is struck, elements in any relationship can go wrong. The main implication for governance is that a principal needs to lock in key players with control over key assets into the operation and decision-making of the principal. In this sense corporate governance structures are relevant for reducing transaction costs, when decisions need to be made which are not or cannot be included in a contract, effectively allowing the firm to internalise these costs. An example of this is Oliver Williamson's 'Markets and Hierarchies' stream of research, which suggests that firms adapt to or internalise high transaction costs by switching between the market and non-market hierarchical structures when the costs of market contracting become too high.

Recommendations for corporate governance: clear principles, unclear results

There are strong themes reflecting economistic principles in the development of practical guidance on issues of corporate governance. What is far less clear is whether the guidance is followed and whether when it is that better corporate performance results.

For much of mainstream economistic thinking about corporate governance, the problem is how the owners can keep control over their capital to ensure that they receive the maximum return. Hart (1995) identifies three common strategies to tackle issues of corporate governance. The first is to organise effective oversight through independent board directors or major shareholders so that managers are encouraged to behave in the interests of shareholders. The second is the threat of take-over of the company; and the third relates to the corporate financial structure and how audit procedures operate. A further form of intervention relies less on the monitoring of outcomes or challenge behaviour and more on bringing agents on board through, for example, giving managers stock options. The logic underpinning the awarding of stock options is that 'aligning the incentives of executives with those of owners is the most direct way to mitigate the agency problem' (Hall and Liebman, 1998:654). Since the manager will not make any money from the option unless the company share price goes up, he/she should have a strong incentive to maximise increase in share price. Since an improved share price also improves shareholder value, the logic is that the incentives of principal and agent have been aligned.

To confirm the impact of theories of corporate governance, Daily *et al.* (2003) argue, it is possible to look at the demands that emerge from shareholder activism. These demands define what the most vocal shareholders regard as appropriate and legitimate governance forms and plainly reflect the basic ideas of economistic theories. Corporations are called on 'to adopt practices that insulate shareholders from managerial self-interest by providing incentives for executives to manage firms in shareholders' long-term interests' (Daily *et al.*, 2003:373). The more notable demands from shareholder activists have included configuring boards so that independent, outside directors have a substantial say; separating the positions of board chair and chief executive officer in order to create a system of checks and balances at the heart of governance arrangements; imposing age and term limits for directors in order to ensure that there is some turn over and directors do not get captured by the corporation interests rather than that of shareholders; and providing executive compensation packages that include contingent forms of pay in order to align outcome challenges to the managers of the corporation in a way that matches the interests of shareholders.

The 1990s saw the start of the introduction of corporate governance codes in a number of countries (Mallin, 2003, Ch3). Codes are often introduced after some financial scandal, corporate collapse or some sort of crisis and are constituted in order to restore investor confidence. So circumstances and contingency reinforce the message from theory that the great goals of corporate governance should be accountability and transparency. While different codes reflect the circumstances of different countries, Mallin (2003: 37) demonstrates 'that there are common core principles that have been influential in the setting of codes across the globe'.

In the US, capital markets have increasingly responded to the demands of investors for better protection. The far-reaching Sarbanes Oxley Act is a case in point. The Act was a legislative response to the uncovering of large-scale corporate wrongdoing in such large US corporations as Enron and WorldCom. In the UK, a more code-based approach has been followed. Self-regulation in capital markets is where the market voluntarily agrees to bond or commit itself to higher standards of business practice. In the UK this is based on the philosophy of 'comply or explain'. Corporate governance codes are non-binding; however companies are required by the stock exchange to explain non-compliance. This is in contrast to the US (New York Stock Exchange) where the company must certify that it is not aware of any violations of the corporate governance rules.

The 'comply or explain' approach has its origins in the establishment of the Cadbury Committee in 1992. The committee was established in the wake of the collapse of several prominent UK companies (such as the Bank of Credit and Commerce International, and Maxwell Communication), which were attributed to weak corporate governance structures. The committee was given a broad mandate to address the financial aspects of corporate governance. In 1992 it published a *Code of Best Practice*. The code was non-binding; however companies were required by the stock exchange to explain non-compliance. The Cadbury Committee developed a list of 'best practice' governance standards to which companies were encouraged to aspire. Companies were then required to disclose how they measured up to the code. This approach also means that companies are free to develop their own governance practices. The Cadbury Code formed the basis for many similar codes around the world. Combining an advisory code with a disclosure regime has been adopted by dozens of countries worldwide. It formed the basis for the current code, the 2003 Combined Code and its proposed follow up the 2005 Combined Code.

The Cadbury Report (1992) in the UK provides an example of an influential report that sets out clear principles of corporate governance that are presented. The proposals conform very strongly with an understanding that the context for corporate governance is one of distrust between managers and shareholders. The overarching aim of the Cadbury principles is to align the interests of shareholders and managers by ensuring that incentives and checks are in place to steer the behaviour of managers. The procedures for composing the board ensure that there are balanced interests and access to resources for all in decision-making. In particular the role of non-executive directors is seen as crucial in maintaining an independent voice on the board that will reflect shareholder interest. Executive directors are constrained in the degree of control they can exercise. Reporting systems are there to ensure accountability and transparency.

By focusing on aligning the interests of management and shareholdings it is clear that reforms have followed a principal-agent/transaction cost agenda – but have they delivered? Here the answer appears to be far less clear. Demands to align interests between managers and shareholders to resolve the agency problems have proved difficult to meet. Minority shareholders are rarely ever in the same boat financially as senior management and directors or major shareholders. No shareholder has ever escaped the burden of capital cost, whereas the manager as holder of a fixed-price option bears no capital cost at all. Secondly, the link between a company's performance and share price is less than clear-cut. Market sentiment and industrial factors account for major movements in share price. As such, stock options may in fact represent an option on the performance of an index such as the FTSE 100 or S&P 500, rather than the performance of an individual company. Daily *et al.* (2003:375) conclude that despite the popularity of stock options to tie managers' interests to shareholders 'extant research has not provided compelling evidence of a strong relationship between executive compensation and shareholder wealth at the firm level'.

Corporate governance practices that reflect the commitment to putting checks and balances at the heart of the design also show no particular benefit. Again, as Daily *et al.* (2003:374) note: 'While agency theorists clearly would prescribe boards composed of outside, independent directors and the separation of CEO and board chair positions, neither of these board configurations is associated with firm financial performance according to reviews of the available evidence'. Of course a lack of evidence does not mean necessarily that effect is not present; it may not have been detected. Overall, however, Daily *et al.* (2003:376) conclude that 'while issues of control over executives and independence of oversight have dominated research and practice, there is scant evidence that these approaches have been productive from a shareholder-oriented perspective'. At the very least, such a finding suggests that there may be a case for looking elsewhere for theoretical inspiration for models of corporate governance.

Resource-based explanation of corporate governance

In this section we point to one of the most prominent alternative ways of looking at issues of corporate governance that challenge agency/transaction cost theories that have come to dominate economics-based conceptions by arguing that corporations are not simply sources of market-based monitoring, but also rely on their boards directors fulfil resource, service and strategy roles as much as oversight functions. Resource dependency theory suggests that boards function as a resource for organisations. Hillman and Dalziel (2003) note the limitations of agency theory and argue that the board of directors function as resource catalysts for organisations by providing linkages to necessary resources, for instance, providing legitimacy, advice and council, links to other organisations, and assistance in acquiring resources. Brown (2005:322) comments that resource dependency insights encourage researchers to examine 'how board members provide connections to influential funders (private and public), bring technical competencies (financial or legal, for example) to an organization, and provide strategic direction for the organization. In addition to performing monitoring and control functions, the board is adding value by bringing resources'.

Besides theoretical innovation, there are empirical and practical factors that drive these alternative ways of viewing the demands of corporate governance. The existence of a wide variety of organisational structures that are not necessarily based on market contracting (e.g. worker and producer cooperatives), and the emergence of new organisational forms where fixed capital is not dominant (e.g. I.T. firms based on intellectual capital), has challenged the conventional view of the firm. In particular, approaches to the firm based on agency or property rights theory typically assume that the organisation adapts to changes in the level of agency or transaction costs. Moreover, they view the firm as a nexus of contracts where issues such as employee monitoring and motivations can be contracted for. More recent thinking has suggested that in order to create such long-term attachment, the challenge is to create an environment where innovative employees know that their pay-off will be greater if they make firm-specific investments (Zingales, 2000).

Lazonick (1991) criticises the *nexus of contracts* approach on the grounds that it assumes the pre-existence of markets. Under the Coasian approach the firm is essentially a passive player that arises out of market failure as opposed to organisational success (Lazonick, 1991). Similar difficulties are also present in Williamson's 'Markets and Hierarchies' stream of research (Williamson, 1973, 1975, 1985, 2002). Because Williamson's framework also assumes the pre-existence of markets, hierarchies will only be used when the transaction costs of using the market are too high. Therefore Williamson's concept of the firm is one of an adaptive organisation, rather than an innovative business enterprise (Lazonick, 1991). This points to an important distinction between the transaction cost and resource approaches to the firm. While the transaction cost approach associates large firms with shirking and increasing monitoring costs (e.g. Alchian and Demsetz, 1972), the resource-based perspectives instead views large firms as a source of greater organisational innovations and efficiencies. The emergence of large firms in the US facilitated easier coordination of mass production, which ultimately permitted greater organisational innovations, lower prices and increased profits (Chandler, 1977). The distinction between both approaches is also important for developing economies, where due to weak institutional structures, the existence of fully functioning markets cannot be assumed.

While the property rights/transaction cost approach has mainly focused on the board of directors as a source of monitoring, a distinguishing feature of the resource-based perspective is that it views the board of directors as a source of innovative capital. The main implication is that where there is uncertainty or changes in institutional structures, each firm is unique and has the capacity to innovate, not just to adapt. Increasing focus on the integrated firm has led to several interrelated approaches that emphasise the organisational learning attributes of the firm (Smyth and Lo, 2000). Central to this analysis is the *resource dependency* view of the firm. Narrowly defined, the *resource dependency* approach focuses on how board capital (which refers to the competencies and experiences of management) leads to the provision of resources to the firm (Hillman and Dalziel, 2003). A broader definition views a firm's resources as linked to previous learning opportunities (Hoskisson and Businitz, 2001). These may include among others, past business and learning experiences, industry expertise, managerial competencies, networks and connections. This is part of an emerging approach to the study of organisations that seeks to understand dynamism within constraints, by paying greater attention to the unique firm (Hagstrom and Chandler, 1999).

What unifies such concepts as entrepreneurship, learning, social networks, and knowledge is that they tend to be firm-specific and intangible resources. Although it could be argued that entrepreneurship is not a firm-specific resource in the strict sense, it may be facilitated or impaired by a firm's resources (Mosakowski, 2002). The possession of any of these resources will affect the cost/revenue structures of the firm, thereby giving it a resource position barrier, allowing the firm to earn economic rents (Wernerfelt, 1984, 1997). The elusive nature of firm-specific resources has been associated with the preoccupation among economists with abstract modelling, which has made it difficult to deal with less easily defined concepts (Leibenstein, 1966), such as resources that primarily refer to unique actions by organisations in response to uncertainty. The standard competition model in assuming a one-to-one correspondence between inputs and outputs hides the vital function of the entrepreneur. The fact that these concepts frequently refer to social and cultural arrangements may explain why sociologists have dominated theoretical discussions of entrepreneurship (Baumol, 1968).

Other important firm-specific resources include learning and knowledge. Aoki (1990) described how horizontal coordination facilitated learning in large Japanese firms by making a distinction between horizontal coordination and the sharing of information or learned results. Amsden (2001) makes a distinction between asymmetries of *information* and *knowledge*. Under transaction cost economics, the development of better corporate governance occurs where informational asymmetries are reduced, but little is said about the contribution of a firm's knowledge-based resources. In this manner a knowledge-based approach is distinct from an information/transaction cost approach. Information is factual, whereas knowledge is conceptual (Amsden, 2001).

The idea of breaking from a narrow economistic perspective is one of the major new ideas in corporate governance literature. In the discussion above much of the focus has been on a resource perspective in which the key questions become: are corporate governance arrangements bringing the right mix of resources and capacity to the leadership of corporations? But there are other potential non-economistic leads as well drawing from legal, historical and institutional governance. It is to those arguments that we now turn as they place an understanding of corporate governance in a wider comparative framework.

Comparative governance systems

We have focused so far on shareholders and managers and only noted in the introduction the option of looking at corporate governance through the perspective of a broader range of stakeholders. The shareholder model is generally characterised by dispersed ownership among multiple investors while the stakeholder model is characterised by concentrated ownership and the presence of various stakeholders that are given some veto rights in terms of the actions of the corporation. A third model that has received less attention in the corporate governance literature, but has taken increasing importance since the Asian Financial Crisis, is the family model of governance. This is generally characterised by family control and a pyramid governance structure. The family-based system of corporate governance is common to such Asian countries as Hong Kong, Korea, Thailand, Malaysia, Philippines and Indonesia. A similar form of ownership is also common to smaller firms in other countries where financing arrangements are less formal. Below we focus attention of the differences between the dispersed shareholder model and the more concentrated forms of ownership associated with the stakeholder model of corporate governance. After drawing a portrait of the stakeholder model in contrast to that of the shareholder model that has been the implicit focus of attention thus far, we move on to look at legal, political and historical explanation of why different forms of corporate governance emerge in different countries.

Operating at a high level of generality it can be argued that the shareholder model of corporate governance is driven by the objective of maximising shareholder value. A firm operating under this model strives to maximise profits through allocative, productive and dynamic efficiency gains. Performance is judged on shareholder value and as such, senior management have an implicit obligation to ensure that the enterprise is run in accordance with the interests of shareholders. The shareholder model is underpinned by the assumption that managers will need to be monitored by weak shareholders and, as we have seen, that corporate governance arrangements will need to be designed to ensure that shareholders can monitor and control the tendency for managers to pursue their own self-interest against the interests of shareholders.

The stakeholder model assumes, in contrast, that enterprise success is dependent on a wide range of stakeholders including employees, creditors, suppliers, and customers as well as investors and management. Blair (1995) defined stakeholders under the 'new' stakeholder model as those actors who have contributed firm-specific assets. Conflict may arise between the goals of shareholders and other stakeholders who have contributed to firm specific-assets, whose value is now tied to the success of the firm. In this regard Blair (1995) argues 'the goal of good corporate governance should be to maximise the wealth-creating potential of the corporation as a whole, rather than just to maximise value for shareholders' (Blair, 1995:275). Following from this Maher and Anderson (1999) see the best firms under the 'new' stakeholder model as those with committed suppliers, customers, and employees. As the actions of suppliers, customers, and employees are all of consequence to economic performance, it is in the shareholders interest to take account of this.

We have suggested already that a narrow concentration in corporate governance arrangements does not always deliver for shareholders better corporation performance and it can also be noted that the stakeholder model also has its drawbacks. Jensen (2001) notes that with no way to keep the score, to know what is being achieved, that stakeholder arrangements can therefore be vulnerable to the self-interest of managers and directors. This is an argument that obviously takes us back to the perspective of shirking management ingrained in economistic approaches. Berglorf and von Thaddon (1999) see deviations from 'shareholder value' as allowing management to hide behind diffuse objectives, possibly allowing individual stakeholder groups to capture excessive rents. Thus, for the success of the stakeholder model it is important that stakeholder concerns do not impede the ability of management to set priorities and objectives.

Although the theoretical literature on corporate governance systems suggests that there is some association between stakeholder governance and profits, surveys on the area have provided mixed results. For example, Demsetz and Lehn (1985) in their survey of 511 large American corporations, find no significant correlation between ownership concentration and accounting profits. Prowse (1992) examines Japanese systems of governance in both independent firms and those that are members of corporate groups (*Keiretsu*), and finds that ownership concentration and profitability are unrelated for both systems.

Demsetz and Lehn (1985) suggest that the concentrated ownership structures associated with the stakeholder model can often enhance the position of shareholders. In particular, the Japanese system of governance provides evidence of this. Many Japanese firms belong to industrial groups known as a *Keiretsu*. Keiretsu firms generally have extensive trading relations with, and own substantial equity holdings in each other. While such a corporate structure is typically associated with the stakeholder model of governance, research by Kang and Shivdasani (1996) shows that the use of corporate governance mechanisms to discipline management increases shareholder wealth in Japanese corporations by analysing the effect of management turnover on shareholder wealth in Japanese corporations.

The emergence of comparative forms of governance systems has led to the emergence of competing explanations for their existence. These competing explanations have centred on the legal and political factors that have been associated with different governance arrangements.

The legal explanation

The legal perspective argues that for the firm, legal systems matter, as in order to attract external finance it must be able to credibly commit to controlling opportunistic behaviour by insiders. The severity of agency costs may be limited by the quality of a country's legal institutions. The legal approach suggests that in order for this to occur, 'there must be an effective legal system that deters violations and that can enforce compensation for infractions' (Dermirguc-Kunt and Maksimovic, 1998:2108).

Much research on corporate governance has focused on examining the relationship between legal origin and governance systems. In particular the work of La Porta, Lopez-de-Silanes, Shleifer and Vishny (1997, 1998, 1999, 2000), hereafter referred to as LLSV, has examined the relationship between ownership concentration and the level of investor protection. Based on a worldwide database of 49 countries, LLSV (1998, 1999 and 2000) find a strong negative correlation between ownership concentration and the intensity of the legal protection of investors. This indicates that countries with a higher level of ownership concentration tend to have a lower level of investor protection. Their studies also show a strong positive correlation between the depth and liquidity of equity markets and the quality of legal protection of investors. Furthermore they show that countries that protect shareholders better have more valuable stock markets, larger numbers of listed securities per capita, and a higher rate of IPO (initial public offering) activity than those countries with weak shareholder rights (LLSV, 1997). They also show that countries that protect creditors better have larger credit markets.

LLSV (2000) apply the 'judicial explanation' to argue that the common law system offers investors better protection. Under the common law system judges apply precedent to deal with new cases that may or may not be covered by existing legislation. This allows them to go beyond existing legislation and thus have greater scope in dealing with expropriation by insiders. By its very nature, the expropriation of investors is a complex issue to legislate for. The flexibility given to judges in the common law system has allowed them to apply legal precedents to such issues as the fiduciary duty of directors and the expropriation of minority shareholders. The fear of such judicial expansion limits the incentives for expropriation by the insiders. In civil law system, laws are made by legislatures, and judges cannot go beyond these statutes. Insiders who find a way, not explicitly forbidden by the statutes, to expropriate outsiders, can proceed without fear of an adverse judicial ruling. Firms operating under the civil law system must therefore rely to a greater extent on insider finance, as outside investors do not have an adequate level of legal protection. Based on the above reasoning, LLSV (2000) argue that legal protection of outsiders under common law judicial systems make expropriation less efficient and explains why in countries with strong investor protection such as the UK and US, stock markets have played an important role in financing economic development, while countries such as Germany and Japan with weaker protection for investors rely more on banks as a source of finance.

Although not without its limitations, this approach, by identifying the important relationship between legal systems and corporate governance structure, has made an important contribution to the debate on the role of institutions in economic development. This should not be surprising given that institutions for dispute settlement are primary to the functioning of society. Yet, economic theory has often chosen to overlook the relationship between legal systems and economic development. The assumptions of the neoclassical model, and difficulties in quantifying legal change, have made it awkward for economists to incorporate the legal discipline in theoretical models. Neoclassical theory in assuming zero transaction costs, paid limited attention to the development of legal institutions, as property rights were assumed to be perfectly specified and costless to enforce. The 'judicial explanation' is recognised as an important contribution in understanding how property rights are allocated in an economy by indicating that better investor protection lowers transaction costs.

The political explanation

The increasing application of the legal explanation has been accompanied by the emergence of other 'political'-based theories, which suggest that legal institutions in themselves do not explain the entire governance picture. Becker (1983) observed that a more general analysis of the influence of interest groups, politicians, and bureaucrats may be necessary to explain how political decisions that affect governance are arrived at. Roe

(2000) argues that European style social democracies press managers to stabilise employment, to forego some profit-maximising opportunities within the firm, and to use up capital in place. Such governance mechanisms as transparency, the market for corporate control, and shareholder value maximisation are therefore weaker in continental social democracies. The absence of these checks on managerial behaviour means that social democratic pressures induce managers to stray further than otherwise from maximising shareholder value. Therefore public firms in these countries will, all else being equal, have higher managerial agency costs. Under these conditions large-block shareholdings will persist as shareholders' best remaining way to control those costs.

Taking a similar approach, Bebchuck (1999) applies a 'rent protection' model to explain share ownership and control. Bebchuck's argument is that when the benefits of private control are high, such as in Continental Europe, concentrated ownership will dominate dispersed ownership. The underlying assumption is that in order to enjoy the private benefits of control, investors are likely to pay a higher price for a controlling block holding. Entrepreneurs will therefore be reluctant to sell voting rights to dispersed shareholders when they can get a higher price from an incoming controlling shareholder who wishes to enjoy the sole rights of control. In other words, controlling shareholders will pay for the economic rents associated with control.

Research on financial development increasingly appears to point to the crucial issue of how these political agents interact in determining how institutions are used. The findings of Rajan and Zingales (2003) that common law countries were not necessarily always more financially developed than civil law countries, indicates that theories regarding the role of legal institutions in financial development may be somewhat incomplete. Rajan and Zingales suggest that the way in which legal institutions are used is what matters. It is the ability of legal and other institutions to limit the actions of powerful interest groups that will determine the corporate governance practice. Indeed, for corporate governance, this approach is indicative of the important function of the state. The government possesses the ability to coordinate standards and aid enforcement; hence if action is necessary, the political desire to carry it out is crucial (Rajan and Zingales, 2003).

A historical perspective

The historical development of legal institutions and the role of the state offer some support for the argument about the importance of political factors. The legislative function of the state has rapidly evolved over the past century. The brief dominance of *laissez-faire* during the 19th century has been countered by the rapidly expanding legal function of the state (Becker, 1983). The state no longer simply protects against basic violations of person and property but now legislates for a range of complex issues such as corporate fraud and public utility regulation to name but a few. Glaeser and Shleifer (2003) argue that a central requirement in the design of a legal system is the protection of law enforcers from coercion. The higher the risk facing law enforcers, the greater is the need for state protection. They apply this concept to explain how both common and civil law system evolved. The civil law system suited France better, as the higher status of magnates in France meant that the legal system could be subject to corruption. Glaeser and Shleifer (2003) see the relatively lower status of magnates in England as resulting in lesser opportunities to subvert the course of justice. This allowed a more hands-off approach to be taken by the English crown and the adoption of a jury system. Giving laymen a role in adjudication was also viewed as a method of improving the efficiency of the legal system.

It is also important that in order for a legal system to be 'efficient' in the first place, a legal system must gain credibility. The concept of law and enforcement is much broader than 'economic' efficiency factors. Legal systems must also be based on trust and credibility. Qian (1999) sees this as concerning the establishment of a credible commitment between government and market. The security of property rights and the development of capital markets were instrumental for England's rapid economic development (North, 1990). The ending of the Crown's arbitrary exercise of power and the establishment of the supremacy of common law courts, helped establish a credible business environment with secure property rights.

The views of Roe (2000) and Bebchuck (1999) are consistent with the perspective of the LLSV team in so far as they agree on the existence of two competing systems: common and civil law. The findings of Rajan and Zingales (2003), however, indicate that the issues of governance may be more complex than either legal or political categorisations. Differences in how states allocate resources mean that corporate governance practice will vary across nations. This variation reflects distinct societal values, ownership structures, competitive environment, and the enforcement capacity of legal systems. Moreover neither approaches addresses the question of which came first: the legal/political system or the economic activity that caused it. Although LLSV find a strong negative correlation between investor protection and ownership concentration, correlation does not imply a cause/effect relationship. For example, did economic organisation occur first and the legal response later? This is not to undermine the legal and political explanations as they provide a highly useful starting points for analysis. There is little doubt that the establishment of credible legal and political institutions matters. The critical question is the order, if any, in which this occurs.

Convergence?

Can convergence between the dispersed and concentrated ownership structures occur? Shleifer and Vishny (1997) see concentrated, as opposed to dispersed, ownership as the rule rather than the exception. Guillen (1999) argues that the success of both German and Japanese Industrial systems has cast doubt on the superiority of the American shareholder model of governance. On the other hand, Coffee (1999) suggests that strong legal protection for shareholders present in the US system, gives it long-term competitive advantages. The benefits of convergence to such systems include lower transaction costs, a factor that may attract corporate migrants from other systems. Coffee suggests that functional convergence may be arrived at through securities regulation, even after convergence in corporate law has been frustrated. Functional convergence is where institutions respond to changing circumstance without altering the institutions' formal characteristics (Gilson, 1999).

Coffee (2001) argues that the evidence suggests that a general movement towards dispersed ownership is already advanced and appears likely to continue, even in the absence of legal change. Legal reform emerges as a response to economic development rather than initiating it. 'The legislature cannot anticipate problems that it has never seen' (Coffee, 2001:65). Under this approach law matters, not because it leads to dispersed ownership in some countries, but rather because it has proved to be more hospitable to the development of dispersed shareholders. The legal and political conditions for the growth of dispersed ownership are of secondary importance to the presence of some mutual interest in improving the quality of securities markets. Accordingly, a motivated political constituency of investors must exist before the political pressure for regulatory intervention occurs. Therefore a reinterpretation of the legal explanation focusing on the issue that although 'markets can rise in the absence of a strong mandatory framework, they neither function optimally nor develop to their potential in the absence of mandatory law that seeks to mitigate the risk of crashes' (Coffee, 2001:66).

Others have argued that the type of convergence in governance systems envisioned by Coffee (2001) may be difficult to achieve. The forces that promote convergence, such as the presence of active institutional investors (both domestic and international), internationalisation of markets (e.g. foreign listings), and competitive incentives, are either partially developed or completely absent in many developing economies. In any event, critics of convergence argue that even among developed economies legal systems, business cultures and corporate structures are simply too different and varied (Allen, 2000). Guillen (1999) argues that a combination of legal traditions, institutional features, and political interests, prevent the convergence of governance systems. Instead, Guillen sees countries developing governance models to suit their legal, institutional and political circumstances. The persistence of a diverse nature of corporate cultures is acknowledged in the OECD Principles.

A report by the OECD (1998) indicates that convergence seems to be a middle ground between the shareholder and stakeholder models.

> As regulatory barriers between national economies fall and global competition for capital increases, investment capital will follow the path to those corporations that have adopted efficient governance standards...philosophical differences about the corporations mission continue, although views seem to be converging (OECD, 1998:83).

Hence, it may be futile to argue which model of governance is best. Convergence is possible in vital areas; however national conditions will ensure that a degree of divergence remains. This suggests a bias towards functional convergence. Prowse (1998), in looking at the lessons of the Asian crisis, suggests balancing the concentrated or insider systems of Asian countries with substantial outside shareholdings as a way of improving governance structures. This approach achieves both a middle ground and improves corporate governance. Shleifer and Vishny (1997) suggest that rather than emulating the corporate systems of the US, Germany, or Japan, it is best to concentrate on identifying and introducing the better elements of each.

Conclusions

Corporate governance has become a matter of global importance in the past two decades. Prior to this, the question of how corporations were structured and in whose interest they were governed was largely taken for granted. The economic transitions of the former centrally planned economies of Central and Eastern Europe, a wave of financial crises and large-scale corporate collapses in the UK, US and Europe have propelled corporate governance to the fore. But have researchers been able to deliver robust formulas for corporate governance? The review offered is this chapter leads us to share the conclusion of Daily and others that it is not always clear 'whether practice follows theory, or *vice versa*. As important, it is not clear that there is concordance between the guidance provided in the extant literature and the practices employed by corporations' (Daily *et al.*, 2003:371).

The dominance of economistic theories that have driven the corporate governance literature has, as we have seen, come under increasing challenge. The dominant theories that have been applied to corporate governance draw on a range of economic understandings, but our study suggests that they have been found wanting in three fundamental ways. Firstly, they fail to deliver recommendations that in turn have enhanced the performance of firms defined, even in the narrow sense of delivering better value for shareholders. Secondly, they neglect other factors that may be the driving factors for effective corporate governance, such as a firm's capacity for innovation and resources for leadership. Thirdly, the debate about corporate governance driven by these economics-based perspectives has lacked an appreciation of the variety of historical forms of comparative corporate governance. We welcome this challenge to economistic framing of corporate governance literature because it opens out the opportunity for more effective cross-disciplinary learning from and to the corporate governance world.

8
Participatory Governance

In the last two decades, 'participatory' governance has become widespread as a practical response to a 'new' context of governing. The formal state apparatus has frequently proved to be inadequate in dealing with growing social complexities and actors from the voluntary and private sectors have become increasingly involved in the governance process. These developments have produced a broad definition of governance as 'institutions and processes, both formal and informal, which provide for the interaction of the state with a range of other agents or stakeholders affected by the activities of government' (Mitlin, 2004:3). This diverse involvement has been hailed as a 'more flexible and democratic way of dealing with public problems' (Fischer, 2006:19). Participatory governance thus manifests a core attribute of governance theory in its attempt to engage with real problems and seek practicable solutions.

At the same time, participatory governance encompasses a bewildering array of diverse practices. These stem from different uses of the idea of participation within particular discourses, which in turn influence the construction of individuals as citizens, community members, beneficiaries, clients, users and so on. These postulations are dissimilar, sometimes contradictory, and reflect the wide range of theoretical traditions that endorse participation. The idea of participation finds favour – for different reasons – within liberal democracy, communitarianism, populism, Freirean empowerment, new institutionalism and also neoliberalism. While such diversity has enriched the normative bases of participatory governance, often imbuing it with irrefutable logic, it has simultaneously yielded complications in practice. These include the misrepresentation of one type of practice for another or equally worrying, the unspecified use of the term leading to ambiguous interpretations. For these reasons, it may even be argued that participatory governance has emerged more as a descriptive term than as a proven methodology (Mosse, 2000:32).

The first section of this chapter is devoted to explaining the meaning of participatory governance. It briefly summarises key theoretical influences on the idea of participation and discusses how these inform the most common forms of participatory governance, and identifies the principal areas of contention regarding definition. Here it shows how these core debates on the description, scope and location of participatory governance are overwhelmingly guided by key arguments played out within two disciplines – politics (including political sociology) and development studies (where economic institutionalism has been influential) – in particular. Historically, the notion of participation has been a vital part of discussion on the democratic ideal. The idea has been keenly revisited in recent times, following the 'institutional cracks of the traditional state' and the proliferation of new forms of social and political association (Fischer, 2006). The practices of participatory governance essentially reiterate the shift from state-centred activities to a proliferation of civil society organisations. They are cardinal to intellectual developments within the politics discipline that have occurred to take on the challenge of governance.

The influence of development studies is more recent and has infused a critical element into the debate, while reigniting old contests on the idea of participation. The explosion of interest in 'community-based' participatory development has certainly brought participatory governance into the spotlight, but it has also aroused concerns over the nature and legitimacy of participation. Is participation a right enjoyed by citizens or a shared experience that stems from being a part of a highly active and mobilised social group? This contentious but extremely important question has its roots in the older rift between indirect and other forms of participation, the first rooted in citizenship and indirect forms of representation, and the second in the community as the social repository of solidarity and popular self-management or direct democracy. Participatory governance is a unique area of practice in that older theoretical conundrums within politics have been re-enacted within the multidisciplinary arena of development studies. The first section reiterates that the worth of a cross-disciplinary perspective on governance theory lies also in appreciating how conceptual dilemmas particular to an older discipline – as politics – underpin debates in more recently evolved disciplines as development studies.

In the second section, the chapter focuses on the seminal issue of power in participatory governance. At a normative plane, participatory governance is fundamentally about a synergistic view of power that combines the best of state and civil society. This perspective is informed by at least four theoretical traditions, which endorse it for different reasons. However, a less nuanced view of power as positive-sum has been readily adopted by the advocates of participatory development, with the discomforting portrayal of participatory spaces as neutral of power relations. Such a view has been fiercely criticised by radical elements within development studies, which use insights from political sociology and anthropology, especially its concern with the social bases of power. These critiques shed light on the processes unleashed by development institutions that continually act to strip participatory governance of politics, presenting it as an apolitical phenomenon that can be easily designed by technocrats and planners. Here too, the use of a cross-disciplinary perspective allows for a more comprehensive narrative of the story of participatory governance.

The third section exposes issues integral both to politics and development studies to focus on the rawest point of contention: namely is it enough to create the 'right' institutions for participatory governance or does participation depend on a particular type of politics to produce desired outcomes? Since participatory governance attempts to remedy the problems inflicted by top-down and hierarchical processes of governing, the literature is rife with discussions on how to 'institutionalise' and subsequently replicate 'successful' practices. Whether or not participatory governance can produce more effective governance is thus of vital interest. The chapter questions the wisdom of debating the effectiveness of participatory governance only in terms of its institutional characteristics. It concludes by discussing the need to rescue the discourse on participatory governance from 'institutional essentialism' and re-link it to radical politics.

The meaning of participatory governance: diversity in theory and practice

The idea of participation is as old as democracy and therefore central to thinking within the politics discipline. The notion of limits upon legally sanctioned political power gripped liberal democrats like Jeremy Bentham, James Mill and J.S. Mill who associated 'liberal democracy with a political apparatus that would ensure the accountability of the governors to the governed' (Held, 1984:42; Macpherson, 1973). Liberal democrats regarded the participation of citizens in political life, whether through voting or involvement through other means, as absolutely essential in creating a direct interest in government. More-over, liberalism regards individuals as 'autonomous' for whom self-determination is what makes life meaningful (Kymlicka, 1990:198). Western ideas of participation include 'pluralism', notably developed by Robert Dahl, who emphasised fair competition among organised group interests, which alone would secure the democratic character of a regime. Dahl calls this 'polyarchy' or 'rule by the many' (1956:133; 1971). Pluralist representative democracy has been formally endorsed and at least intermittently practised by the majority of states since World War II. As a result, electoral participation has received wide-spread acceptance as the ideal mode of participation in the consti-tution and functioning of government.

Liberal representative democracy received its staunchest challenge from communitarianism, This theoretical tradition dates to Jean Jacques Rousseau, who was critical of the liberal democratic notion that 'demo-cracy is the name of a particular kind of state which can only be held accountable to the citizenry once in a while' (Held, 1984:50). For Rous-seau, these communes were 'societies organised in bodies not too big, so that they can be governed, and not too small, so that they can have their own life' (Rousseau, 1968). Such ideas of direct democracy pri-vilege participatory decision-making by consensus over representative deliberation. Yet, pluralist representative democracy has largely pre-vailed over direct democracy the world over for three principal reasons: the sheer increase in the size of populations; the influence of colonial-ism; and finally, the collapse of communism following which powerful western countries promoted democratisation (of the representative multi-party variety) through aid (Doornboos, 2001; Leftwich, 1994). Other communitarian theorists like Alasdair MacIntyre (1981) and Charles Taylor (1979) have criticised the liberal view of the self as false and argued that individuals should be referred to in their socio-cultural and historical contexts and are an integral part of a 'community'. Participation in this theoretical tradition stems from membership of a community, further understood as a 'unity' with its own 'intrinsic value' (Avineri and De-Shalit, 2001:4).

Participation also has its theoretical roots in 'populism' which in general celebrates the 'virtue that resides in simple people, who are in the overwhelming majority, and in their collective traditions' (Wiles 1969:166; Laclau, 1977; Peet and Watts, 1996). Populism espouses a particular type of politics, authority, structure and ideology in which an effort is made to manufacture a collective 'popular' will and an ordinary subject. Populist arguments have been used successfully to counter the claims of populist democracy especially when electoral participation has widened but without narrowing the gap between the elites and the majority. As a sustainable method of participatory practice, however, populist regimes have been less successful. While they may have commonly brought about some changes in the composition of elites, they have not usually achieved significant redistribution of power to the majority. Their propensity to coherent economic policies, arbitrariness and corruption has typically brought about their breakdown and replacement by overtly anti-participatory regimes (Stiefel and Wolfe, 1994:24).

A radical conception of participation arises from the notions of Paulo Freire who essentially sought to 'liberate' people through empowerment for which he saw education as an essential tool. Freire (1972) believed in the power of the human agency to challenge existing power structures, and advocated a critique of existing power relations to go hand-in-hand with learning a 'language of possibility' for creating a new society, a process he referred to as 'conscientisation'. This concept of self-liberation has led its proponents to valorise a limited role for external allies in the development of local groups or organisations, although this has been harder to execute in practice. Local social movements based on Freirean ideas of empowerment have often developed complex ties with national and international movements, raising difficult questions on the role of external agency in self-empowerment through individual participation.

These four theoretical influences have mainly characterised thinking on participation within the politics discipline. Albeit distinctive in their respective emphases, they are united to the extent that they each espouse distinctly political objectives. These include the proper functioning of democracy (through the accountability of government and fair representation), the deepening and broadening of democracy (whether through direct participation, reduction of distance between the elites and the majority, or indeed, changes in a *status quo* of power), empowerment (through the realisation of individual freedom and the fulfilment of the human agency) and the contestation of domination (variously through electoral competition, community-based action and conscientisation). In recent years, two other theoretical influences on participation – neoliberalism and new institutionalism – have gained in significance, particularly within the economics discipline and have subsequently dominated the discourse on participation in mainstream development. These influences have been particularly significant in the extension of participation to the construction of individuals not as citizens, but as beneficiaries, clients and users. They are also testimony to the rising influence of neoliberal economics within mainstream development studies as compared to politics, especially political sociology and anthropology. The latter has been home to radical voices within development studies, which are vehemently opposed to an 'apolitical' view of participation, with an impoverished view of power and accountability (see Bastian and Bastian, 1996; Cooke and Kothari, 2000; Mosse, 1994 for some strong critiques).

Neoliberalism has its conceptual roots in the new political economy that depicts the individual as a rational utility maximiser both in the political as well as in the economic sphere (Mueller, 1979). The state is viewed as predatory and also as less efficient than the market in satisfying individual wants. This viewpoint has led to the dual policy prescription for reducing the size of the state (especially in economic decision-making) and increasing the participation of individuals in market-led forms of decentralisation ostensibly in order to curb government excesses (see Mackintosh and Roy, 1999). The last decade has seen the proliferation of user-fees based service delivery and public-private contracting, aiming to allow individuals greater choices as 'consumers'. However, while participation through 'marketisation' may allow 'citizens to let their opinions be known through "exit" options, it prohibits their active participation in government' (Ackerman, 2004:447). Participation along these lines has been criticised for 'downgrading accountability' as citizens are left with 'consumer entitlements' in the market place but not rights. It has also been observed that such participatory policies may even threaten community capacity and social capital in the developing world (Cunill, 2000; Wallis and Dollery, 2001 as cited in Ackerman, 2004:447).

The second key influence on contemporary notions of participation stems from new institutionalist communitarianism. Elinor Ostrom and others theorised the community – as opposed to the state or the market – as a potential agency to tackle the collection action problem defined by Garrett Hardin (1968) in his landmark paper titled 'The Tragedy of the Commons'. A range of scholars have commented on the conditions that enabled collectivities to evolve institutions to overcome problems of collective action (Ostrom, 1986, 1990; Erickson-Blomquist and Ostrom, 1984; Runge, 1981, 1986; Ruttan and Hayami, 1984; Wade, 1987). While these works in the new institutionalist tradition are empirically rooted and rigorous, they have contributed to the predominant orthodoxy in development thinking regarding the virtues of 'community-based' participatory development. In this formulation, 'communities' remain historically as well as spatially unspecified, but their apparent 'abilities' to evolve institutions, either endogenously or with some support (through development practitioners) are emphasised.

The key problem with this approach, as stated earlier in the chapter on economic institutionalism, is that it is profoundly apolitical (see Bates, 1995). As a theory that explains the origin and formulation of institutions in society, new institutional economics underemphasises the role of politics, political power and the state. As a paradigm that dominates contemporary development, it seriously obscures power relationships within and outside the 'community', simplifies the over-arching role and presence of the state to an ahistorical state-community dichotomy and presents misleading notions regarding self-help, self-reliance and reciprocity to solve the problems of poor people. It has led to enthusiastic endorsement of civil society as the site for community-based participation and of NGOs and other voluntary organisations as its favoured agents (Clark, 1991; Korten, 1987; Uphoff, 1993). A rosy picture of civil society has followed in which an array of different organisations, ranging from labour unions to religious organisations and grassroots associations contribute to the dynamic vibrancy of social life, and synthetic ties of trust or 'social capital' bind civil society together (Putnam, 1993, 2000). This view has been criticised for denying social conflict (Hadiz, 2004) and for simplifying the relationship between the civil society and the state (Kaviraj and Khilnani, 2001). The coming together of neoliberalism and neoinstitutionalism has wor-ryingly produced a brand of 'market' and 'community'-based parti-cipation that is seen to reduce government costs and responsibilities. Ackerman writes, 'Participation suddenly appears to be "practical" and attractive when governments can offload service delivery to non-governmental organisations and community groups or convince local residents to donate volunteer labour or material' (2004:447).

It is clear that a range of theoretical traditions from politics and eco-nomics inform participation. These are contemporaneously manifested in lively debates on the nature of participation within development studies. A case can therefore be made that a cross-disciplinary per-spective helps to appreciate the different contours of participatory practice that exist. But do all types of participation qualify as parti-cipatory governance? A common view is that participatory governance necessarily entails and enables the collaboration of the 'public' with the state. This is deemed to be necessary following the 'inability of the traditional state to cope with a range of contemporary social problems'

(Fischer, 2006:19). Participation is regarded as integral to the concept of governance itself, as wider than government, 'to evolve and identify new modes of problem solving and decision-making that fill gaps created by the failure of traditional forms' (Fischer, 2006:19). Reflecting the original thrust on democratic participation, it is argued that participatory governance can 'make for better citizens, better decisions and better government' (Cornwall, 2004:78; Mansbridge, 1999; Gaventa, 2002). However, contemporary forms of participatory governance reflect thinking beyond representative democracies and the establishment of 'new voice mechanisms which argue for more direct connections between the people and the bureaucracies that affect them' (Gaventa, 2004:28). Participatory governance has thus been linked to community-level governance as also with more active forms of 'citizenship'. Direct forms of popular participation have combined with representative forms of democracy to yield a variety of participatory governance initiatives: local participatory planning in India, participatory budgeting in Brazil, citizen monitoring committees in Bolivia and citizen consultation in Europe (Gaventa, 2004).

These examples have inspired further conceptualisations of participatory governance. An influential journal *Environment and Development* (2004) used the following criteria for definition: the arena of action should go beyond a specific neighbourhood or single development, and the extent of government engagement should surpass individual consultation (Mitlin, 2004:5). Others have offered more radical formulations. Fung and Wright (2001) describes participatory governance as a form of experiment in the design of democratic governance that attempt to address the challenge of a loss of democratic vitality; a concern to which both the Left and the Right have not adequately responded. They favour substantive engagement with the state, especially from the left of the political spectrum, in order to develop 'transformative democratic strategies' that advance values of 'egalitarian social justice, individual liberty combined with popular control over collective decisions, community and solidarity' (Fung and Wright, 2001:6). Heller refers to participatory governance as a 'distinctly democratic version of decentralisation, defined by an increase in the scope and depth of subordinate group participation in authoritative resource allocation' (2001:133). Ackerman argues that despite the popularity of participation, most experiences of participatory governance have not allowed 'the direct involvement of citizens and societal groups in the core functions of government' (2004:448). The trend, as he crisply writes, has been to 'send sections of the state to society' rather than inviting 'society into the inner chambers of the state' (2004:448).

Ackerman's point focuses on an important tension following contradictory objectives between the different forms of participatory governance that exist. As we discussed, an important thrust towards participatory governance has come from within a neoliberal approach which sees participation as an instrument for reducing the size of the state and the responsibility of government, inhibiting any holistic programme for citizen involvement. Further, other initiatives for participatory governance have been restricted to community-level initiatives in development programmes. These have been localised in scope and restricted in potential precisely for the obscuring of links between community-level participation and wider structural relationships with higher levels of the state and markets. On the other hand, other initiatives – notably in Porto Alegre in Brazil and Kerala in India, which we will shortly discuss – have been more political in their scope and inspired calls for even greater radicalisation of participatory governance. At this stage, it is possible to understand these tensions through a cross-disciplinary lens: participatory governance dominated by ideas stemming within economic institutionalism and neoliberalism has gravitated away from full-scale involvement with the state on core functions, but participatory governance dominated by influences stemming from within the politics discipline (democratic thought, communitarian theory, Freirean empowerment philosophy) has veered towards a potentially radical type of collaboration with the formal state apparatus. In recent times, these progressive views have received greater attention with calls for bringing citizenship to the core of the participatory agenda.

State or civil society: where does participatory governance begin?

The question of how participatory governance can be effectively initiated is a perplexing and contentious one. Should it to be initiated by the state (meaning government agencies but also international organisations), or should it arise from 'popular initiatives' located within civil society? This debate is cardinal to politics, but has resonated more recently in the arena of development studies with changing perceptions regarding the respective roles of state and civil society in development. Development is a resilient ideology and has favoured predominant roles by different agencies to avert continual challenges: first the state (1960s, early 1970s), then the market (1970s and 1980s) and more recently the civil society (in the 1990s) successively, before arriving at a more synergistic view of their mutual relationships (see Moore, 1995).

Civil society has grown in significance as a 'site for governance' for its role in facilitating public deliberation and problem-solving in non-hierarchical ways by a range of new actors, from NGOs to social movements. These have 'invented and experimented with' a variety of 'new participatory mechanisms' particularly in the fields of environmental politics and community development (Fischer, 2006:20). In a more nuanced approach, the state-civil society distinction is elided over; a distinction is made instead between 'invited spaces' and 'claimed/created spaces' (Gaventa, 2004; Cornwall, 2002; Brock *et al.*, 2001). These authors refer to invited spaces as 'those into which people (as users, as citizens, as beneficiaries) are invited to participate by various kinds of authorities, be they government, supranational agencies or non-governmental organisations' (Cornwall, 2002:24). This view privileges the *processes* by which people are induced to participate and recognises that all initiatives for participation initiated by 'civil society actors' are not identical. So, while NGOs are crudely located within civil society, they frequently act in collaboration with official development agencies (whether governments or international development organisations and donors) and invite participation within already created spaces, whose scope and potential may also have been pre-determined in the context of an overarching governance initiative. In contrast are 'claimed/created spaces' described as 'organic' and emerging 'out of sets of common concerns or identifications' and 'may come into being as a result of popular mobilisation, such as around identity or issue-based concerns, or may consist of spaces in which like-minded people join together in common pursuits' (Cornwall, 2002:24). The authors also identify 'closed spaces' within the formal decision-making process of the state that are still out of the remit of participatory governance. However, they emphasise that these spaces are not rigid, 'exist in dynamic relationship to one another' and can actively enable their mutual transformation (Gaventa 2004:35). We will return to this important point a little later.

Notwithstanding the promise of civil society, the role of the state in fostering participatory governance has come in for close scrutiny. This may partly be explained by the remarkable conjugation of similar conditions involving the coming to power of left-of-centre political parties in two well-known initiatives, i.e., that of participatory budgeting in Porto Alegre, Brazil and democratic local governance in two Indian states, West Bengal and Kerala. Participatory budgeting, among the best-known initiatives for participatory governance, started in Porto Alegre and spread to other cities in Brazil as well as Latin American countries like Peru, Ecuador and Colombia and even Europe (Spain and UK). In essence, it means more scope for citizens and community based representatives in setting priorities for local government expenditure, and also implies a local government budgeting system that is more transparent and available to public scrutiny (Abers, 1998; Cabannes, 2004). The coming to power of the Left Parties coalition led by the Workers' Party (*Partido dos Trabalhadores*) is widely credited for the success of participatory budgeting in Brazil. Cabannes (2004) clarifies that the Left-led coalition benefited from a number of key historical occurrences including the adoption of some participatory policies by the minority Brazilian Democratic movement during the military regime, the steady increase in municipal revenues brought about by the 1988 constitution, and the increasing presence of leftist parties in local governments.

In India, locally elected bodies in urban and rural areas (panchayats) have been denied power and resources since independence in 1947, and have been successively denied opportunities by national and state governments to evolve as robust institutions for local governance. The 73rd and 74th constitutional amendment 1993 have tried to tackle this situation by granting constitutional recognition to these bodies, but in practice, a number of subsidiary clauses have allowed the empowerment of panchayats to be a matter of state discretion. West Bengal and Kerala have proved to be notable exceptions to this general scenario. When the Left Front Government of West Bengal took over in 1977, it saw panchayats as opportunities for popular mobilisation and empowerment and launched a definite policy of using panchayats as vehicles of structural reorganisation of land-based relations, and adopted a range of measures to galvanise these bodies (Kohli, 1989; Webster, 1992). In Kerala, panchayat reform was part of a much broader process of popular mobilisation and campaign, complemented by active initiatives of the Communist Party of India (CPI) led Left Democratic Front (LDF) government for financial devolution and decentralised planning (see Isaac and Frank, 2000; Heller, 2001). In fact, in an unprecedented measure, the LDF government devolved 40% of the state public budget from traditionally powerful line departments in the bureaucracy to nearly 900 village panchayats. A large scale political and administrative mobilisation effort has been organised to support the reform process, wherein the architects of participatory planning have consciously banked on Kerala's celebrated history of popular movements (in particular the mass-based Kerala Peoples' Science Movement or KSSP).

While these initiatives are celebrated as pioneering, it is also accepted that the political and institutional conditions that have facilitated them are 'exceptional, and in most of the developing world improbable' (Heller, 2001:133). Both in the Indian cases and in Porto Alegre, left-of-centre political parties acting on the strength of intense grassroots involvement constituted socially progressive governments that could 'colonise state power and transform formal governance institutions' (Fung and Wright, 2001:23). The Porto Alegre experiment, it is claimed, has resulted in the creation of a 'public sphere' where 'collective discussion' aids the production of a 'public will' (Baiocchi, 2003:56; see also Baiocchi, 2001). Here, the role of 'state-sponsored' settings in fostering a sense of 'public' is hailed for empowering participants 'otherwise relegated to subaltern spheres' (Baiocchi, 2003:69). These initiatives, and others around the world, have contributed to a 'consensus' that a 'strong state and a strong civil society are the needs to develop both "participatory democracy" and "responsive government"' (Commonwealth Foundation 1999 cited in Gaventa, 2004:27).

Yet, the literature abounds with scepticism of such sanguine perspectives. There are numerous descriptions of how state-sponsored experiments in participation have tended to push civil society leaders and institutions into roles as brokers of interests that may in turn neglect people's real needs (Cabannes, 2004). Others have pointed to the lingering 'technocratic' vision associated with state-led initiatives which privileges experts and planners in participatory processes, thus producing tense relationships with local people and local knowledge. The attempt to control participation through itemisation and channelisation into well-defined forms has been observed in different locations (Stiefel and Wolfe, 1994; Chhotray, 2004). State-managed participation has frequently reflected the paradox between the familiar mode of time-bound target orientation and the 'messy' social relations that often inhibit quick results. At the other end of the spectrum is 'anarcho-communitarianism', where the problem is not too little but too much democracy (Bardhan, 1999 as cited in Heller, 2001)! This viewpoint favours radical democracy through social movements and dynamic civil society organisations, but the problem here is one of institutionalisation. Social movements and community initiatives confront problems of social divisions and internal power struggles, and the sustenance of momentum is notoriously hard. Thus, the development of necessary managerial, organisational and technical capacities is as much an imperative for participatory governance as the nurturing of intimate association with grassroots organisations by a committed political agent.

Citizenship versus community engagement

The debate between the virtues of indirect, representative democracy and direct democracy that is central to political theorising has been vigorously re-enacted, albeit in a modified way, within development studies. This follows the virtual explosion of interest in participation within development programmes in the guise of 'community-based' participatory development. Here we refer mostly to the 'invited' spaces typically created within government, NGO or donor-led initiatives. As discussed earlier, this approach is clearly dominated by new institutionalist theory, one that has been criticised for producing generalised and prescriptive ideas regarding communities and their abilities to evolve institutions for direct self-governance (see Mosse, 2003). As communities are regarded as harmonious entities, the formation of community-based institutions is typically expected to occur through consensus, not contest. Frequently though, and quite unlike the direct democracy envisioned by early communitarian theorists, participation as imagined within such community-based programmes has no explicit link with political representation or citizenship. This follows the lack of consideration of wider structural links between the problems experienced at the community-level and higher levels of the state or markets. Further, participatory processes are conceptualised in excessively procedural terms with little or no reference to the power relations that underpin them. In short, community-based participatory development has, all too often, been conceptualised in strikingly apolitical terms. Little wonder then, that it has earned staunch critiques from the votaries of political participation through representation in elected bodies.

Scholarship within development studies in the last two decades has focused on the need to consider 'local knowledge and understanding' as a basis for 'local action', and on 'direct forms of participation through the development project cycle' (Gaventa, 2004:28). As a result, a range of participatory tools and methodologies have proliferated to aid the collection of multiple forms of knowledge for planning and policy processes. In contrast, work on political participation and participatory governance carried out within political science has often focused on issues 'largely underplayed by those working on participation in the community or social spheres'; these include 'critical questions dealing with legitimate representation, systems of public accountability, policy advocacy and lobbying, rights education and awareness building, and party formation and political mobilisation' (Gaventa, 2004:29). Yet, this literature has under-emphasised issues of local knowledge, or 'direct and continuous forms of engagement by marginalised groups' (Gaventa, 2004:29). Nevertheless, insights from politics scholarship have been utilised by radical critics within development studies to criticise excessive procedural emphases on community-based participatory development that do not take larger issues of political mobilisation seriously.

This apparent rift between a more 'political' emphasis on participatory governance and a 'developmental' thrust on community-based participation has been used in certain contexts to describe different types of local institutions in contrasting terms. For instance, this sort of contrast has dominated the debate on decentralisation in India, where elected local bodies (panchayats) have been compared to non-elected 'community' bodies that have proliferated in a number of development programmes in the last decade. The latter are seen by the advocates of political decentralisation as yet another attempt by the bureaucracy (in charge of development policy-making) to deflect powers away from constitutionally mandated local bodies, which have been created explicitly to facilitate participatory governance (see Baumann, 1999). This critique has its merits, but what is worrying is the tendency to view panchayats and other community-based local bodies (like local forestry or watershed committees) as different *purely* on the basis of their projected institutional attributes. Their often identical social context, which clearly impacts upon their actual character, is disregarded. This has led to an obscuring of the diverse empirical realities that influence the functioning of panchayats and other local bodies. This analytical trend has, rather unfortunately, led to the transposing of the debate on institutional effectiveness into rivalry between key actors following their particular interests. In the process, there has been little or no consideration of the potential of these institutions to foster participatory governance that facilitates continuous involvement of 'marginalised groups' at the community-level while also promoting a broader sense of citizenship (Chhotray, 2007).

A number of authors have commented on the dangers of this approach. Gaventa (2004) and Cornwall (2002, 2004) rightly point out that participatory spaces exist in a mutually constitutive dynamic relationship with one another. By not appreciating this point, we would be guilty of underestimating the unpredictable, and often, chaotic processes that simultaneously existing local bodies can and do unleash upon one another. So 'closed spaces may seek to restore legitimacy by creating invited spaces; similarly invited spaces may be created from the other direction, as more autonomous peoples' movements attempt to use their own fora for engagement with the state' (Gaventa, 2004:35;

Cornwall, 2004). This point is fundamentally about the 'horizontality' of power, ever fluid, entering, shaping and moulding coexisting spaces (more on this in the next section). Therefore, the 'transformative' potential of participatory governance 'must always be assessed in relationship to the other spaces which surround them' (Gaventa, 2004:36).

In this viewpoint, promoting citizenship or political representation is not the exclusive responsibility of any one institution, nor is it out of bounds of others. Indeed, this point is simply illustrated by the less-than-satisfactory performance of so many elected local bodies around the world that do not foster inclusion in mainstream political representation. There are calls for a more holistic notion of citizenship as 'practised rather than given' (Gaventa, 2004:29). In this view, citizenship is conceptualised differently from its liberal incarnation as 'individual legal equality accompanied by a set of rights and responsibilities, bestowed by a state on its citizens' (Gaventa, 2004:29). Instead, an 'active' notion of citizenship is proposed, where the right to participate in social and economic life precedes all other rights. The idea of 'participatory citizenship' combines the liberal notion of citizenship together with citizenship based on dynamic membership within a socioeconomic community. At least conceptually, participatory governance underpinned by this enhanced notion of citizenship is derived both from the formal political right of citizenship and the lived experience of citizenship which precedes and legitimates the former.

Janus-faced power: the normative and the empirical in participatory governance

Participatory governance is fundamentally about transformative power. It is about opening up decision-making processes conventionally dominated by hierarchical and top-down state structures to new social actors. It follows the demonstrated lack of effectiveness of these conventional methods in a changing and complex social context within a globalising world. In this sense, participatory governance is not a type of governance, but the essence of governance itself, since governance without participation would be etymologically anomalous. This being the case, the quest for a synergetic arrangement of power wherein actors from state and society (the former refers to the official state apparatus) can harmonise their capabilities, defines participatory governance.

The trouble however, is that power in the context of participatory governance is rather Janus-faced. In theory, power is conceptualised as expansive and positive-sum. It has also been imagined to act as a practical bridge between radical power (as symbolised by progressive social movements) and authoritative state power (as represented by rigid bureaucracies), tapping the dynamism of both, to enable fundamental transformations in governing. In this respect, what is regarded as participatory governance would not sit comfortably with Freirean notions of power for example, or even populism, where a very sharp line is drawn between people power and state power. 'State-society synergy' has been argued as one of the 'best' ways to strengthen government accountability (Evans, 1996a, 1996b). In practice however, participatory governance fully reflects the unequal and asymmetric relations of power that characterise social relationships, bureaucratic hierarchies, as well as the mutual interface between state officials and social actors. So while the theory of power in participatory governance is synergetic and progressive, the practice of power can be exclusionary, oppressive of the relatively disadvantaged and reinforcing of dominant social elites and privileged state officials. The two faces of power, like the two faces of Janus, coexist.

We will argue that a cross-disciplinary perspective allows us to see these two faces clearly and make sense of them within the broader context of theoretical influences that inform participation. Even as far as the theory of power is concerned, there are subtle differences that can be traced back to four principal theoretical traditions characterising political and economic thinking: liberal-democratic thought, communitarianism, neoliberalism and neoinstitutionalism. Each of these influences arrives at a positive-sum view of power through participation for different reasons.

The liberal-democratic tradition emphasises public deliberations amongst rational individuals in the public sphere, which are mediated by a 'neutral state' (Kymlicka, 1990). Participation in public affairs is thus cardinal to liberal-democratic philosophy. Power is viewed in terms of the ability of individuals to impact upon public decision-making through their best judgement. Since the state has the public interest at heart, the exercise of such power positively aids individual fulfilment and is positive-sum in nature. The liberal-democratic perspective recognises the diversity of interests amongst individuals, but regards that these are resolved by liberal-democratic institutions which continue to provide successive opportunities for resettling political equations (Kaviraj, 1996). In the communitarian tradition, unlike liberal individualism, no hard distinction is made between the state or political society and the social or civil society. Communitarian thinkers have focused on the role of the state to enhance the life of the individual in society (Kymlicka, 1990). Their view of participation is derived from the organic membership of an individual within a community, and the notion of power therefore is synergetic rather than exclusionary. In recent decades however, the proponents of neoliberalism have replaced this 'public interest' view with a 'private interest' view of the state as predatory, and individual participation in government activities is prescribed to increase economic efficiency and reduce rentseeking. In this context, a second view of the liberal 'public' sphere has become popular, especially amongst the proponents of market-based reform. This sphere comprises 'voluntary organisations and NGOs, universities, trade unions and professional organisations' that 'can act as intermediaries between the government and the people' (Williams and Young, 1994:87). This idea of the public sphere as an arena of intermediaries has dominated contemporary usage of the term civil society. Subsequent popularisation of the civil society as a site for participation has also received tremendous boost from new institutionalism, which valorises the ability of community-based institutions for self-governance. These influences have endorsed the power of participation to check state excesses, but also to organise collectively and affiliate with the state to achieve a range of objectives, from improved service delivery to reduced poverty. They have together produced a language of participation that obscures the power relationships within 'civil society' and consequently, projects participatory governance as a positive-sum experience. This is highly suspicious given the starting point both of neoliberalism and new institutionalism to trust markets and 'communities' rather than the state for the provision of public goods, and the rather limited scope of so many experiments with participatory governance.

Whatever the rationale, the theory of power often varies considerably from the observed practice of participatory governance. There is an exhaustive literature on the subject, but it is possible to delineate the principal critiques that have emerged. First of all, participants in these processes face each other from highly unequal positions of power, stemming from class and gender inequalities, material differences, asymmetries of information and personal capacities for deliberation amongst other factors. While deliberation aims to generate positive-sum solutions in which nearly all participants reap benefits from cooperation, such power differentials may and frequently do result in unfair decisions. Participatory governance attempts to widen the representation of excluded groups in decision-making, but the 'strong' may nevertheless use tools at their disposal to advance collective decisions that

favour them (Fung and Wright, 2001:33–34). Beyond unfair representation and direct force, powerful vested interests may seek to improp-
erly and unreasonably exclude issues that threaten their interests, from
the scope of deliberative action. This is particularly a problem with
development projects that attempt to promote participatory governance. Such projects typically equate participatory deliberation with
decision-making in ostensibly neutral public settings, which in turn
may hide the real structure of power (Mosse, 1994; Chhotray, 2004).

Second, deliberative institutions for participatory governance do not
function in a vacuum and are part of a larger state structure. Thus,
even if deliberative norms prevail and diverse participants cooperate,
the powerful may turn to measures *outside* of these 'new' institutions to
defend and advance their interests. Besides, participatory procedures
may also be conducted as 'ritual' within the newly created institutions
without affecting or in any way changing the 'business-as-usual' of
social elites. New institutions may suffer explicit resistance from interests firmly ensconced within the existing power structure, i.e., elected
politicians, bureaucrats, traditionally dominant interest groups, and
suffer a loss of real legitimacy. Of course, it may work the other way as
well, as in Kerala and Porto Alegre, when locally dominant left-wing
parties have sustained participatory governance granting it widespread
legitimacy. Bureaucrats and politicians, who may have ordinarily
resisted such initiatives, have supported these instead, in an attempt to
ride on the success of participatory governance (Fung and Wright,
2001:35).

Third, although participatory governance is claimed to reduce rent-
seeking, the creation of participatory processes in practice may in fact
increase the opportunities for 'rent-seeking participants' to advance
private or factional gains. This would affect the provision of public
goods through participatory governance, by skewing the benefits in
favour of those who can control its mechanisms. Ironically enough,
participatory forums may allow vested interests to mask their self-interest
through the 'benign' façade of participatory discourse (see Chhotray,
2004). And finally, participatory governance initiatives may also lead to
what Fung and Wright (2001) have called the 'balkanisation' of politics,
and therefore power. The concern here is that participatory governance
initiatives by 'constituting and empowering hundreds of groups, each
focused on a narrow issue within cramped geographic boundaries' might
aggravate the problem of factionalism (Fung and Wright, 2001:36). The
aggravation of ethnic conflict through decentralisation is certainly a real
possibility. However, on a more positive note, the balkanisation of power

may be the first, and indeed necessary, step to empower lives that would otherwise remain dominated by particular concerns. These critiques have been inspired by scholarship broadly within a political sociology tradition. They take on dominant theorisations of power, which in part flow from classical political theory (liberal democratic, communitarian) but more prominently from newer theorisations in economic thinking, particularly neoliberalism and neoinstitutionalism. Here attention to disciplinary crossovers is particularly helpful given the increasing dominance of new economic thinking on development. It becomes possible to appreciate the ways in which classical propositions within politics have been revisited within the more recent arena of development studies which is cross-disciplinary in itself. Radical elements within development studies have resorted to essentially political notions – notably citizenship – to tackle the rather impoverished notions of participation and accountability that have dominated the governance discourse.

Within politics too, it is possible to highlight the rising accent of post-modernism. The post-modern literature has subtly shifted the 'understanding of politics to culture, social meaning and identity politics', extending analysis beyond the 'structures, practices and methods of state institutions that organise the play of power' to 'the discursive constructions of the meanings and identities of the actors, institutions and practices inherent to it' (Fischer, 2006:25). This general trend has prompted a re-theorisation of power within participatory governance taking into account lived asymmetries, and moving away, considerably, from the prevailing rigid normative positive-sum view. In this formulation, the theory of power is much more closely aligned with its practice, and is not Janus-faced after all!

This re-theorisation of power has focused on the use of 'spatial metaphors' in relation to participation and within contemporary development discourse more generally. These refer to spaces or arenas as the site for processes such as 'widening', 'extending', or 'deepening' of participation, citizenship or democracy, and to the ways in which individuals are represented, whether they are 'situated', 'positioned', 'dislocated', 'displaced' and so on (Cornwall, 2004). Foucault argued that 'space is fundamental to any exercise of power' (1984:252). It is a 'social product...it is not simply "there", a neutral container waiting to be filled, but is a dynamic, humanly constructed means of control and hence of domination, of power' (Lefebvre, 1991 as cited in Cornwall, 2004:80). Space is a 'practised place', it is argued, and 'it is those practices that come to constitute particular spaces that infuse them with power' (de Certeau, 1984 cited in Cornwall, 2004:80).

This view casts a drastically different light upon participatory spaces, whether these are 'invited spaces' or 'claimed/created' spaces. While there has been much stress on 'inviting' people to participate within spaces created by governments, NGOs and donors, these spaces have been mistakenly regarded as neutral and harmonious, within which all individuals would be equally willing and able to participate (see Chhotray, 2004). In fact, numerous empirically grounded studies have shown that 'spaces in which individuals are invited to participate, as well as those that they create for themselves, are never neutral' (Cornwall, 2004:81). Power relations 'help to shape the boundaries of participatory spaces, what is possible within them, and who may enter with which identities, discourses and interests' (Gaventa, 2004:34).

While this view of power may present a less sanguine view of the prospects for 'empowerment' for the 'marginalised' than the 'positive-sum' approach might suggest, it simultaneously opens up new ways of considering the relations between coexisting spaces. As we discussed in an earlier section, this implies that invited, closed and claimed spaces can and do potentially impact upon one other. This means that creating new institutions (spaces) on its own may not be sufficient to over-turn the *status quo* in favour of the marginalised. But it may mean that radical developments within some spaces can horizontally affect the way people perceive their 'subaltern' positions in other spaces, often encouraging them to resist domination and transform the nature of participation altogether. Here, the 'spatial metaphor' perspective links well with an older formulation of coexisting social relations put forward by Laclau and Mouffe (1985) to emphasise 'how different social relations react reciprocally, either to provide each other with mutual conditions of existence, or at least to neutralise the potentially destructive effects of certain social relations on the reproduction of other such relations' (Mouffe, 1988:30). Inspired by Alexis De Tocqueville, Mouffe argues that 'as soon as the principle of equality is admitted in one domain, the eventual questioning of all possible forms of inequality is an ineluctable consequence' (1988:94).

Participatory governance and effectiveness

Effectiveness is a vital part of the discursive claim of participatory governance, since it evolved in response to widespread discontent with the 'ineffectiveness' of traditional methods of governing in dealing with growing social complexities. Nevertheless, while there is much concern about how effectiveness is to be defined and attained, there is less consensus on the precise terms in which it ought to be discussed. It is possible to delineate two broad strands of opinion: the first that tries to simplify from a range of empirical experiences to arrive at generalisable principles that primarily emphasise issues of institutional design and the second that resists this simplification by emphasising the specificity of local political spaces that are created or that emerge in relation to participatory governance.

This difference in approach can be understood in terms of an old disciplinary divide between economics and anthropology. While the first favours parsimony in explanations of economic and social change, the second pursues complex explanations (Bardhan and Ray, 2006). This is because economics 'looks for patterns in economic life that, while not universal, are widely generalisable', critically underpinned by the assumption of the 'self-regarding, choice-making individual'; and also 'parsimonious theories explain many observations with few assumptions, and this feature has come to be regarded as elegant' (Bardhan and Ray, 2006:670). In contrast, the anthropological research tradition does not regard parsimonious explanations highly, precisely because there are no universalisable evolutionary laws or grand theory of change. The 'project', as the authors succinctly argue is 'to complicate, rather than simplify, question the unquestioned, and be wary of neat and tidy parsimonious explanations' (Bardhan and Ray, 2006:672).

This issue of parsimony versus complexity has resonated also in relation to the important issue of what constitutes useful policy advice. The clear preference amongst policy-makers for simplified assumptions and generalisable conclusions has contributed to the pervasive sway of economics on a range of matters. Earlier in the chapter, we discussed the domination of new institutional and neoliberal economic thinking on the theorisation of participatory governance, and also argued that critical voices against these influences have emanated from within a broad political sociology and anthropology tradition. It has been argued that while it may not matter as much for economic models – like the new institutionalist model – to 'generalise outwards across a population', it is far more worrying when these are used to 'generalise downwards' to 'predict' practice (Mosse, 2006:707), since they are ill-equipped to do so. It would perhaps be unfair to club all discussions within the first strand of opinion on the issue of effectiveness as simplistically parsimonious in nature, especially since these may be based on rigorous and sophisticated academic research from a variety of disciplines, cross-cutting economics as well as politics. However, the process of transposing research into policy advice entails the danger of reductionism, and it is with this cautionary element in mind that we discuss the issue of institutional design.

Those interested in participatory governance broadly agree that for participatory governance to last, it must be institutionalised. Ackerman writes, 'Once initiated, the best way to assure the sustainability of a participatory framework is through its full institutionalisation' (2004:459). This is true irrespective of whether the origins of participatory governance lie in popular initiatives (as in Porto Alegre) or within state institutions and hierarchical political party structures (as in Kerala, where the ruling communist party transformed existing local bodies through its participatory planning initiatives). The concern with the former is particularly to avoid 'bureaucratisation' and 'political co-option' (Cabannes, 2004), while preserving their vibrant social dynamics. Fung and Wright (2001) reviewed five experiments in participatory governance (neighbourhood councils in Chicago, regional job training partnership in Wisconsin, a habitat conservation planning project under the US Endangered Species Act in addition to participatory budgeting in Porto Alegre and local participation reforms in Kerala and West Bengal in India) in order to isolate a number of characteristic that lead to empowered deliberative democracy. The principles they draw have been most widely cited in discussions of institutional design that can facilitate the '"progressive colonisation of the state" and its agencies' (Fung and Wright, 2001, 2003; Fischer, 2006:23).

Fung and Wright (2001) identify political principles as well as 'design characteristics' and a primary background condition that is common to these initiatives. The background condition states that there 'should be a rough equality of power among the participants' (Fischer, 2006:23). In each experiment, the authors regard that the political principles include the existence of a practical and identifiable problem, the 'empowered' involvement of ordinary citizens and the presence of 'reasoned' deliberation to address the problem under deliberation. The institutional design characteristics that have followed on comprise, firstly, the devolution of decision-making to local units, active connections between these units and higher levels of the state to ensure proper supervision, resource allocation, innovation and problem-solving and secondly, the remarkable restructuring of administrative agencies responsible for dealing with the identified problems. Each of these points reiterates the broad state-society synergy view that Fung and Wright espouse of participatory governance. Similarly commenting on institutionalisation,

Ackerman identifies three levels: the inclusion of participatory mechanisms into the 'strategic' plans of government agencies, the further creation of agencies to assure 'societal participation' in government activities and the inscribing of participatory mechanisms into law (2004:459). He is also similarly optimistic of the state-society synergy view, but is more insistent than Fung and Wright on the need for opening up the 'core functions of government' to 'the direct involvement of citizens' (2004:447–448).

The chief merit of this type of scholarship is to highlight the principal features that have contributed to the vibrancy of a few chosen experiments in participatory governance. In focusing on how these initiatives came to dealing effectively with their identified problems, they offer vital guidance to reformers who aim to follow in their footsteps. However, stripped of their particular contexts, these principles can contribute to misguided assumptions that have been abundantly criticised by others who favour a more nuanced and empirically rooted understanding. There are two principle issues here: one is that of institutions and the second is that of power. Taken to its logical extreme, the institutional reform position places faith in matters of procedural design concerning the carving of new institutions (so, typical keywords within Fung and Wright's principles that lend themselves to easy generalisation are 'devolution', 'resource allocation', 'restructuring of administrative agencies' and so on). It commensurately devalues the explanatory role of power, by reducing it to a constant variable: so, the 'enabling' background condition mentioned by Fung and Wright (2001) presumes a broad equality of power amongst participants. Furthermore, this approach has contributed to a particular brand of institutional 'essentialism' precisely by attributing particular characteristics to new or re-created institutions, presuming that the *process* or *procedure* of institutional reform would necessarily yield the desired characteristics in practice. As we discussed earlier, this approach has also contributed to misleading debates that contrast old with new institutions and disregard the overarching social context that invariably shapes their mutual character.

Following on, a number of scholars have extended their critical approach to power in relation to participatory governance to discuss the issue of effectiveness. Simply put, the question they raise is whether designing institutions along the principles abstracted from 'successful' initiatives elsewhere in different contexts is enough to guarantee effective participatory governance. This business of 'importing' principles from other contexts and using them to 'design' participatory institutions has been very popular in international development. The birth of the participatory development project is perhaps the most important turning point in development planning in recent years. As a result, the formulation of participatory tools and methodologies has been a key priority for development practitioners. In fact, participation has fostered a whole new type of knowledge creation within development studies (participatory appraisal, participatory planning, participatory budgeting and so on).

However, a number of empirical studies on the actual experiences of participatory projects have revealed a variety of problems. There is a wide literature on this subject (see Bastian and Bastian, 1996; Chhotray, 2004 and 2005; Cooke and Kothari, 2000; Mosse, 1994 and 2000, among others). The most common experiences these studies observe include elite capture of participatory spaces/forums, the marginalisation of possibilities by which the poorest and most vulnerable sections of a community may be represented and the disturbing enactment of a ritual of participation that is not substantiated in reality. Similarly, while participatory planning has been at the heart of plans to challenge the top-down pattern of institutional mechanising, in reality, such planning has frequently preserved the need for expertise in project planning, putting project officials at an inherent advantage over the locals they seek to 'empower'. These experiences have further problematised the description of participatory development as an aseptic technical process that is apolitically designed. This symbolic taking away of the 'colour' of politics, innate both to the theory and practice of participation hints at the recent rise of neoliberal and neoinstitutional economics. These theoretical influences, as amply discussed through the chapter, have led to ahistorical conceptualisations of markets and communities where participation is ostensibly located, and an impoverished view of the state that plays no significant part in participatory processes save for sub-contracting functions to private and voluntary agencies.

The growing opinion expressed within radical quarters of the development studies discipline can be summed up succinctly: '...simply creating new institutional arrangements for participatory governance will not be more inclusive or more pro-poor. Rather, much will depend on the nature of the power relations which surround and imbue these new, potentially democratic new spaces' (Gaventa, 2004:25). Effectiveness here is not being weighed in purely temporal terms, since there is not much point in extending the life of a participatory governance initiative if it cannot make a qualitative difference to the lives of the most disadvantaged persons, both in material and symbolic terms. Quite in contrast to the first viewpoint which ultimately favours the conceptual reduction of varied experiences into a set of stylised principles, this viewpoint does the opposite. It rejects any such intellectual contraction and favours the reverse: greater specification of the local political conditions that vitally impact upon the performance of participatory governance.

Moreover, proponents of this viewpoint are far less certain about the precise conditions in which participatory governance initiatives can work as 'transformative participation', in the interests of the poor and disadvantaged. Using spatial metaphors of power, they emphasise how power 'puts boundaries on participation' and in its 'more insidious forms, may be internalised in terms of one's values.....such that voices in visible places are but echoes of what the power holders who shaped these places want to hear' (Gaventa, 2004:37). This view is *political* in the central emphasis it accords to power, and is commensurately hesitant in arriving at easy prescriptions for policy-makers. However, it does not entirely reject *all* attempts at institutional design. Fung and Wright's attempts at delineating the essential attributes of 'empowered deliberative democracy' have been generally supported even by those critical of pursuing the institutional design project indiscriminately (for example see Fischer, 2006; Gaventa, 2004). At the same time, these authors emphasise the need to 'supplement the structural and procedural design principles with an examination of the underlying social and cultural realities in the political contexts to which they are applied' (Fischer, 2006:24). They place stress on establishing the pre-conditions of participatory governance in the form of 'prior awareness building so that citizens possess a sense of their own right to claim rights or express opinions' and also strengthen their own 'capacities for exercising countervailing power against the "rules of the game" that favour entrenched interests', all of which are imperative for new institutional mechanisms to produce a change in *status quo* (Gaventa, 2004:7). Cornwall cautions that while the 'first' element in fostering transformative practice may lie in innovations in institutional design, it is important to remember that the broader literature on design has 'less to say about dealing with difference, either in positionality and status or in knowledges' (2004:86).

Yet, interestingly, not all voices in this tradition are pessimistic about the possibility of transformative participation. The same contingency of conditions that complicate the 'intentionality' of institutional design may also produce unexpected results that are progressive in nature (Cornwall, 2004). This reiterates the need to regard the connections between old and new institutions seriously, without confining particular objectives – whether community development, empowerment or citizenship – to a single institution. Cornwall draws from feminist experiences to argue that 'effective' participation within the 'public sphere' may be linked to the access that marginalised actors have to 'other spaces' which may be 'sites of radical activity' (2004:87). She recommends more strategies that allow participants to actually 'reframe' the debates within which issues cardinal to participatory governance occur. These 'practical' pointers notwithstanding, this viewpoint concludes, somewhat inconclusively, that a lot more needs to be known about how participatory governance can be effective.

The question of effectiveness thus links with contentious and unresolved issues that are to do as much with disciplinary differences as with the question of how to link academic scholarship to policy guidance. However, this discussion has illustrated the significance of a cross-disciplinary perspective in appreciating this subject in a multi-dimensional way. The enduring challenge lies in promoting more frequent conversations between those who do empirically rooted and nuanced research on the politics of participatory governance, and those who try to look 'above' this politics to pursue a programme of reform. It is imperative that the two camps do not talk past each other. The consequences of such isolation may be too damaging for us to afford.

9
Environmental Governance

Recent concerns posed by environmental changes have led to a serious consideration of how the environment ought to be governed. The environment encompasses issues that are simultaneously local and global in character, and its governance continues to pose both theoretical and practical challenges across a range of disciplines. Environmental resources are essentially shared in nature. As such, the interdependence of those who depend on these resources is inevitable. The need for governance, broadly understood as collective decision-making, is widely agreed upon but there is little consensus on either the scale at which such decisions must be taken or the wisdom of the actors that dominate the process at different levels.

Equally, the discussion is underpinned by a fundamental paradigmatic shift from limitless and extractive growth to sustainable development, with a focus on intergenerational equity and justice. However, this shift is by no means uncontested and deep-seated tensions between different interests within the developed world and even more acrimoniously, versus the developing world, continue. These tensions are regularly manifested in global forums, which serve as the institutional expressions of environmental governance. Here too, there are opposing pulls: between the oft-repeated need to pool resources at a 'global' scale evolving 'global environmental regimes' involving civil society(ies) and the less easily articulated, but ever present fears of the infringement of national sovereignty. Further, a deeper schism exists between those who warn against imminent scarcity of environmental resources and others who espouse technological innovation and market-based regulation. There are also radical critiques of the cooptation of the idea of sustainability by the latter group, with the rise of 'green capitalism' and its institutionalised pursuit by powerful organisations like the World Bank.

The environment is a contested terrain, the desirable nature of its mechanisms of governance is widely disagreed upon, but the purpose of governance itself is not in question. The eclectic range of studies on the subject have led to the rise of environmental governance as a 'discrete area of policy and research' devoted to expanding the wide 'theoretical and knowledge base of sustainability and environmental justice' (Duffy, 2005:825; Agyeman, Bullard and Evans, 2003:15). The first section of this chapter sets the context for critically appraising key strands of thought within environmental governance. It explores the transformation in values and outlines major epistemological developments which have shaped current perceptions of the environment. The second section presents an overview of contemporary discourse on environmental governance. Here, an attempt is made to sift through a large and rather unwieldy literature using three focal points that seem to have concerned theorists and practitioners alike: the nature of the environment and its governance as a 'global' issue; environmental governance as a collective action problem eliciting institutional responses from states, markets and communities; and the tense governance dialogue between the developed and the developing world. The section reveals the array of multi-disciplinary influences that have enriched thinking and investigation in these three respects, opening up critical spaces being continually used to challenge orthodoxies in thought and practice. The third section elucidates the centrality of power to normative conceptualisations of governance arrangements for the environment, but equally, to the lived realities of negotiating and experiencing environmental governance. The final section discusses the tricky issue of governance effectiveness, given that environmental concerns continue to grow.

Shifts in values and epistemological developments

Since the 1960s, there have been steady attacks on the dominant socio-economic paradigm (nicknamed 'exclusionist' for excluding human beings from the laws of nature) of 'free' market-led economic growth, supported by infinitely available natural resources and sinks for waste disposal (Porter *et al.*, 2000). A wave of public concern about problems such as the dispersion of DDT and acidification in the early 1970s in North America and Europe marked a distinct environmental consciousness, leading to key landmarks like the passage of the National Environmental Policy Act of 1969 in the United States and the convening of the first worldwide environmental conference in history, the United

Nations Conference on the Human Environment in Stockholm in 1972. In the same year, the Club of Rome published the highly influential *Limits to Growth* study, which was to become the intellectual forerunner of an alternative environmental and, correspondingly also economic, paradigm (Meadows *et al.*, 1972). At its core was an intense scepticism of unchecked growth and neo-Malthusian predictions of imminent doom sparking off concern for the well-being of future generations (McCarthy, 2004).

Such environmental activism however was almost entirely located in the industrialised world. Developing countries viewed economic development and poverty alleviation as far more pressing. They were also suspicious of the new environmental agenda for fear of losing the right to develop 'high-consumption' economies on environmental grounds (Najam, 2005; Soroos, 2005). They therefore initiated demands for a 'new international economic order' that would be underpinned by major reforms in global economic institutions and doggedly refused to converse with the developed world on the environment. Thus, the economy and the environment were two sides to a bitter 'North-South' divide: one was inextricably bound to the other.

In recognition of this inter-linkage, the idea of 'sustainable development' attempted to allay the fears of the developing world by emphasising in turn the inseparability of development from the environment (Paehlke, 2004). The spotlight on 'sustainability' revealed a strong concern for equity, not only between wealthy and poor nations, but also within societies and between generations. Sustainable systems of renewable natural resource management, radically efficient energy, a stabilising world population and (less explicitly) limits on total consumption were emphasised (Porter *et al.*, 2000). It was hoped that such a discourse, couched in an idiom of 'global' urgency, would be harder for the developing world to ignore. Used for the first time in 1987 by the Brundtland Commission on Environment and Development in its much cited report *Our Common Future* (Brundtland, 1987), this term has become the principal environmental catchword of our times. The 1992 UN summit on Environment and Development held at Rio de Janeiro further represented the highpoint of international consensus-building on sustainable development. Preceded by two years of hectic discussions around global environmental issues as well as North-South inequities, the summit yielded a clear plan of action – Agenda 21 – in addition to other major treaties on climate change and biodiversity. Indeed, the 1990s witnessed a number of global conferences – on human rights in 1993, population and development in 1994, and both social development and women in 1995, which included talks on the environment. The World Summit on Sustainable Development was convened in 2002 in Johannesburg, not to advance any new agendas, but to revitalise the Agenda 21 recommendations.

Sustainable development also represented a move away from the 'exclusionist' paradigm by focusing on 'market failure' in the sustainable use of natural resources (Sheehan, 1999; Porter *et al.*, 2000). The market failure model argued that prices ought to reflect the real costs to society of producing and consuming a given resource, but conventional free-market economic policies systematically under price or ignore natural resources (Dasgupta and Maler, 1990, cited in Porter *et al.*, 2000). It follows that public policies that do not correct such market failure encourage over-consumption and correspondingly more rapid depletion of renewable resources. This critical streak notwithstanding, it has been alleged that sustainable development does not seriously challenge 'the free market juggernaut, collapsing in policy circles into light-green capitalism' (McCarthy and Prudham, 2004:327, more details later). 'Promethean promises of abundance' through technological innovation and the pursuit of self-interest through 'efficient' markets have continuously obscured environmental concerns (McCarthy and Prudham, 2004:327). Advocates of the 'environmental Kuznets curve' hypothesis argue that industrialisation does cause rapid environmental degradation, but posit that once economies mature, production becomes more efficient and wealth increases, people can worry less about survival and choose to direct resources towards environmental protection (see Stern, 2001 for a critical review). The argument is that the dynamics of capitalist modernity can ultimately be harnessed to improve environmental quality.

Despite a clear transformation in values relating to the environment, growth and development, the debate continues. On the one hand, modernity itself, with its attendant emphases on extraction, industrialisation and growth, is being critiqued, with the call for re-evaluation of 'many of the central meta-narratives of the affluent industrialised Western world' (Durant et *al.*, 2004:509). On the other, the rise of international environmentalism and its appeal for attention on issues ranging from global warming to climate change has been dismissed as fear mongering, ideologically motivated, and often based on politically distorted interpretations of science (Sheehan, 1999). Another twist in the debate is provided by the Stern Review (Stern, 2006) on the economics of climate change by a committee headed by eminent economist Sir Nicholas Stern. This report has provoked urgent concerns amongst the advocates of free-market-led economic growth by arguing precisely that unless checked, climate change could cause tremendous economic loss. By focusing on economic arguments Stern may have caused those who have dismissed environmental concerns as secondary to growth, to take notice of the environment.

As a result of these clashing values, the very notion of global environmental change has become contested. An important issue in this respect is whether the concept of environmental change ought to be treated simply as physical change or in fact as a 'social' phenomenon resulting from particular human activities or institutionalised practices (Lipschutz and Mayer, 1996). It is to the subject of human social institutions and their relationships with the environment that we now turn.

The environmental governance discourse: multi-disciplinary influences

The discourse on environmental governance is rich in terms of the sheer expanse of issues across which it traverses: recognition of the environment as a global concern, but also awareness of the complex global-local relationships that complicate its governance; the significance of states as key governance actors, but also their inadequacy, and the rise of new actors from the voluntary and private sectors; the enactment of debates on the institutional appropriateness of states, markets and communities to tackle the collective action problems embodied in environmental governance; and not least, the fierce contests of interests between the developed and developing worlds. These issues resonate at the heart of intellectual developments regarding governance in a number of disciplines: notably international relations, politics and public administration, economic institutionalism and development studies. In fact, a case could be made that the environment has served as a key site of the *practice* of governance posing real challenges that a variety of disciplines have had to contend with.

Global environment, global politics: global environmental governance

'The environment has become a key site of global governance because of its transboundary nature' (Duffy, 2005:825). Until the 1980s however, it was relatively uncommon to discuss environmental problems as 'global' as these were viewed as 'marginal to national interests and international politics' (Porter *et al.*, 2000:1). This changed subsequently, with the highly publicised appearance of 'global environmental threats', from ozone layer depletion to global warming, that could profoundly affect all humanity. The transboundary nature both of the cause and effect of such problems signalled that it was clearly beyond the authority of individual nation-states to solve (Durant *et al.*, 2004). While conceptualising the environment as a global concern, a useful distinction was also made between international commons (physical or biological systems that lie wholly outside the jurisdiction of any one state), shared natural resources (both renewable and non-renewable resources shared by two or more states) and transboundary externalities (where activities located in one state produce consequences that impact other states) (Young, 1997:8). Further, crises impacting upon each of these (global warming, reduced fish stocks in particular places and the Chernobyl disaster respectively), arose from issues that lay at the heart of a 'global environmental politics' (Porter *et al.*, 2000). Intense economic development, population growth, urban migration, inefficient production and soaring consumption all constitute the meat of such a politics. While states are regularly engaged in intense competition over economic growth, aid and trade, an integral aspect of global environmental politics is also an emerging 'global civil society'. This new element has been described as 'a realm of actors who increasingly engage in transnational politics that is often, but not always, characterised by a high degree of autonomy from the states in which they are based' (Lipschutz and Mayer, 1996:77). It is viewed moreover as an active element of the growing system of global governance, rather than just as 'an agent of reform, resistance or rebellion' (Lipschutz and Mayer, 1996:49).

The experience of global environmental politics reiterates a core element in what has been described as 'global governance', in that it highlights a 'move away from a state-centric view of global politics' (Hewson and Sinclair 1999, cited in Duffy, 2005:827). That the state-centric system now coexists with a decentralised multi-centric form of organisation is increasingly accepted (McGrew, 1992; Rosenau, 1990). The literature on global governance refers to this pluralisation of actors in different ways. Hardt and Negri (2000) famously referred to this 'decentralised' and 'deterritorialised' regime of power as 'empire' while others suggested that global governance only extends the power of states in the global system. Whatever the opinion, there is a strong sense that global governance is:

> normatively about dispersing power away from hegemonic centres of power, especially states; about extending and overcoming resistance

to liberal democratic values and procedures; and about ordering people and things through recourse to reason, knowledge and expertise (Duffy, 2005:827).

In this context, global environmental governance is loosely understood as that 'which focuses on the regulation of environments and the actors that impact upon them' (Duffy, 2005:827).

It follows that a necessary feature of global environmental governance is the absence of a single authority to direct environmental matters (Bryner, 2004). Environmental policy scholars have commonly turned to the concept of 'international regime' as the basis of environmental governance. They refer to a multiplicity of different regimes comprising:

> international treaties and agreements, intergovernmental organisations, binding and non-binding norms and principles, relevant national and local government institutions, and associated non-governmental and private institutions that define and implement policies in different issue areas such as climate change, maritime oil pollution and endangered species protection (Vig, 2005:4; see also Axelrod, Downie and Vig, 2005; Porter *et al.*, 2000; Young, 1997).

The notion of an international regime can be used in two senses: in the first, it is a set of norms, rules or decision-making processes, whether explicit or implicit, producing some convergence in the actors' expectations in a particular issue area; in the second, however, it is a system of norms and rules specified by a multi-lateral agreement amongst relevant states (Porter *et al.*, 2000:13).

The first usage is critiqued for lacking both 'predictability' and 'stability', and it is the second usage that predominates. Regimes (as for whaling, climate change, protection of endangered species and the prevention of ozone layer depletion) are always created and operated through multi-lateral negotiations. Most regimes take the form of a binding agreement or legal instrument (called the *convention*) agreed upon by its constituent members. There are also *framework conventions* followed by the negotiation of one or more *protocols* which spell out specific obligations. The negotiation of a framework convention may take several years, as in the case of trans-boundary acid rain, ozone depletion and climate change. A non-binding agreement could also be viewed as a regime to the extent that it establishes norms that influence state behaviour. So for example, guidelines for global environmental problems such as forest management, are referred to as *soft law*, and could be considered regimes with varying degrees of effectiveness (Keohane and Nye, 1977). In this sense, the Agenda 21 plan of action at the 1992 Rio Summit could be regarded as an 'umbrella regime' for worldwide sustainable development, defining norms of behaviour on a wide range of environment and development issues (Porter *et al.*, 2000).

There is a great deal of theoretical debate in explaining the emergence and formation of international environmental regimes. These debates are central to theorising within the international relations discipline. The basic divergence here is between two schools of thought: realism and liberalism. Realism views the world as an anarchic collection of sovereign nation-states, each of which is a unitary actor in pursuing its unique national interests (Vig, 2005:3). In this perspective, nation-states do not cooperate with one another, unless it is clearly in their interest to do so, and cooperative behaviour will continue only so long as the parties perceive this condition to be met. Also known as the 'structural or hegemonic power' approach, it suggests that strong international regimes are a function of the existence of a hegemonic state that can exercise leadership over weaker states and that the absence of such a hegemonic state is likely to frustrate regime formation. Liberals, on the other hand, believe that states are interdependent, and in fact, have many common interests that lead them to cooperate; moreover, they believe that international institutions not only serve these common interests, but also create further incentives for cooperation (Vig, 2005). Game theory and utilitarian models of bargaining depict the process of negotiation of global environmental regimes differently from the structural-hegemonic approach. As bargaining situations are distinguished by the number of parties involved; the nature of the conflict and the assumption that the actors are rational, this approach suggests that small groups of states or coalitions are more likely to be able to successfully negotiate an international regime than a large number because each player can more readily understand the bargaining strategies of other players (Hampson, 1989–90). However, others hold that the significance of veto power in global environmental politics implies that relatively small groups of states are no more likely to form regimes than larger ones (Porter *et al.*, 2000).

A further debate is drawn on the importance of agency versus structure in explanations for regime formation. New institutionalists regard agents as ontologically superior to structures, viewing state behaviour as shaped by rational interests pursued in institutional bargaining forums. They claim that state behaviour is modified over time through the experience of pursuing regular exchanges with others to meet long-term common objectives as also the subordination of short-term interests for longer-term mutual advantage (Yahuda, 2001). This view is countered by the structuralists (or constructivists) who hold agents and structures in equal ontological standing. They assert that actors have interests or goals only in the context of social relations that produce meanings and values, and argue that institutions cannot simply be viewed as forums for bargaining between agents with autonomous preferences (Sandholtz, 1999).

These perspectives are regarded as overwhelmingly state-centred and thus fall short of the analytical challenges presented by the requirements of global governance. They have been roundly criticised by scholars broadly grouped together as 'pluralists', although views within this category may vary greatly with some viewing states as more insignificant than others. State-centred perspectives are held guilty of presenting all states as 'unitary' actors with a single internally consistent set of values and attitudes. As a result, the role of domestic politics, which may vitally impact upon negotiating positions, is utterly disregarded (DeSombre, 2005; Porter *et al.*, 2000; Rabkin, 1999). State-centred views have also been criticised for underplaying the roles assumed by international organisations in the creation of global environmental regimes (Brietmeier, 1996). An alternative 'institutional bargaining' model of regime creation accords greater emphasis to international organisations, hypothesising that states are fundamentally incapable of tackling environmental concerns as the protection of national security and promotion of economic growth are their primary concerns (Porter *et al.*, 2000). While acknowledging that explanations for the formation of international regimes have been largely state-centric, others have been critical of the deliberate 'attempt' to create a system of global governance on the back of state-led initiatives. This is leading to states 'being reconfigured within new regulatory regimes and hybridised transnational state actors' (Goldman, 2001:515). Concerns that global governance 'can and has been used to thwart private rights, local self-rule and the ordinary give-take of domestic politics' have followed (Sheehan, 1999:55).

Given the inadequacies of state-centred perspectives of global (environmental) governance, it has been proposed that the concept of the global or transnational regime is not quite adequate to capture the complexity of the rules, principles, norms and practices of a very large number of rather dissimilar actors. Instead, the notion of a 'global civil society' is suggested as more apposite (see Lipschutz and Mayer, 1996). These authors persuasively argue that the term provides 'convenient shorthand' to describe a multiplicity of overlapping processes, but also that it underlines the grounding of environmental protection, sustainability and governance in 'societal' processes as opposed to state-centred and institutionalised political ones. This recognition of the wider society, and numerous social actors, as a site for social action is in keeping with the new governance challenge being debated within the politics and international relations disciplines. Lipschutz and Mayer take their point far, suggesting that this approach suggests a form of social action 'somewhat parallel to the holism that is found in some ecological models, without implying the indivisibility of the planet that is characteristic of much environmental analysis' (1996:2). A related theoretical approach referred to as the 'epistemic communities' model emphasises the role of international learning in the formation of environmental 'regimes' (Brietmeier, 1996). Such learning is primarily based on scientific research and disseminated through 'transnational networks of groups', which influence public perceptions of key issues and impact upon decision-making.

Despite these theoretical advances, global governance theorists have been criticised for being too preoccupied with the mechanisms of governance while being blind to the challenges that it continually faces. The experience of global environmental governance in sub-Saharan Africa has been used to illustrate how 'invisible global networks' flow through developing states, constituting important political and economic interest groups, and are able to 'challenge or subvert attempts to manage, control or govern the environment' (Duffy, 2005:825). In the context of Madagascar for instance, Duffy powerfully illustrates how illicit sapphire mining is carried out by 'complex clandestine or shadow networks that include international actors and local Malagasy from all sections of society' in a country where the formal apparatus of global environmental governance are visibly present (donor consortium, international NGOs, Malagasy state) (2005:832). Her incisive analysis rests on Reno's notion of the 'shadow state' which exists alongside the formal state apparatus and is constituted by powerful interest groups both within and outside the country (see Reno, 1995, 1998; Duffy, 2005:928). This point brings home the limitations of adopting too sanguine a view of 'global civil society' to comprehend global environmental governance.

Institutional responses to the environment as a collective action problem

It is an inescapable fact that most environmental resources, especially air, water and forests, share attributes of 'common-pool' (widely referred to as common property) resources. They are *non-excludable*, which means that it is costly and difficult to exclude individuals from using the good, either through physical barriers or legal instruments, as also *non-subtractable*, meaning that the benefits consumed by one individual subtract from the benefits available to the others (Ostrom, 2000:337). The problem of their governance has served as essential fodder for new institutional theorists, eminently Elinor Ostrom and others, who have sought to put forward a theory of human cooperation that produces institutions which can effectively govern common-pool resources. Following this 'common-pool' character, the environment presents fundamental governance challenges that strike at the heart of the problem of collective decision-making. As such, the history of institutional responses to environmental governance has encompassed states, communities and markets. The debates on the appropriateness of these institutions have occurred in several disciplinary contexts: politics and economics, international relations, as well as development studies.

The classic description of the environmental collective action problem is owed to Garrett Hardin's 'Tragedy of Commons' paradigm. Using the metaphor of a 'pasture open to all', Hardin argued that individual rational action based on self-interest under conditions of geometric population growth, threatens a common resource with irreversible degradation. Hardin's (1968) two solutions were absolute privatisation or absolute state control. Mancur Olson (1971) referred to this self-interested action vis-à-vis a common resource (specifically a public good) as 'free riding', arguing further that such a problem cannot theoretically exist in the state as it has the distinguishing attribute of possessing the legitimate authority to coerce should the need arise. The clear policy prescription that arose from this paradigm was simply that 'swift and sure government intervention was needed to resolve and prevent commons tragedies' (Schlager, 2004:148). At the time, it dovetailed nicely with the goals and purposes of modern state-building that was occurring in newly liberated developing countries. Such emphasis on state action contributed to the predominance of state-led initiatives in the process of international regime formation and global environmental governance more generally.

As already discussed, the sweeping dominance of state-centred approaches to environmental governance has merited critical responses on a number of grounds. The indispensability attributed to state-led governance further suffered on account of the wide discrediting of the 'tragedy of commons' paradigm. New institutional theorists paid theoretical and empirical attention to the attributes of 'communities' to evolve their own institutions to govern common-pool resources. Ostrom (1986,

1990) notably focused on identifying the conditions under which 'appropriators' are expected to cooperate to devise governing arrangements. In this tradition, great emphasis has been placed on the institutions that are most likely, and able, to facilitate cooperative behaviour to promote desired values such as sustainability of growth and development and conserve the earth's environmental resources (see Erickson-Blomquist and Ostrom, 1984; Runge, 1981, 1986; Ruttan and Hayami, 1984; Wade, 1987 for other empirically rooted works on 'self-governing' institutions). However, new institutionalist advocacy of community action has been countered by a rich critical tradition for being a 'predictive and generalising theory' of the economic and institutional conditions of collective action (Mosse, 2003:274). A number of authors have shown how, in practice, 'community-driven' approaches may produce expectations of 'community-like' behaviour that are unsubstantiated in practice, and also, that the state and community are mutually constitutive, as opposed to being simply dichotomous (see Mosse, 1997; Li, 1999 for excellent ethnographic analyses). Nevertheless, others argue that even if common-pool resource theory does not, and cannot, predict that collective action will always be successful, it has contributed significantly to developing more complete explanations of cooperation and resource users' ability to coordinate and govern their behaviour (Schlager, 2004:169).

Market-based solutions to environmental governance have also been staunchly advocated. They endorse Hardin's recommendation of privatisation as one way of dealing with the collective action problem. The proponents of formal markets argue that well-defined, private and exclusive rights to resources not only create entitlements where none exist, but also allow for the exchange and purchase of these entitlements, serving essential environmental purposes. The state-market dichotomy with respect to the environment has its roots in a long-drawn ideological battle, between classical liberalism and Keynesianism. The main role of the liberal state is to protect the property rights of 'free, equal, landed individuals', which contrasts starkly with the Keynesian state, which strived to bring about environmental protection leading to 'the proliferation of environmental laws, regulations, constituencies and norms' particularly in advanced capitalist countries (McCarthy and Prudham, 2004:278). The subsequent rise of neoliberalism has been characterised by assaults on Keynesian-era environmental regulation, also referred to as 'first generation approaches' to environmental governance (Durant *et al.*, 2004:2). Neoliberalism draws closely from classical liberal ideas regarding private property, which now resonate in a host of contemporary schemes for environmental management that attempt to protect nature through the price mechanism (McAfee, 1999).

A number of market-based environmental measures have been conceptualised and put into practice. Tradable environmental allowances are now widely practised in a number of developing countries (Dailey and Ellison, 2002). Other schemes include the environmental certification of commodities, eco-based taxes and payment for environmental services for watershed protection (to pay people in upstream reaches to change destructive land-use practices through charging downstream water users) (Bulas, 2004; Mansfield, 2001). The proliferation of market-based measures has created its own impetus for global regulation, as industries and businesses feel that 'standardising environmental regulations is necessary for global markets to function effectively' and 'many regulators anticipate that standards will ease their enforcement and compliance costs' (Durant *et al.*, 2004:496). In this framework, governance is fundamentally about regulation to derive the maximum benefits from capitalist modernisation through the crafting of international environmental laws, policies and institutions. The role of states in this framework is a facilitatory one as opposed to that of direct regulation in the Keynesian era. This, furthermore, is rationalised as 'global environmentalism', capable of restraining the excesses of capitalism, and steering growth along more environmentally benign paths (McCarthy, 2004:328: Buttel, 2000; Sonnenfeld and Mol, 2002).

Market-based measures have been criticised on many grounds, including that they do not suit all contexts and all types of environmental resources and have very questionable effects on equity. Water for example, being a *mobile* common-pool resource is obstinately difficult to privatise (Ostrom, 2000; Bakker, 2005; Bruns and Meinzen-Dick, 2005). While we cannot go into the detail of these critiques here, it is important to summarise the main propositions of a dissident perspective that has arisen of neoliberal environmental governance. Its proponents focus on the links between neoliberalism and environmentalism as ideologies, discourses and class projects (McCarthy and Prudham, 2004:276–278). They contend that the rise of 'free-market environmentalism', once an oxymoron, has proliferated since the Thatcher-Reagan years, and contemporary forms of environmental governance ranging from tradable permits to transferable quotas essentially reflect that environmentalism and neoliberalism have incorporated elements of one another. These critics also warn against the growing convergence of sustainable development with 'green capitalism, the greening of the World Bank and corporate green-wash' (McCarthy and Prudham, 2004; Goldman, 2001). They argue that the concept of *ecologically* sustainable development has been transformed into *economically* sustainable development, focusing on how a larger range of goods and services can be accessed through improved management of natural resources. Indeed, the last decade has witnessed the rise of 'corporate environmentalism', with the initiation of 'eco-friendly business practices' by prominent corporations, and the use of these to 'influence the behaviour of environmental activists, legislators and regulators' as well as to secure 'ancillary benefits such as attracting "green" consumers and reducing costs' (Lyon and Maxwell, 2004:262). Transnational corporations have increasingly partnered with the United Nations and other international organisations to address serious environmental problems.

All this is dismissed as illusory. Broader critiques have been levelled at environmentalism as a component of the World Bank's agenda for good governance for treating 'natural resource issues poorly' (Batterbury and Fernando, 2006:1853). Echoing a persistent theme on governance debates within development studies, it is argued that new environmental governance regimes alter the range of powers and the capabilities of state and civil society actors in ways that even conflict with the ostensible goals of 'good' governance. Batterbury and Fernando (2006) reason that the good governance framework does not capture the reality of environmental governance, and lend their support to the emerging literature on 'eco-governmentality' (see Goldman, 2001, 2004). This approach targets the World Bank in particular, for 'targeting resource based populations...and compelling them to participate in the neo-liberal process of eco-government' within the larger context of globalisation (Goldman, 2001:499). This is described as part of a larger process of the 'construction of transnationalised environmental states' by the World Bank, whose policy interventions dominate the globalisation agenda, to prompt easier integration with its environmental institutions and interests. The idea of the 'governance' state has been put forward in this context to denote 'a product of social engineering' by World Bank policies since the onset of structural adjustment in the 1980s (see Harrison, 2004). Nevertheless, these new transnationalised states are often bypassed by resistant networks comprising powerful interests both locally and globally (Duffy, 2005).

Recent work has focused on the development of a 'third-way' approach to environmental governance, which is not purely market-, community- or government-based, which is neither results or outcomes focused, and is devoted instead to building 'complementary and synergistic roles for markets and mandates, for experts and laypersons...bureaucrats and communities' (Durant *et al.*, 2004:2). This approach recognises that it is not merely a question of which institution (state, market or community) resolves the collective action problem of environmental governance, but also the level or scale at which governance is organised (see Batterbury and Fernando, 2006; also World Development special edition, 2006). This issue reveals a distinct discomfiture amongst some scholars about the pooling of all environmental issues at a 'global' level. Lipschutz and Mayer write that the term 'global environmental change' conceals as much as it reveals, since it seems to relegate 'local' environmental problems to another realm of behaviour and politics, and presumes that 'global' problems can somehow be handled through a top-down process of centralised management (1996:22). Besides, 'first generation' common and control type approaches are viewed as inappropriate and politically unsustainable for dealing with contemporary environmental problems, such as those caused by 'small, diverse, and numerous non-point sources of pollution', including greenhouse gas emissions, emissions of ozone-depleting chemicals and so on (Durant *et al.*, 2004:3). In contrast, governance approaches that are based on flexibility and adaptability to a myriad of local circumstances, diverse regulatory targets, interdependent actors and knowledge bases are favoured.

In the same vein, Lipschutz and Mayer (1996) make a powerful case against treating *all* environmental problems as unbounded and transnational. They argue for primacy to the local, on the basis that the physical environmental effects of certain activities may be based on access to a shared physical resource, the activities contributing to these impacts tend to be bounded in social, economic and even physical terms. Drawing from Ronald Herring's notion of nesting, i.e. 'all local arrangements for dealing with natural systems are embedded in a larger common interest defined by the reach of ecosystems beyond localities', they envision local systems of production and action as being 'nested' within larger ones (Herring 1960, cited in Lipschutz and Mayer, 1996:24). They propose the notion of 'resource-regimes', signifying hundreds of thousands of resource-using institutions, which function at varying geographical and social scales, and are not only 'material', but also 'ideational' involving collective cognition, ideas and explanations.

No lived process of governance demonstrates the significance of the scale of institutional responses to the collective action problem better than decentralisation (see Larson and Ribot's excellent 2005 edited collection of studies on decentralisation in natural resources management from around the world). Natural resources are economically valuable, cardinal to the livelihoods of both the rich and the poor, and physically present in the local sphere, all of which make decentralisation a volatile and contentious process. The actual restructuring of governance arrangements through decentralisation has frequently led to the heightening and widening of conflict between old and new interests on land, water and forest regions around the world (Larson and Ribot, 2005). These experiences have reiterated that questions where should power lie – public, private or collective – and at what spatial level – central, state, regional or local. The issues raised have immense practical relevance for environmental governance.

A tense environment: whose governance is it?

If 'good governance' is a fundamentally transformative project orchestrated by the developed west in the developing regions of the world, then the environment is a prime arrow in its quiver. The World Bank's pursuit of environmentally sustainable development and its efforts to restructure and 'environmentalise' states to this end have been viewed by critics as a particular exercise of power for governance, which they describe as 'eco-governmentality' (Goldman, 2001, 2004). The Bank has been consciously trying to 'green' project funding since the 1980s, and a series of 'green conditionalities' now accompany infrastructure projects as a result. These have led to the rewriting of laws relating to environmental regulation and property rights, restructuring of state agencies and the creation of a new hybridised network of transnational actors that act to mobilise the Bank's green epistemology, which is fundamentally neoliberal to the core. Eco-governance by the World Bank and other influential international organisations is thus excessively normative along neoliberal principles, which obscures the cultural specificity of different contexts. It is significant that governance of the environment, through its association with property rights and state regulation, has become an important component of the wider 'good governance' agenda. However, as with the rest of good governance, this sort of eco-governance is presented as a politically neutral phenomenon with little reference to the deep inequalities of power between the developed and developing worlds that contextualise it.

Indeed, the history of environmental governance is one of conflict between the developed and developing worlds, and is a paradigmatic case for consideration within the critical development studies discipline. This stems from the inextricable links between environmental issues with growth, development and trade, all contested issues in the iniquitous North-South relationship (Stiglitz and Charlton, 2005). As one author aptly summarised, while 'northern' environmental issues were climate change, ozone depletion and the loss of biodiversity, 'southern' environmental issues were drinking water and sanitation, urban pollution, desertification and so on (Porter *et al.*, 2000:47). From the early days of the 1970s, many developing countries perceived the North's environmental governance initiatives (for example the Stockholm Conference in 1972) as 'efforts to sabotage the South's development aspirations' (Najam, 2005:231). Although southern states won a symbolic victory with the legitimisation of their demand for a new international economic order (NIEO) by the UN General Assembly in 1974, the next two decades saw the NIEO agenda rapidly receding from international attention, and the onset of decades of aid conditionality and structural adjustment. It was at the Earth Summit in 1992, with the broad ranging ideological emphasis on 'sustainable development' that attention was refocused on southern aspirations and the need for North-South negotiations once again.

In addition to endorsing a global commitment to sustainable development, the Rio Summit also provided an emphasis to three critical, subsidiary principles: 'Additionality', 'Common but Differentiated' principles, and 'Polluter Pays'. This emphasis was important, as it addressed southern fears that even though they had not been historically responsible for producing the major environmental problems of today, they would somehow be made to bear the costs of global environmental action either through lost development opportunities or real costs of remediation and adaptation. However, the last ten years or more since Rio have seen a considerable dilution of these concepts and fostered a tremendous dissatisfaction of environmental governance within the developing world (Najam, 2005:326–238). The principle of additionality sought to ensure that new monies would be made available to deal with global environmental issues. And yet, soon after Rio, during negotiation of the Desertification Convention (UNCCD), it became clear that few new funds would be made available for implementation of the treaty. Since then, negotiations on several other multi-lateral environmental agreements (MEAs), have seen the Northern countries argue that utilising market forces and managing existing resources better substitutes for some portion of the original promise for additionality. This is also the case for the 'Common but Differentiated Responsibility' principle, which acknowledges that some nations have a greater responsibility for having created, and therefore, addressing global environmental problems. This principle has arguably been undermined in the context of the Climate Convention, with the United States taking the position that it would not accept mandatory greenhouse gas reduction targets unless India and China did likewise, even though industrialised countries account for the vast majority of greenhouse gas emissions. Finally, although the 'Polluter Pays' principle is rooted in fairness, many in the South believe that an increasing pattern of pushing the implementation of MEAs southward (as in the climate, biodiversity and desertification regimes) by seeking relatively fewer changes in behaviour in the North, waters down the principle considerably.

In this context, the formulation of environmental trade measures or ETMs (laws that authorise restrictions on trade for a variety of policy objectives related to domestic and international environmental issues) have been viewed suspiciously by developing countries. Perhaps it is not surprising that the United States has taken the lead in defending the right to use ETMs for both domestic and international environmental objectives, and it is no accident that it has been the target of a number of cases brought before the GATT/WTO dispute panels. At Rio, India and South Korea proposed that unilateral actions to deal with environmental problems outside the jurisdiction of the importing country should be avoided, to which the US objected, but agreed while submitting an 'interpretative statement' justifying the use of ETMs in 'certain' situations (Porter *et al.*, 2000:187). The last decade has witnessed an interesting and increasing rivalry between the US and large developing powers such as India and China, which together continue to frustrate international cooperation on environmental governance. This has been countered by a more pro-active stance towards environmental governance within the European Union. An interesting role reversal is underway, with countries like the UK lobbying with India and China for help with tackling climate change and other issues. These trends have considerably complicated the picture of a simple North-South domination with respect to environmental governance, legitimately raising the question: 'whose' governance is it?

Power and environmental governance

Power is central to the theory and practice of environmental governance. It impacts upon the form (how governance is structured), content (how governance is imposed) and ethic (whether governance is fair) of environmental governance. It is significant that the discourse on power is itself shaped by multi-disciplinary influences, with ideas from within international relations, politics, economics and development studies playing a crucial part both in guiding the major debates around power and in offering the conceptual and linguistic tools through which these debates are carried out. These influences are not clear-cut and it is hard to discuss them separately. Besides, critical traditions – notably political ecology, an 'interdisciplinary... strategy....[that is] seeking to describe the dynamic ways in which, on the one hand, political and economic power can shape ecological futures, and, on the other, how ecologies can shape political and economic possibilities' (CEEP) that have enriched the critical discourse on power are themselves derived from different disciplines.

The idea of environmental governance is fundamentally about how to use power to influence critical decisions about the environment. The nuts and bolts of the governance process have meant that convincing states to 'give up' power over traditional areas of decision-making to supranational or even global bodies, has been the key dilemma. The reasons for this have varied, depending on key issues in the location of respective states in international political economy: the United States on the one hand, and India and China on the other, have each shown a measure of recalcitrance towards the crafting of environmental governance arrangements for their own particular reasons. In theoretical terms, state-centric explanations for the formation of governance arrangements have traditionally dominated, but this is changing with a growing perception that such explanations are limited in the face of increasing diffusion of power beyond state agencies, to large and diverse networks of 'civil society' actors. Other alternative theorisations like the 'global civil society' and 'epistemic communities' approaches have emerged to capture this novel exercise of power in the execution of environmental governance.

Equally, the lived reality of environmental governance at a number of levels, from the local to the global, demonstrates that 'struggles over resources lie at the centre of struggles over power' (Peet and Watts, 2004:xiv). There is a clear link between politics and social relations, and 'the larger processes of material transformation and power relations' in the environmental domain (Peluso and Watts 2001, cited in Batterbury and Fernando, 2006:1857). There is a strong thrust in this critical tradition (some of it described as 'political ecology') on viewing environmental change as a 'social' rather than a purely 'physical' phenomenon, as resource degradation shares a mutual relationship with political and social change, therefore explanations for such changes must be sought at 'multiple scales, and across the human and non-human worlds; from the international economy down to the systems of rules governing local access to forests' (Batterbury and Fernando, 2006:1857). Thus, the wider literature on environmental governance regards the issue of power not merely in terms of *agencies* (states, international organisations, NGOs, advocacy groups and so on), but also in terms of *structural conditions* informing agency action.

In this context, the discussion on power has grown to highlight the struggles underlying the process that leads to the definition of environmental problems (such as climate change), environmental goals (such as sustainability) and thus environmental governance itself. The meanings attached to environmental resources and their uses are negotiated, not in the sense of 'legislative bargaining or environmental mediation' but instead of a social and political interaction that involves a fundamental reworking of the 'cultural meanings of things elemental to society' (Gamman 1994, cited in Lipschutz and Mayer, 1996:60). These can be thought of as the 'intellectual framework' to which our material systems are anchored and from which they derive social purpose and legitimacy. Thus, we see a continuous confrontation between the scientific-technological paradigm of nature and ecology on the one hand, and culturally rooted evocations of nature and 'mother earth' to privilege indigenous knowledge on the other.

Whatever their basis of knowledge, modern environmentalists are accused of politically distorting science and using 'environmental fears' opportunistically to generate public support. The 'dubious' role of pro-environment NGOs in influencing the climate change agenda at Kyoto, by forging links with national and international environmental agencies has been decried (Sheehan, 1999). The trenchant, even ugly, confrontations on climate change reveal that the science behind climate change is widely contested. These affirm the prescient remark that 'science by itself cannot provide a community with values; only politics can do that' (Lipschutz and Mayer, 1996:44).

No environmental principle or objective is beyond the purview of accusations of self-interest. The issue of 'sustainability' is most illustrative of this. In the years since the 1992 Rio Summit it has become clear how, precisely on account of its consensual character, the concept of sustainability is extremely general, lacking specific content on how sustainable development is to be attained or who is responsible for achieving it. Such vagueness is described to be deliberate, as it 'allows the idea to be adopted by virtually everyone as a way of bringing people together to seek common ground' (Axelrod, Downie and Vig, 2005:7). In this formulation, the authors add, 'it is clearly a political and social construct, not a scientific concept or blueprint' (Axelrod, Downie and Vig, 2005:7; Baker *et al.*, 1997; Parris, 2003). Others view that although sustainability has its merits and demerits, it helps and has helped 'morph environmental issues into the decidedly more conflictual politics of livelihoods issues' (Durant *et al.*, 2004:516). Implicit in the notion of sustainability is the conviction that the 'pie cannot grow indefinitely' and this 'whether ultimately theoretically defensible or not, logically points to questions of distribution *and* equity', either within or across nations and within and across the developed and developing worlds (McCarthy and Prudham, 2004:279; Durant *et al.*, 2004). In fact, radical critiques have targeted the cooptation of the idea of sustainability by the international environment establishment. Sustainability is central to the exercise of eco-governmentality by the World Bank. It thus constitutes the basis for a highly sophisticated form of power that unfolds within an uneven and contradictory process of 'global inclusion and social exclusion' (Goldman, 2001:516; see also Frank *et al.*, 2000; Buttel, 2000).

Ultimately, the future of environmental governance rests in a contest for power between the developed and developing worlds in this highly unequal, though rapidly changing, context of globalisation. The actions of the United States and the European Union, as two vitally important actors, will have a bearing on the extent of international cooperation that is possible with the developing world. The recent past has shown a striking contrast between US and EU approaches to international environmental governance (Rabkin, 1999; DeSombre, 2005; Axelrod, Vig and Shreurs 2005). While the EU has emerged as a leading actor in global environmental diplomacy, backed by common internal policies for its member-states and the delegation of authority to centralised administrative units; the US has pursued increasingly unilateral strategies, often unwilling to exercise leadership or even participate in multi-lateral environmental efforts. Some believe that this attitude can be explained by the nature of influence exercised by domestic politics, especially domestic Congressional regulation, that make it extremely difficult for the US to submit to international regulation on matters that have not been approved domestically (DeSombre, 2005). More generally, the stand-off on key environmental governance measures, like the Kyoto Protocol, between the US and emerging global players like India and China, has ironically created an interest based alliance that works against international cooperation on the environment.

The effectiveness of environmental governance

The question of effectiveness repeatedly surfaces within the literature on environmental governance, albeit implicitly, with concerns regarding the ability of environmental regimes to 'solve' the problems they set out to resolve. However, demonstrating effectiveness in relation to the environment is very difficult. It is not sufficient to observe that after a regime was created, the problem that led to its creation subsequently subsided; 'as both the problem and the apparent solution can be attributed to other causes, the danger of ending up with spurious correlations is great' (Young, 1997:13). With the science of environmental change being contested as the politics of its governance, effectiveness can hardly be understood as a temporally definite outcome. Nevertheless, there is the view that irrespective of whether regimes prove 'effective' in solving the problems that motivate their creation, international and transnational institutions can, and often do, produce consequences that transcend their particular issue areas with unintended effects, which may bear important implications for international society as a whole (Levy, Young and Zurn, 1995).

However, effectiveness is regarded in practical terms with respect to the difficulties experienced in orchestrating environmental governance. At heart, this issue points to a fundamental collective action problem: even if the forging of international agreements would reduce uncertainty in interaction and make everyone better off, then their very creation poses a collective action dilemma (referred to as a '"second" order of rationality problem', see Elster, 1979). Environmental regimes are essentially negotiated by states which are 'highly resistant to imposing on themselves an enforceable obligation to alter domestic social institutions' (Lipschutz and Mayer, 1996:39). As described earlier, the history of state-led initiatives on environmental governance is a chequered one. Perceptions of national interest, the influence of domestic party politics, interest groups and business lobbies can all work to restrain the enthusiasm of states for international environmental governance, as most notably seen in the US case. Conversely, pro-active public opinion in EU countries has noticeably complemented the EU's institutional drive for common internal policies amongst its member states, and subsequently a strong unified position enabling it to act as an international facilitator for environmental governance.

The scale at which governance issues are sought to be resolved is also viewed as a major variable impacting upon effectiveness. Here, effectiveness is seen in broadly spatial terms, in terms of the relevance of governance arrangements to those who are *most* involved in their implementation and in the negotiation of outcomes (see Adger *et al.*, 2001 for an illuminating discussion of the appropriateness of temporal and spatial scales of governance in relation to climate change). In this respect, the logic of environmental problems transcending particular localities and thus necessitating transnational, even global, regimes is held to account by those who find fault with the 'stickiness of large-scale institutions' (Lipschutz and Mayer, 1996:39). They argue that 'no matter how much is learned about environmental change, either as a physical or *global* phenomenon, it will never be enough to "solve" the "problem(s)" of environmental change at any level' (Lipschutz and Mayer, 1996:68). The authors concur that it is only by reconstructing our understanding of the global environment as the outcome of myriads of micro-level practices, which consequently requires changes in micro-level practices, can we even think about problem-solving.

Despite the strong thrust towards globalising conceptions of the environment and its governance, there is uncertainty, not consensus, on the wisdom of such an approach. Haas (2004) comments on the utopian nature of the idea of a centralised global environmental organisation and questions the appropriateness of decentralised networks of institutions to deal with complex and uncertain policy environments. Some more recent writings have tried to present a compromise solution, a third approach, which involves:

> inspiring, arranging, coordinating, and monitoring community-based partnerships of public, private and nongovernmental stakeholders who mutually define problems and co-produce consensus based solutions with environmental agencies (Durant *et al.*, 2004:12).

But as our previous discussions reveal, this seemingly harmonious approach contains veiled asymmetries in power – both within and between countries – that would continue to inform, if not determine, the success of cooperation.

Finally, and perhaps most significantly in terms of future thinking, is the issue of the relationship between the rules underlying governance regimes and their manifestation in practice. If the environment is not just a physical, but also a social phenomenon, then there is no reason why rules underlying regimes must remain fixed, or subject only to change through state sanctioned or negotiated institutionalised procedures. This is especially true if we are to accept – as in the socio-legal tradition of analysis – that individual behaviour is mediated not by official laws or formal rules alone, but by a range of official and unofficial rules and norms. Indeed, it is the tension between reconciling particular cultural transformations in resource meanings and use with aggregated, institutionalised collective decision-making, or governance, at different levels, from the local to the global that will remain the biggest challenge to the effectiveness of environmental governance.

10
Governance: From Theory to Practice

Governance is concerned with the practice of making collective decisions. Governance theory, as such, has both an explanatory dimension and an advisory character. This twin theory-practice focus justifies the core intellectual pursuit of the book, which is to delineate not only the development but also the application of governance theory. The book explores governance theory from a cross-disciplinary perspective and offers those interested in governance access to some of the valuable analytical tools that each discipline has to offer in its distinctive treatment of the idea of governance.

In the first part of the book we identified five key disciplines to focus our investigation: politics and public administration, economics (particularly economic institutionalism), international relations, development studies and socio-legal studies. The second half of the book looked at governance theories that have developed in application in complex settings. It examined the three critical areas of corporate, participatory and environmental governance and investigated whether these practical areas of governance have been enriched by theoretical developments from a range of disciplines. We found that environmental governance is an area that is shaped by ideas and debates on governance originating with international relations, development studies, economic institutionalism, politics as well as socio-legal studies. Participatory governance has attracted valuable insights from political science and development studies. Corporate governance practice, in contrast, displayed a tendency to draw from particular branches of economic institutionalism and much less from other disciplines, although it might have benefited from doing so.

Our general position is, therefore, that governance practice is best understood when viewed through a multi-disciplinary lens. We argue

214

that a cross-disciplinary focus delivers a more subtle and complex understanding of the challenges involved in designing governance solutions than those that are derived from a single discipline base. Understanding the multi-disciplinary basis of governance is necessary if we are to equip ourselves to better analyse and appreciate the practice of governance. Knowledge of the wider intellectual resources that have been applied to governance, drawn from a range of disciplines, allows those interested in reforming governance to move beyond a narrow vision and to counter their disciplinary biases. It also enables a more realistic appraisal of the sorts of problems 'governance solutions' can actually solve and what those solutions might be. In this concluding chapter we ask what has our cross-disciplinary tour delivered in terms of enhanced understanding; and what in the way of advice for designers of governance systems does our book provide?

In addition to a commitment to cross-disciplinarity our approach argues that governance challenges can usefully be met through an investigative approach rather than by way of a check list of normative principles against which any system is checked. The normative approach can establish some valuable guidelines for governance systems and therefore offers a valuable starting point but if you want to understand what might work in a particular setting it is necessary to develop an approach driven by empirical as much as normative theory and one that recognises the subtlety of some of the normative challenges involved in governance and does not simply call for more transparency or more accountability. In short to change the world for the better you need to understand it in a superior way and apply normative principles with care and in balance with one another.

The first section of the chapter focuses attention on the core disciplines that we have examined to bring out diverse ways in which the nature of governance problems have been perceived and the solutions that are on offer from each of the disciplinary bases. But knowing that a range of mechanisms are available to you does not mean that it is obvious which one or which mix to choose. The second section of the chapter explores this issue and begins by arguing that the search for governance solutions involves practical judgement rather than the application of simple formulas of best practice drawn out from indicator-driven audits. Moreover we argue that most governance solutions are likely to be untidy rather than neat formulations and need to be designed in context rather than simply derived from abstract principles. A complex appreciation of the prospects for institutional change lies at the heart of the governance search for solutions and the chapter offers some guidelines for that search, drawing on and developing insights from our cross-disciplinary tour.

The third section of this chapter focuses on the contradiction between the ways that governance debates have developed over the last two decades or more in academic fields compared to those read by practitioners and policy-makers. The former have more insights than have so far been incorporated into 'real world' governance debates. In particular we argue that politics needs to be taken more seriously in these practical discussions and much favoured blanket solutions – such as the call for a greater transparency – need to be treated with greater scepticism. Again our over-arching point is that our cross-disciplinary tour reveals a richness of understanding that the practice of governance cannot afford to ignore.

Advances stemming from a multi-disciplinary approach

We draw our prime lessons in understanding from the five disciplines covered in Part I of the book. In *political science and public administration*, even those doubting the depth and focus of the governance literature admit that the governance turn has made a major impact. The strength of the political science literature is the range and variety of its empirical studies, and its capacity to throw up useful new conceptual insights. A variety of theoretical frameworks are displayed, ranging from rational choice to post-structuralist approaches, but none of these can claim particular origins or focus on the governance debate as such. The novelty and originality of governance theory in political science comes in particular conceptual developments. These include the concept of the hollowed-out state; the investigation and understanding of the concept of governance failure; and the idea of meta-governance as a reference to the over-arching capacity of state bodies to steer governance. It is worth dwelling on each of these insights in turn.

The governance turn, for political scientists, signalled an increased awareness of the multi-layered nature of decision-making – with local, national and supranational institutions intertwined in (often complex and over-lapping) collective decision-making challenges. From public administration scholars there has been comment on a 'hollowing out' of the nation-state. This has meant an overall fragmentation of its structures and institutions, matched by a move of decision-making powers to international and supra-national bodies, and a new dynamism and energy around local and regional politics. Within work focused on the European Union, the governance turn has involved a shift in focus away from the EU as a negotiated partnership between a group of nation-states, to a complex set of policy relations stretching down to local and regional levels and internationally outwards in trade and foreign policy arenas – incorporating a wider range of public and private actors.

The idea of governance failure draws upon a recognition that organising governing through networks is far from unproblematic because it operates in the context of conflict and uncertainty. In this light, governance failure might occur because of irresolvable conflicts between interests, a lack of trust between agents, inept steering by state actors, as well as differences in time-horizons between participants and the challenge of working at different spatial scales. The odds, in some respects, seem stacked against governance and although political scientists have seen examples of governance success, they have in many respects a greater focus on identifying the circumstances for governance failure. Along with other political mechanisms, governance has a considerable capacity to disappoint participants, especially relatively unorganised citizens, but at the same time there appears to be no alternative but to try and mix together the ingredients of a governance solution again and to keep on trying.

A further key debate in political science is between those who have argued that we are witnessing the emergence of governance without government, and those that see the issue as governments having to operate in a new context. The two perspectives might best be seen as opposite ends of the spectrum rather than in conflict with one another. Since those that take the governance without government perspective, while emphasising the role of relatively autonomous networks of societal-based actors in collective decision-making, still give credence to a governmental role in steering or providing a meta-governance framing by political representatives and governmental officials. And those who take a stronger line about government still being a powerful actor nevertheless recognise the distinctive and substantial role for non-governmental actors in governance arrangements. For them governance is about new conditions leading to governments remaining influential, perhaps even dominant actors in collective decision-making, but having to operate in different ways, with different tools. The group of writers that have developed a focus on the new tools of governing have done so in a way that emphasises the variety and flexibility of soft tools of governing available to governors. This school can be linked, in turn, to a more explicitly normative set of writers who use governance to refer to the need for government to re-invent itself, to become better at steering and more willing to share the 'doing' (or 'rowing') with other agencies under contract, or at arms-length in some way (Osbourne and Gaebler, 1992) and see governance as closely connected to the rise of New Public Management (NPM). Others challenge whether NPM techniques provide an inadequate guide to operating in the context of governance, and they argue that another concept – public value would be a better guide (Moore, 1995; Stoker, 2006b). Public value management matches the demands of governance because it demands a public sphere based on the building networks of deliberation, matched by networks of delivery, driven by an underlying concept of shared value.

The political science approach to governance recognises that what can be achieved by governments is mediated through a complex web of institutions and a dispersed range of networks. The problem that governance addresses for political scientists might be summed up as: we are all affected by each other more than before, but we lack the tools to hold each other to account. The integrated and complex policy networks that are characteristic of governance mean that responsibility for action cannot easily be tied to mechanisms to hold decision-makers to account since responsibility is shared and diffused. Put boldly: modern governance creates a world where 'nobody is in charge'. This dilemma is a core concern for the political science literature. Politicians do not sit, as some media commentary implies, at the top of one consolidated, bureaucratic, machinery of government with all the levers of control just sitting in front of them. Rather, a multitude of special interests and lobbies both inside and outside the government machine put up ideas and projects for their consideration. Moreover, in the world of modern governance, to achieve many desired changes requires that governments do not simply act on their own, but instead in concert with other governments or with citizens or specialist and sectional interests. Environmental issues provide a constant example of these complex processes of governance in action. They often require a mixture of global and local action; interventions around energy saving or recycling need the active support of businesses, community groups and citizens in general. Modern politics takes place through the medium of governance. But constructing accountability and effective intervention in that medium is not straightforward (Stoker, 2006a).

Governance emerged within *economics* as part of a challenge to the classical orthodoxy which carries the general label of economic institutionalism. North, Williamson and others were instrumental in encouraging economics to look beyond exchanges between rational actors and to focus on the context in which these exchanges were taking place. Institutions matter, according to all these economists, and that focus places governance at the heart of their programmes of work. The complexity of the task undertaken by actors will impact upon the attributes of a transaction and make it more likely that some governance routes will be pursued – rather than sticking to a market-like system. Alternative structures emerge to deal with those situations where market-like relations become more problematic. That is when market incentives cannot be provided with sufficient intensity and bite; when administrative controls of audit and accounting need to be more developed; and where the most likely form of workable redress is forbearance and development, rather than legal sanction or dispute resolution. If an asset in the exchange cannot be easily specified, and if there is great uncertainty over its management, then a formal institutional response is more likely to emerge. Firms (and by extension government bodies), it would seem, exist because of the need to get beyond the limitations of the improvised and makeshift nature of relationships constructed through market exchange. Firms and other organisations look to build predictability and trust.

Creating institutions to support predictability and trust is a key theme of economic institutionalism. Elinor Ostrom, for example, applies this approach to examine the problem of dealing with shared resources in common pool settings. The management and supply of water, for example, runs the risk of over-use or exploitation, unless some constraint is provided on the exploitation of resources by individuals. But that constraint does not need to be in the form of state regulation and control, or privatisation of ownership or use rights – it can come from those who use the common pool resource, providing they have the right institutional framework or set of rules to steer their actions. Basically, the solution offered in Ostrom's work is that norms, information-sharing and incentives can, if aligned, ensure that cooperation becomes possible. The key is to be able to provide a credible commitment, a framework that enables all those interested in a decision to be able to predict the basis for future decisions and regard the governing criteria as legitimate.

The economics literature is, in many ways, more optimistic than the political science literature about the prospects for finding effective governance solutions. The area of the literature where a sense of the potential for failure comes through is in the discussion of path dependency. Here, following the work of Douglass North in particular is found a sense that past choices can constrain present choices. North introduces an important temporal dimension into the discussion of institutions and governance by identifying how a particular way of organising adopted in one period may provide a constraint with negative consequences on future practices because it becomes ingrained into a system through habit or because interests are tied to it. Deciding everything through committees of employees with a few outsiders, for example, might have made sense when UK universities were small private institutions, but as their scale and external funding has increased so committees as a form of decision-making are no longer so appropriate. This insight brings into focus a core dilemma in the governance debate – today's institutional solutions may be tomorrow's problems.

In the *international relations* governance literature, under the influence of James Rosenau, has developed new terms such as 'fragmegration' to signify an era in which globalisation encourages a seemingly contradictory dynamic of greater localising and regionalisation of differences, and at the same time a drive to provide more integrated processes that erode the capacities of states and the meaning of territory. There is a strong recognition in the literature of the simultaneous growth of soft forms of legislation with the spread of a stronger and more hard-edged form of regulation in a globalised world. Globalisation and governance are seen as closely connected. The central claim of work on international relations and governance is that in a period of globalisation the number and type of sites of where governing decisions have been made has multiplied to create a complex, multi-dimensional ensemble of institutions.

As well as exploring emerging institutions and regimes of global, the international relations literature is also noteworthy for its focus on the hegemonic dynamic of developments in governance. The fundamental understanding here is the way that ruling ideas can come to limit the choices open to actors. In particular, neoliberal ideas with their commitments to free trade, markets and limited government, have provided much of the framework for thinking about governance choices in the last decades, and they are reinforced in the everyday exchanges, rules and communication that guide global governance. To understand governance, these writers suggest it is vital to see the wood as well as the trees, and recognise how neoliberal thinking has provided the defining backcloth to the rise of governance debates in the world of practitioners, but in a way that also feeds into academic debates. However, the neoliberals have not had it all their own way and there are a number of actors that have sought to explicitly challenge a neoliberal agenda and suggest that public, private and civic actors working together could tackle global issues of concern. The role and importance of hegemonic power is one the key insights international relations literature offers to governance theory.

What is also clear from the literature on international relations is that the future is unclear. There are various scenarios about what might emerge from a form of world government, from strong regional groupings, to a new era of democratic involvement led by civic organisations and NGOs. Debate rages between those who think that global governance will be anarchic and those that argue a new order will emerge. But most writers are pessimistic, or at least cautious, about the prospects for bringing popular accountability and oversight to decision-making at the global level.

The development studies literature starts with what can be referred to as a 'project of governance' literature aimed at promoting a particular type and form of good governance. The principles of good governance are not new in that they tend to restate the virtues of a tradition vision of effective public administration that can be stretched back as far as the writings of Max Weber on bureaucracy. The principles represent a wish list of good practice with a clear separation of politics and administration, with the former conducted according to the rules of accountability, and the latter according to the highest standards of integrity and efficiency. Not many have criticised the principles, as such, in that they have the character of platitudes but what has been commented upon is the way that the principles have played a key part in establishing conditions and limits on the provision of development aid to developing countries. The principles have been elaborated in a range of ways and extended to include a commitment to multi-party democracy and a broader process of democratisation. The role of governance in development, therefore, has a strong political dimension despite claims that it is apolitical. At its worst it has a sort of hectoring tone and at its best it helps to identify how effective governance – the capacity of states to manage aid and support the processes of economic and civic renewal – is an essential ingredient in any development programme. The importance of getting the institutional framing right is a message that the good governance debate shares with the literature on economic institutionalism, and it would not be contradicted by the literatures of political science and international relations.

The more explanatory literature in development studies challenges the exhorting, propagandising literature in development studies. First, there is widespread expressed doubt on the efficacy of the use of political conditionality as an instrument for bringing about good governance. A variety of empirical studies challenge the idea that a set of conditionalties associated with aid would have enough driving power to straightforwardly change established institutional practices and power relations. Maybe some of the more naïve institutional donors might have believed that change could occur by the simple installing of the right institutions (with perhaps academic support from some parts of the institutional economics literature), but the essence of much of the work of development studies has been to suggest that the processes of change are more complex and difficult. The critical point is that the way that politics works through governance to achieve collective action cannot be contained under the rubric of good governance. There is also a critical literature on whether it is at all feasible to link donor attempts at creating good governance with the constitution of democratic political systems. There are disagreements both on whether it is at all right for donors to intervene in the constitution of democracy, as well as what might be the best way of doing so. Finally, there is an extensive literature that suggests that although the good governance debate refocused attention of the state and its role in development, it failed to fully understand the role of the development state in East Asia or incorporate into the development of its principles. The good governance debate, it is claimed, is driven by ideology rather than a clear understanding of what kind of governance processes have, in other locations, driven rapid economic growth and might therefore provide effective guidance to other developing countries.

In development studies the governance debate has proved somewhat of a Trojan horse in raising a wider set of issues. Fundamentally, the criticism of good governance is that it hides a wider set of power relations between North and South, and it fails to examine the construction of relationships in the context of structural inequality and disadvantage. Good governance principles are not adequate to the task of readdressing developmental imbalances, and as such, they are a smokescreen behind wider issues of fair trade, power redistribution and social justice are hidden from view. This line of argument is not to suggest that the institutional frameworks and politics that drive governance are unimportant. It is rather to suggest that governance debates need to take place with due recognition given to the undermining effects of structural inequalities as a core part of the picture.

The literature within socio-legal studies is even more dissident in tone than critical development studies. It argues against a top-down view of governance, with the law as a key tool for the enforcement of social order. Official state law is only one amongst plural normative repertoires in society that govern social conduct. Governance from this perspective becomes more a description of social reality than an objective aim to be pursued. The socio-legal school diverts attention away from formal laws, rules and regulations as the site in which analysis ought to be located. It takes the individual, positioned at the 'intersection' of many different legal domains or spheres, as the focal point for investigation. The socio-legal approach stands apart from some of the other literatures reviewed here, but it offers a valuable challenge to those perspectives. It offers a more bottom-up view. A key analytical feature is its focus on the individual and it would seem reasonable to argue that the way a law or a regulation works depends to a degree of the way that an individual understands that intervention. The individual self-regulates by taking upon norms about the need to work and the importance of taking responsibility. In short, writers within the socio-legal perspective are hinting at elements in the governance lexicon that might not be easy to manipulate or influence. It becomes possible to see how different individuals are constrained by laws, but also enabled by them to further their own interests. Most socio-legal studies are dismissive of a view of the law as a coherent instrument through which social behaviour can be intentionally controlled. Instead, the understanding that social behaviour has many underlying causes, which are often not within the conscious control of individuals, runs through the heart of the socio-legal tradition. Within a Foucauldian perspective, the most effective governance, it would appear, is that in which individuals are most willing to be actively involved in their self-regulation. Though judgements of whether such self-regulation is necessarily in their interest is altogether less easily determined.

Combining insights from a number of disciplines give a clearer sense of what governance options are available (see Table 10.1), although we exclude socio-legal studies from this exercise, viewing it instead as asking all would-be reformers to be sceptical of what they are trying to achieve and how they set about it. Institutional economics sees the issue of governance as about securing the voluntary cooperation of actors to meet collective challenges. Things go wrong when individuals cannot oversee the action of others and thus overcome their fears of opportunistic behaviour and the solution is seen in developing mechanisms that enable more effective communication and mutual oversight. But insights from political science would suggest that there is a danger of crowding out intrinsic or moral motivations if the intervention is designed alone around the assumptions of institutional economics. Institutional economics again identifies the challenge of giving a credible commitment. People need, it could be argued, to be

Table 10. 1 Governance problems and solutions: insights from different disciplines

Main Discipline(s) for source of insight	Perceived governance problem	Mechanism for governance solution
1. Institutional Economics and Political Science	Communication and information failures lead to fears of opportunistic behaviour.	Development of more transparent systems and institutional arrangements that ensure mutual oversight. Try to avoid crowding out of intrinsic or moral motivations.
2. Institutional Economics and Political Science	Inability to make credible commitments means that cooperation cannot be sustained.	Provide scope for power to be held by arms-length or independent institutions but do not deny role of power and politics.
3. Political Science and International Relations	Accountability mechanisms are misaligned and as a result actors lack responsibility to each other and the capacity to join up.	Clarify responsibilities and develop new accountability procedures that stress power-sharing and joint learning.
4. Political Science and International Relations	Trust and legitimacy are not present in the governance setting and as a result the effectiveness of governance arrangements is compromised.	Develop reconciliation measures and practices of representation and participation.
5. Development Studies and Political Science	Structural inequalities and ingrained power relations block path to effective governance.	Move beyond hectoring principles to engagement with the realties of politics by providing scope for the mobilisation of new political forces.
6. Development Studies and International relations	The hegemonic influence of key ideas and powers lead to forced agreement rather than shared ownership and commitment of challenges.	Provide space for the challenge to hegemonic forces and provide opportunity for a more open exchange.
7. International Relations, Political Science, Development Studies and Institutional Economics	Enforcement and regulation failures mean that agreements when reached cannot be implemented.	Strengthen the state or role of regulators, but beware of undermining the voluntary and committed engagement of others in finding governance solutions.

able to see the institution on offer as part of a governance solution and one that has the context and incentives to act in a predictable and acceptable way. Creating something at arms length, or with an in-built independence, can do the trick in terms of convincing others to engage with the decision-making process and grant it legitimacy. But again there are fears from political science and other disciplines that such processes should not be pushed too far and so try to deny the appropriate role of politics and power in decision-making by claiming that decisions are of a technical nature when many would deny that claim.

Political scientists, and others, tend to see governance problems as created by the failure of governance arrangements to deliver what traditional or more established forms of government based on authority and territory have in the past provided. Governance then is seen as beset with accountability problems that need to be addressed by the greater clarification of roles and responsibilities and new mechanisms of accountability. The key challenge though is not to try to restore accountability mechanisms of the past, but those that promote a new understanding of power-sharing and learning as the essential ingredients of decision-making. Trust and legitimacy are also seen as essential elements that a governance system may lack and will need to obtain through political processes of reconciliation and more effective and varied mechanisms of both representation and participation.

A number of disciplines, along with development studies, also recognise the central importance of the capacity for effective action by the state or its agents in governance and the problems created by its absence. As such, more so than institutional economics, there is a greater interest in and commitment to regulation and enforcement as part of the rubric of governance. What institutional economics cautions against in these circumstances is the danger of an over-extension of state power which could be undermining to governance.

Development studies, and to some degree international relations, more than other disciplines bring into focus the way that structural inequalities and asymmetries of power condition governance problems and will need to be addressed if governance solutions are to be found. Both disciplines are more aware than others how hegemonic ideas can also limit and undermine governance capacity and how they need to be challenged. These disciplines bring more of a critical edge to their approach to governance because their governance turn took place in response to official projects around the promotion of good governance and in the context of a particular neoliberal conception of the construction of process of economic development and globalisation.

Combining the insights from different disciplines enriches our understanding of the challenge of governance. Regardless of the formal constitutional, legal or managerial rules settled upon according to circumstances and objectives, it is critical for those involved to retain reflexivity both about how to act and the boundaries for their action. No single blueprint will serve as a template for the actions of, and interactions between, the many stakeholders involved in modern governance. What works now may need to be changed in the future. But an awareness of the diversity of insights from across discipline and practice boundaries we are convinced will aid the process of establishing legitimate and effective governance in complex settings.

Searching for a governance solution: some design principles

The multi-disciplinary approach we offer suggests a range of understandings of governance problems and solutions. In this section of the conclusion we go on to argue that effective governance solutions are likely to involve a clumsy mix of mechanisms. Governance challenges can usefully be met through an investigative approach rather than by way of a check list of normative principles offered by mainstream audit models. In order to decide what mix could work, in what setting, requires a subtle process of political judgement. We offer a design approached premised on a subtle understanding of how institutions work and can be changed. We conclude with a heuristic that could aid the choices of reformers.

Governance solutions may be clumsy

The art of effective governance design is getting the mix right of different mechanisms. It can be suggested that a sustainable governance system needs to have a requisite variety of coordination mechanisms drawing on a range of social forms. Thompson *et al.* (1990:96) comment that Aristotle was onto a profound truth when he concluded that a balance of political cultures was the key to good government. Institutional sustainability, itself, requires an element of robustness and flexibility, not an eternal sameness (Goodin, 1996). For example following the discussion in Chapter 2 it could be argued that an institution needs hierarchy to ensure that some basic rules are set and followed; individualism to give drive and initiative; communitarian spirit to give a sense of team and commitment and even fatalism to allow scope for cooling down and a limit to hyperactivity. Any one cultural form has certain pathologies built into it, which need to be corrected and held in check by other forms. Hierarchy can degenerate into mindless rule-setting and following. Too much individualism limits the ability of collective goals to be followed.

The implication of the argument is to pour considerable doubt on whether governance arrangements that are developed around a single set of self-consistent principles are either viable or desirable. It suggests instead that what is required is a relationship between different cultural forms that enables the 'disorganising positive feedbacks dynamics of each of the solidarities to be held in check by the negative feedback dynamics between them' (Perri 6, 2003:37). The real challenge in the governance then is the search for clumsy solutions (Verweij and Thompson, 2006). Ultimately 'the case for clumsiness rests on the idea that a limited number of collective ways of organizing and thinking exists, each with its particular strengths and weaknesses, none of which should be allowed to gain the upper hand. This is an old view going back at least to Weber and Mill, indeed even to Aristotle' (Verweij and Thompson, 2006:22).

What is required is governance set up that allows for a mix of mechanisms. The creative tension between these forms is likely to yield the most sustainable and effective long-term results. The need to find the right mix is a theme in other discussions of governance (Rhodes, 1997b; Jessop, 2003). But we argue in particular that there are limits to the extent to which any one governance principle could or should be applied. To make governance happen it needs to be given institutional expression through rules that can stick. Usually the challenge involves a process of institutional change since most reform movements do not start with a blank sheet. Insights from a range institutional theory do not lead to the inevitable view that reform will fail or that it is pointless. This is not to deny what all practitioners and policy-makers already know: it's hard to change the world. It is to argue that if the processes of institutional change were more fully appreciated and the available governance options better understood then reform could be smarter and the prospect of redesign success increased. Our cross-disciplinary tour has, hopefully, added to that depth and breadth of understanding essential to better practice.

The limits to mainstream approaches to governance audit

Mainstream approaches assess governance achievements or prospects against benchmark standards. A thoughtful essay for the World Bank (Kaufmann and Kraay, 2007) reviews these approaches to governance. Their focus is very much on the conditions for good governance – a capable state, accountable to citizens and subject to the rule of law – and the aim is to find various surrogate measures to judge whether these conditions are present or absent in a particular case. The measures can either be obtained through an assessment about what are the formal rules that are in place or by more nuanced judgements in part driven by an understanding of outcomes achieved by the system of governance. The judgements in the case of rules-based work may be seen as driven by objective information but may lack a grasp of the realties of practice. Outcomes-based judgements whether they come from business people, experts or polls of citizens are more subjective in character. All systems of measurement are subject to an element of error and can lead to various results or judgements. Reviewing attempts to judge the range of democracies in Africa, Berg-Schlosser (2008:3) notes that various established methods reveal substantially different estimates in numbers. For one the figure is a low as 4, for another 10, another finds 12 and one gets as high as 26. In short a lot depends on what you propose to count and how you propose to count it. Mainstream approaches are normative in focus and then driven by judgements about measurement approaches. They can offer valuable insights but need to be explicit about the basis of their measurement and clear about their limitations (Kaufmann and Kraay, 2007).

Mainstream approaches rely on a definition of governance by reference to a set of outputs or political goods. Such an approach does not fit easily with our understanding as offered in Chapter 1 where we provided a process definition of governance. For us governance is about the rules that guide collective decision-making. A regime of governance is likely to address a range of issues and find institutional expression for its preferred options. It will need to answer three questions: how should power be distributed, who should be involved in a decision and how should rules, once agreed, be enforced? These are the three big questions that recur in political life (Gamble, 2000) and it is appropriate that governance structures and processes should be designed to deal with them. Moreover we are less interested in judging the governance of a particular country or system but more with understanding what governance arrangement might be appropriate, given a particular policy challenge or problem. We think the mix of theoretical and empirical insights from our range of disciplines have something to offer in the search for governance solutions in complex settings.

Governance rules need to find institutional expression. They may be formally stated, informally established or informally by-passed. Institutional forms, the behaviour of actors and the surrounding context of meaning and culture are the building blocks of regimes of governance. The challenge is a dynamic one. History also matters. In most instances governance reforms do not start with a blank sheet but instead require the redesign of existing institutions. The establishment or enhancement of democratic governance is invariably a battle of institutional change. Any audit of governance from our perspective needs therefore to reflect further on how institutions can be changed. It should start with insights from empirical theory as much as normative theory and focus on institutions can be designed better to meet governance challenges.

The prospects for institutional design

Some traditions within institutional theory present a relatively pessimistic view of the possibility of intentional change. In particular we noted at the end of Chapter 3 how the concept of path dependency shared between some economic institutionalists and political scientists presents us with a relative pessimistic of the prospects for intention-driven change. The key theoretical insight to emerge from the path dependency literature is that increasing returns experienced by the involved actors that keeps them along the same path. Actors have learnt to deal with the system in a certain way, they may find coordination easier as the behaviour of others becomes predictable under the agreed policy or institutional umbrella and their behaviour can be better adapted to new contingencies as they are better placed to guess what the response of others will be. If we follow path dependent arguments there could be one design principle: 'don't' bother'. Or to put it in a more nuanced way 'don't expect too much'.

Of course one central reason why reformers like institutional reform is that it is very difficult. Reformers wish to lock-in a style of governance that will persist, but in order to lock-in their own values reformers have to break-in to existing institutions. Sometimes, with the help of a little smooth talk, they are invited in. So, without path dependency, intentional design would be less attractive. Design is risky because institutions are hard to change, and it is valued because institutions are hard to change. The seeds of weaknesses in the path dependency argument can be found in its greatest advance, namely the argument about increasing returns (see Gains *et al.*, 2005). A key problem for the theory is that is has over exaggerated the impact of increasing returns. In short, factors beyond increasing returns may affect policy development. Institutions can in turn be affected by a realignment of power. The institution that seemed set in concrete may not to be able to defend itself from attack. The world of politics may be murky and evaluation a difficult task but that does not stop processes of learning and adaptation. A change in direction may result from an uncertain sense of best practice or even from following fashion but there are clear incentives for actors that have the prospect of career movement built on the reputation of being a reformer to go for change, even if its advantages are not clear-cut. Further short-term time horizons may make policy-makers risk adverse to change but equally it could make them prone to going for spectacular reform on the grounds that they can get the credit for the scale and imagination of the reform and not have to worry too much about the long-term impact.

Path dependency is driven not by a sense of history but by the incentives that are provided to people. Change the incentives and you will change behaviour. That is the central insight of a second great school within institutional theory: the rational choice approach that as noted in Chapters 2, 3 and 4 has had a great influence in politics, economics and to some extent in international relations. A rational choice account of political action suggests that political agents will act according to the incentives and constraints that are provided to them. In the world of governance studies Elinor Ostrom's work covered in Chapter 3 is perhaps the greatest exemplar of this style of thinking. In the right circumstances, new rules can promote different sorts of political behaviour, making the interesting question whether the principles behind the design can be realised in the behaviour of the political actors who are part of the design process. Agents, who have clear incentives, then can sign up to the norms being offered by the reformers. The issue is how clever is the design and how responsive is the reform process. The rational choice gives hope to reformers in search of better governance solutions.

But other traditions in institutional theory suggest insights from rational choice need to be applied with some caution. Social or cultural institutionalists do not view people as simply or even primarily instrumentally calculative but rather they argue that people tend to act on the basis of their values and their beliefs as noted in Chapter 2. What people want and the way they behave are determined by whom they think they are and where they are, where their life is embedded. At a minimum these theorists argue individuals are not rational egotists alone. Institutions mould individuals in a variety of complex ways. Different understandings and meanings inhabit the institution and provide an organic and subtle framework for individual decision-making. Moreover, individuals have a range of motivations beyond those of the rational egotist. They can see norms not as sanctions but as commitments (Taylor, 1996:229–230). The norms reflect a way of understanding life. Action for individuals is not based on a weighing of costs and benefits but rather on their commitments (their beliefs and values) which imply that they could not act in any other way. In this sense they are expressive of their understanding of themselves. Certain actions may be motivated by this acting out of deeply held beliefs or values. There are other motivations that could be seen as highly relevant to the study of cooperation and collective action that are also ignored by rational choice theory (Taylor, 1996:230–231). The first is people's sense of social identification; how and to what extent they define themselves as members of a group. People are, it might be argued, more likely to follow a rule if they regard themselves as members of a group from which the rule emanates. The second is intrinsic motivation; the reward for doing something is the doing of it. This observation again challenges rational choice perspectives that assume people will need an incentive. Indeed it may be that incentives, providing extrinsic rewards, will undermine rather than bolster motivation.

In pouring doubt on the attempt of rational choice to manipulate people through selective incentives and or guiding rules, many social institutionalists come close to seeing institutions as incapable of conscious design. Institutions 'are certainly the result of human activity' but 'not necessarily the products of conscious design', according to DiMaggio and Powell (1991:8). March and Olsen (1989) argue that most institutional reorganisations do not achieve the purposes of the instigators and designers. To be sure institutions do change they suggest but usually in incremental steps and without a conscious sense of direction. We think that social institutionalists are right to claim that institutional reforms are complex affairs with unintended consequences but mistaken to suggest that intentional reform is possible.

Cognitive, social and motivational filters: towards a heuristic

We see a positive rather than a negative in the range of beyond rational motivations that drive individual behaviour. Namely, that there are more opportunities for the potential reformer to seek to influence than a straightforward rational choice framework allows. People's preferences and their management strategies to realise these preferences, are shaped by a range of beyond rational factors, as all non-economistic literature recognises. If we are to engage with citizens as reformers then we should do so with a better and deeper understanding of their motivations and decision processes.

The first element of complexity is introduced by cognitive filtering. Subtle theorists, such as Elinor Ostrom (1990), allow for the development of schemas and heuristics, tacit theories about the world and the way it works, which are used by individuals to ease decision-making in the context of a complex environment and a corresponding complex array of strategic responses. This in turn links with the literature on bounded rationality discussed in Chapter 2. But as also noted in Chapter 2 cultural institution theory, for example, sees the decision-facilitating devices used by people as not purely cognitive but also as socially influenced and embedded. The second element of complexity is introduced by recognising how people's choices are socially framed. An individual's choosing is shaped by their social context and an associated set of understandings connected with a way of life. So designers of governance solutions need to reflect on how the problem and solutions are socially framed. What are the main social and cultural parameters that will be used to think through a governance settlement by the actors involved?

Cultural institutionalists, in particular, as noted in Chapter 2, argue that your social situation becomes tied to explanations of the way that the world works, the way that you and others should be judged. In the ordered, role-bound world of hierarchy following the rules becomes both a depiction of what you do and what you should do. In a world of many rules and much imposition but where you no have fixed position and social status fatalism guides your actions and becomes your motto: life is beyond your control. Where rules are thin on the ground and where your social connections are weak you are left with only your individualism to stand on, the only choices that matter are your own. Where rules and detailed regulation is thin on the ground but where your sense of group loyalty is high you understand the world through the eyes of your group: its norms, rules and views are what give your life meaning.

What provides the analytical efficiency of cultural institutional theory, as noted in Chapter 2, is its argument that certain ways of life are regularly to be observed and that those ways of life in turn enable people to make decisions in the context of limited information and extensive complexity in a range of social settings. As noted in Chapter 2 the empirical claims and practical applications of institutional cultural theory may leave something to be desired but their concept of social filters does provide us with a heuristic for judging what social filters might be in play. Cultural institutionalists focus on four filters: hierarchy, communitarian, fatalistic and individualistic and only the latter fits neatly with the assumptions of rational choice.

The implications for those interested in governance design is that what would seem right for someone from an individualist culture would not necessarily seem right to someone from a hierarchical, communitarian or fatalist culture. Thinking back to Ostrom's discussion of environmental management in Chapter 3, it now becomes possible to see the rationality that she identified operating in a particular individualist social context (see Table 10.2). Both decision procedures and substantive value stances reflect a particular social framing. For an individualist the perception of time is short-term; there is a limited sense of any responsibility to future generations; and only where a credible commitment to substantial future benefits can be made does it makes sense to extend the cost/benefit calculation over environmental matters. But other social framings might produce other ways of thinking through the issues. For those embedded in a more communitarian setting the decision rules and underlying values can be fundamentally different. The time frame when looking at environmental matters is not just short-term it is urgent; a strong sense of intergenerational responsibility exists and there may well be a willingness to take a short-term loss in order to deliver a long-term gain. The social frames of hierarchy and fatalism as Table 10.2 shows also offer distinctive paths to follow. The point of Table 10.2 is simply to illustrate what needs to be investigated in the case of any particular governance choice: namely the dominant social framing of the issue and the players that need to be engaged.

The final element in our search for design principles is premised on recognising the motivational complexity that can be brought into play in governance settings. As noted earlier one predominant assumption is that actors are driven by an instrumental rationality. What if we assume instead that individuals have innate tendencies to cooperate with others and reject the assumption of opportunism built into instrumental rationality models? Why assume that unless firmly bound by external constraints and steering incentives people will choose options in their narrow short-term self-interest when most of us would claim to live and make choices in some moral universe? The assumptions of pure self-interested rationality embedded in rational choice theory creates what Bryan Jones (2001:120–121) calls a rationality trap, a perceived problem that will plague human interactions that might be illusionary if there is a tendency built into humans to over-cooperate. Social psychological research suggests there are good evolutionary grounds and much evidence to suggest that such a cooperative tendency does exist (Jones, 2001:Ch5).

As argued earlier by Taylor (1996) it is important to recognise the possibility of the internalisation of moral principles which cannot be

Table 10.2 Four rationalities-perspectives on environmental matters

Rationalities	Individualistic	Hierarchical	Communitarian	Fatalistic
Time perception	Short-term: cost/benefit choice	Long-Term: institutional responsibility	Compressed: urgent need for action	Short-term: coping
Intergenerational responsibilities	Weak: responsibility lies with each generation	Balanced: needs of current and future generation of equal concern	Strong: needs of future generation and sense of responsibility high	None: no sense of long-term community responsibility
Discount Rate	Diverse: if substantial benefits in future can be guaranteed may defer, if not will discount	Technically calculated: rules and experts to make the judgement	Zero or Negative: future benefits may even be traded off against a short-term loss	High-future benefits will be discounted

Source: Adapted and developed from Rayner (1999).

traded, which means viewing an individual can have moral code principles – sacred and separate – and using them as a core guide to decision-making (see also Goodin, 1982). In short, what is being suggested is a micro-foundational assumption that people are capable of exercising moral as well as instrumental judgement and that the two forms of judgement cannot be collapsed into one another. In particular, for policy-makers, there is a danger that by focusing on crass material or instrumental incentives they may undermine moral motivations. Crucially in designing institutional interventions as if agents are treated as knaves means running the risk that 'good works which were formerly produced out of the goodness of people's hearts must now be compelled through more expensive and inefficient external mechanisms of social control' (Goodin, 1982:114–115). Frey (2007), drawing on a range of social psychological research, has developed this insight to argue for a different approach to changing behaviour which recognises that the incentives and constraints favoured by instrumental rationality can crowd out intrinsic motivation. 'The 'holy cow' of modern economics needs to be reconsidered. External and, in particular, monetary incentives, do not mechanically induce human beings to act in the desired way, because they crowd-out intrinsic motivation under identifiable conditions (Frey 2007:4–5). Three psychological processes account for the hidden costs of stimulating behaviour through external incentives and constraints. When people feel that they are being controlled, especially through intensive oversight and regulation, they may feel impelled to forego intrinsic motivation because the external framework is too overwhelming that it makes maintaining an intrinsic motivation pointless. When people find their perceived intrinsic motivation overlooked or ignored this situation can lead to loss of self-esteem on their part, and a loss of sense of purpose. Finally, when they are not encouraged to display their cherished intrinsic motivations they can experience a sense of anger at this deprivation. The implications for policy-makers in choosing their governance strategies and interventions are potentially substantial in the light of these arguments. We need to design with a mix of motivations in mind.

So far in this section we have added to the complexities facing the designer of governance responses but ultimately our aim is to add too a better understanding of the opportunities available to reformers. Let us conclude with a heuristic that pulls together the insights on offer and might help designers meet the challenge of thinking through design principles to tailor institutional expressions of governance to specific settings. Drawing on and developing a framework offered by Brennan

on the possibilities of global governance. Chapter 5 argued that the good governance literature too often attempts to deny the role of politics and power in the advocacy of governing arrangements as a precondition to international aid and development support. In Chapter 8 we commented that participatory governance is sometimes mistakenly promoted as a way of trying to take the politics out of governance.

In this conclusion we want to labour the point further because in our view the attempt to exclude politics from governance is rampant in practices in both the developed and developing world. In the developing world critics ask why it becomes possible for the experts, planners, bureaucrats and consultants that constitute Ferguson's (1990) 'anti-politics machine', to shun or appear to shun politics. How did development come to be associated with such a strong antipathy to politics, and why does politics become such an easy theme to manipulate a negative image of, especially for the purposes of development? Where did the idea of 'anti-politics' originate? Lets us offer two propositions to respond to this question (Chhotray, 2008). The first is that development has been closely associated with the economy. A number of historical factors have contributed to the conceptualisation of the economy as a domain that is principally autonomous of society, culture and politics. The second is the lingering influence of a tradition of thought about politics which depicts political behaviour in very dark and unflattering terms, and appears to dominate over other traditions of thinking about politics. A very negative view of politics has further abetted the zealous restriction of development to this 'autonomous' economy. At the core of these two conceptualisations also lie judgements about individual economic behaviour as rational and necessary for development, and in contrast, about individual political behaviour as irrational and unnecessary for development.

The shadow of the 'anti-politics machine' can also be seen to dominate thinking about governance and partnership in the developed world as well. Current reform trajectories in the UK and other western democracies tend to push in other directions, by focusing on the development of technocratic capacity rather than political dynamics. Governance solutions are seen as somehow best if placed beyond politics. Faced with the complexity of modern governance there is always the temptation to look for technical fixes rather than embrace politics in the round (Stoker, 2006a). And paralleling debates about development, politics is seen in a negative light and as having failed to cope with the complexities of modern governance. People no longer trust politicians or politics and so the best hope for reform lies in by-passing politics.

This denial of the role of politics is evident in the rise of partnership arrangements and in the enhanced role given to expert bodies and commissions.

Partnership is assumed to work best in situations where the heat of politics is taken out of the situation. Skelcher and colleagues (2005) in their study of partnerships in the UK identify a number of discourses about partnership that shape and limit the way these processes are understood by those engaged in them. The two dominant discourses have no place for politics. The first views partnership as an extension of the realm of management. It places great value on managerial autonomy and increased discretion for managers from the processes of politics. According to this view, partnerships are the arenas where the real priorities of an area can be addressed in a long-term and stable manner without the disruption of short-term politics considerations. All that is required from leading politicians and citizens is their explicit endorsement of the long-term strategic objectives of the partnership, agency arrangements or governing framework in order to legitimise the practices of the managers. Citizens, too, may be called upon to move beyond an implicit to an explicit level of endorsement of this management-controlled form of governance through thin and weak forms of public consultation that involve them endorsing the strategic plans of the partnership or agency.

A second common discourse also tries to deny politics by creating governance arrangements that provide a buffered zone for decision-making that is free or independent of politics. There are a number of variations in this line of argument. One is to emphasise the importance of elite exchanges between partners away from the gaze of the public so that negotiation and compromise can be facilitated. This image of good governance practice is long-standing and is reflected in many mechanisms used to reach agreement in governing arrangements. Again, the argument is that if the heat of politics is removed then sensible long-term decisions can be negotiated.

A similar line of argument is used to justify an increased role for independent commissions and bodies. Governments in recent years have taken the lead in a seemingly concerted process of 'taking the politics out of politics'. Politicians, it seems, no longer trust themselves – offloading many of their previous responsibilities to a bewildering range of independent and, above all, non-political, authorities and agencies. One justifying argument involves defining issues as matters of technical or expert concern rather than ideological or value-driven conflicts; when so defined the issues can therefore be left to the technocrats to decide. This would appear to be the rationale used to justify handing over decision-making power in the NHS to a care quality commission, leaving house-building to a new homes and communities agency and giving power over major planning issues to an independent planning commission. There is a further interesting variation of this governing practice in which the system creates a deliberately insulated form of agency that delivers a credible commitment that decisions are going to be made in the long-term public interest. The most well known example in the UK is that of delegating control over the money supply and interest rates to an independent decision-making body to insulate it from short-term political interests.

Our position is that to understand governance, and make appropriate decisions about which governance practices to adopt, requires an acceptance of the role of power and politics in governance. Contrary to the view that governance is assumed to work best in situations where the heat of politics is taken out of the situation we favour an approach to governance reform that offers a realistic but positive view of the world of politics.

An essential feature of the changing patterns of governance analysed in our book is that governing takes place through multiple agencies, relations and practices. Decision-making power is dispersed across a range of new sites for action. Politics is to be found in the dynamic of the relationships between officials and managers, politicians, citizens, lobby groups, non-governmental bodies, think-tanks, advisors and the media. Politics here is understood as the processes of collective decision-making that help us manage conflicts and create conditions for cooperation. It is to be valued as a mechanism for social coordination for at least three reasons. First, it enables people to cooperate and make choices on the basis of something beyond the individualism of the market. It treats people, and encourages them to treat others, with recognition of the full roundness of their human qualities and experience. Second, political decision-making is flexible so it can deal with uncertainty, ambiguity and unexpected change. Politics is an essential coping mechanism in an uncertain and unpredictable world. Finally, politics can move beyond a distribution of benefits – a rationing function also offered by markets – to establish a process of social production in which interests are brought together to achieve common purposes. Politics can influence the basis for cooperation by changing people's preferences and creating an environment in which partnership is possible.

But our understanding of politics does not deny its connection to power. Bernard Crick (2000:21) in his *In Defense of Politics* comments:

'Politics ...can be simply defined as the activity by which different interests within a given unit of rule are reconciled by giving them a share of power in proportion to their importance to the welfare of the whole community'. Politics is about getting interests to come together in the sense that they have to take account of each other. These interests are reconciled, not bound, by a new, jointly discovered consensus. The preferences associated with interests are malleable; shaped as they are by norms and values and the context of what is achievable. This definition also places power at the centre of politics, a share in the collective decision is granted according to the interest's importance to social welfare. Those that control key resources are likely to have increased decision-making clout.

Normative principles, democracy and governance

We offer, then, a realist understanding of politics in which governance has to be pursued. Accommodation is achieved in a variety of ways: sometimes by mutual understanding driven by deliberation but more often through hard bargaining, vague specification of outcomes, divide-and-rule, obfuscation, the use of rituals and symbols and the exercise of hegemonic influence. Politics is driven not by mutual admiration but rather by the necessity of pursuing a common direction in an interconnected world where one cannot choose one's neighbours.

We are therefore sceptical about those that argue that governance has to be done through some advanced form of deliberative democratic engagement. Governance for some is tied to a discourse of participatory democracy that takes a utopian view of politics. This discourse demands the direct engagement of many citizens in decision-making and puts a strong faith in the ability of deliberation to bring about social cooperation rather than to encourage conflict.

We reject also those that favour magic single bullet solutions to the challenges of governance. A case in point is the way that '(t)ransparency is a term that has attained quasi-religious significance in debate over governance and institutional design' (Hood 2006:3). The promotion of transparency of the core governance virtue can, according to Hood, be traced back to the political reflections of Jean-Jacques Rousseau and the economic logic of Jeremy Bentham. The former train of thought tends to argue for transparency as a basic feature of a good society in which governors, citizens and officials are willing to open themselves out to investigation and challenge from others as part of a broader republican duty to think beyond their self-interest and act in the common good. In the latter, the line of reasoning is less high-minded and more driven by a sense than unless people are subject to inspection they will misbehave, so it is better to design institutions as if people were knaves.

The idea that 'sunlight is the most powerful of all disinfectants' is one of the great truisms of governance thought. The guidelines on good governance produced by the international agencies and discussed in depth in Chapter 5 are full of calls for greater transparency in governing arrangements. The cry is regularly heard in the developed world as well and as noted in Chapter 2, concerns about lack of transparency and accountability haunt discussions about emerging new governance arrangements in this context. A focus of transparency fits well with our set of design measures, namely those that are virtue enhancing. Transparency encourages good behaviour because it demands that ultimately that behaviour will have to be justified in a public setting. Transparency works against corruption and abuse of power. So it is right that it is lauded as a governance tool.

But the argument over transparency is more complex than might be first thought and provides a good illustration of the subtlety of the challenge facing those who design governance systems. Transparency can mean a range of things when it is applied to governance and it has a close relationship to other concepts such as openness and accountability (Heald, 2006). For the sake of the clarity of our discussion let us define transparency as the capacity to observe and check the behaviour of others. Stated as such you might ask: can you have too much of it? The corporate governance literature reviewed in Chapter 7 would appear to have a preponderance of advocates for this position. But we argued there that the dominant theories that have been applied to corporate governance draw on a range of a narrow economic understanding and have failed to deliver recommendations that in turn have enhanced the performance of firms. Moreover, they have neglected other factors that may be the driving factors for effective corporate governance, such as a firm's capacity for innovation and resources for leadership. The lack of trust implied by an obsession with transparency can be debilitating – in that it can lead to the neglect of other factors that could drive forward effectiveness.

In particular, it could be argued that an over-emphasis on transparency, that in turn carries messages about lack of trust, can lead to a crowding out of more positive motivations for politicians, officials and stakeholders to determine their actions. Faced by perceived excessive demands for information and audit actors may react by operating according to the demands on the monitoring systems in a way that follows standard procedures and achieves formal compliance, but in a way that may undermine innovation and the ambitions of the monitoring itself in terms of achieving more effective services or programmes. Another related perverse effect may be the generation of so much information that it becomes impossible for anyone to judge its quality or determine its intelligibility. Rather than demystifying governing processes in the name of democracy, an excessive focus on transparency may have the opposite effect (O'Neill, 2006). As Hood (2005:223) concludes, transparency may therefore be 'good in some conditions and manifestations but also capable of taking negative or degenerate forms'.

The critics of the good governance debate in development studies come up with another line of attack. Jenkins' (1999) study of the success of India's economic reforms reflects, he argues, the government's ability to pursue what he describes as reform by stealth. Reform was put in place in the 1990s, despite previous failed reform attempts, by a process of gradual and incremental reforms undertaken quietly and furtively, through a combination of underhand tactics and essential political skills by governing elites in order to manage or defuse any resistance that might have occurred. As Jenkins comments that success came not from following the open governance and transparency arguments of the good governance agenda but by an effective political approach that gave political leaders enough breathing space to put the reforms in so that interest groups and special interests could not block them Jenkins (1999:52) criticises good governance principles that naively associate state 'capacity' or 'competence' to take decisions around policy reform with 'accountability' which among other things requires transparency of decision-making and relationships. He exposes the rather 'unrealistic' and 'sanitised' view of politics (Jenkins, 1999:45) that sees governance as always marked by open flows of information allowing public opinion, facilitated by a committed governing elite, to coalesce around an optimal solution. Rather he recognises that too open an accountability process can be preceded by the identification of clear winners and losers that in turn makes change not possible. Politics works in more subtle ways than the simplistic application of assumptions about transparency suggest.

Transparency is an essential element in any governance system. It is an essential element in establishing the vigilance appropriate to overseeing the exercise of governance. But if it is reduced to procedures for collecting and checking information about the performance of others it can become a rather unhelpful tool. Our point here is about the need for thinking transparency more broadly as accountability through genuine power-sharing rather than 'narrowly' as simply displaying information. Even when understood as part of an accountability system it needs to make its contribution in a way that allows political leaders the space to breathe and act while supporting the engagement of citizens in decision-making.

The literature of political science worries immensely about accountability in the context of governance. The key problem about governance arrangements is, from this perspective, that they lack the transparency of traditional public administration where we know who is making decisions and therefore how to hold them to account. Several authors as a result, argue that there is an accountability deficit at the heart of governance, as noted in Chapter 2. But as also noted in Chapter 2, the extent of the problem depends on the type of accountability that is viewed as at stake. If accountability is about ordinary non-engaged citizens monitoring and controlling governance processes, then many governance processes would appear to have a massive accountability deficit and are crying out for more transparency. However, if accountability is seen as enhanced by the sharing of power and learning, then perhaps governance processes have something to offer. The obsession with transparency is in this light premised on an over-simplified understanding of the way that governing processes work and it is driven by the fear of being duped and a lack of trust. We need to embrace politics more openly in governance and the structure of democratic inputs in a realist light.

So in trying to reconcile governance and a realist understanding of politics with some concept of democracy two factors need to be borne in mind (see Stoker, 2006a). First, it is vital to recognise the variety of issues that people think are important. An important issue to one person can mean nothing to another. This is so because politics rests on a fundamental truth about human beings. Because we and only we can live our different lives we all see the world through the lens of that experience. Most of us probably carry around in our heads a set of (usually unarticulated) understandings of what range and type of issues matter to us; they will be different to those held by others. We need a politics that allows citizens to have a say over what is important to them, not what professional politicians, lobbyists, journalists or scientists tell them is important. The second is that having a say does not mean, for most people, having a veto or being the final judge. As amateurs, citizens are cautious about claiming decision-taking responsibility. 'Having a say', generally means wanting to influence, but not having to decide. The institutional implication is that we need to revive representative politics as much as we need to develop new participative forms of engagement if governance is going to work. We should give representative politics the space it needs to work. We need to move beyond a conveyor belt conception of the way that representation works. This model rests on trying to ensure that the way the representatives are elected guarantees they will be held to account for giving voice to the expressed preferences of their constituents. In reality, the relationship is more complex than that (Saward, 2005). Elected representatives can and do select parts of their constituency and choose to give prominence to their needs and concerns. They may highlight some aspects of their constituents' lives over others. Moreover, they seek to shift the preference structures in their constituencies and persuade them that they are right to focus on some issues and not others. In short, representation is not a process of holding a mirror up to a constituency and faithfully reflecting back the image; it is a more creative process than this, and one that is shaped by power.

To see representation in this way means that all claims to be representative are 'partial and contestable' (Saward, 2005:182). This is not to deny the value of elected representatives. They can make a strong claim to democratic legitimacy (indeed, we would argue the strongest claim) by virtue of being directly elected in a system of mass voting. However, this process does not recognise the legitimacy of others' claims to represent people's interests, from 'private' actors, voluntary associations, community groups, ethnic minorities and other groups that find alternative ways of representing a constituency of citizens. Constituencies are not necessrily given or permanent. They are all constructed and may indeed be short-lived. To be represented in the modern world, citizens, with their complex identities and interests, need to be represented through a range of elected and non-elected means. Modern governance demands a subtle appreciation of the complexity of the practices of representation.

Beyond a recalibration of what constitutes representation we need to have more opportunities for direct engagement (see the discussion in Chapter 8). We need a variety of ways that people can engage in politics directly. An excellent pamphlet by Graham Smith (2005) for the *Power Inquiry* suggests a way forward in terms of more participative forms of engagement. Smith highlights innovative forms of public engagement from across the world and offers the following categorisation for these schemes: consultative, deliberative, co-governance, direct and e-democracy schemes. The range of options for engaging people is considerable (see Table 10.3). The goal should be to take examples of effective practice from several countries and test them further.

Table 10.3 New forms of citizen engagement

Form	Description	Illustrative case	Key reference or source
Consultative innovations	Informs decision-makers of citizens' views through a combination of methods to explore public opinion.	Public debate on the future of GM technology in the UK in 2001.	Smith, G. (2005)
Deliberative methods	Enabling a cross-section of citizens to have the time and opportunity to reflect on an issue by gathering opinion and information in order to come to a judgement about an issue or concern.	The British Columbia Citizens' Assembly in Canada was established in 2004. Over 11 months 160 people were given the task of reviewing the province's electoral system.	http://www.citizens assembly.bc.ca
Co-governance mechanisms	Arrangements aim to give citizens significant influence during the process of decision-making, particularly when it comes to issues of distribution of public spending and implementation practice.	Participatory Budgeting started its existence as a form of engagement in Porto Alegre, Brazil in the late 1980s but by 2004 it is estimated that over 250 cities or municipalities practiced some version of it.	Cabannes, Y. (2004)
Direct democracy	Referendums called by citizens that come in two broad forms. Popular initiatives allow the recall of decision made by elected representatives. Citizens' initiatives – allow citizens to set the agenda and put an issue up for public decision.	Quite widely practiced in Switzerland and the United States.	http://www. iandrinstitute.org/
E-democracy	The use of information and communication technology to give citizens new opportunities to engage.	MN-POLITICS is run by a non-partisan, independent organisation established in 1994 that aims to enable internet-based dialogue and debate between citizens and groups in Minnesota.	www.e-democracy.org

In short, we need an active strategy for engaging or re-engaging people in governance that is built on realistic premises as well as normative concerns about the range, quality and equality of the engagement (Macedo *et al.*, 2005). To a degree, the legitimacy of governance rests on the range and variety of opportunities for public participation, at least in some elements of the political process. Moreover, given the complexity of modern governance, citizens' input is often not only required in the initial phase of policy-making, but also in their implementation. Environmental change, sustaining healthier lifestyles and improving education are all areas that require an input from government but also from the citizen if positive change is going to be achieved. The quality of engagement is also a relevant issue. Political engagement does not always have to be intensive or deliberative but it should not be uninformed and divisive either. We need to think hard about how to design our systems to incorporate an element of competition and challenge, whilst at the same time allowing scope for participation that binds people together and supports the overall legitimacy and health of the political system. Finally, issues of equality are important. We should be concerned if the evidence points to obstacles blocking particular groups from engagement: the poor; the less well-educated; racial and ethnic minorities; young people or women. To achieve all these objectives governance need not deny politics, but embrace it and to do so in the context of a realist understanding of the dynamics of power that surround governance.

References

Abbott, A. (2001) *Chaos of Disciplines* (Chicago: University of Chicago Press)

Abers, R. (1998) 'Learning Democratic Practice: Distributing Government Response Through Popular Participation in Porte Alegre, Brazil', in Douglas, M. and Friedmann, J. (eds) *Cities for Citizens* (Chichester: John Wiley and Sons)

Ackerman, J. (2004) 'Co-Governance for Accountability: Beyond "Exit" and "Voice"', *World Development*, 32(3):447–463

Adger, W.N., T.A. Benjaminsen, K. Brown, H. Svarstad (2001) 'Advancing a Political Ecology of Global Environmental Discourses', *Development and Change* 32(4):681–715

Agyeman, J., Bullard, R.D. and Evans, R. (2003) 'Introduction', in Agyeman, J., Bullard, R.D. and Evans, R. (eds) *Just Sustainabilities: Development in an Unequal World* (London: Earthscan)

Alchian, A. and Demsetz, H. (1972) 'Production, Information Costs, and Economic Organisation', *The American Economic Review*, 62(5):777–795

Alchian, A.A. (1959) 'Private property and the relative cost of tenure', in P.D. Bradley (ed.) *The Public State in Union Power* pp. 350–371 (Charlottesville: University of Virginia Press)

Alchian, A.A. (1961) *Some Economics of Property* (Santa Monica, California: The Rand Corporation)

Allen, J. (2000) '*Code Convergence in Asia: Smoke of Fire?*' Asian Corporate Governance Association (ACGA). Available online http://www.acga-asia.org/loadfile.cfm?SITE_FILE_ID=25 Accessed 13 March 2008

Amsden, A. (1989) *Asia's Next Giant: South Korea and Late Industrialisation* (New York: Oxford University Press)

Amsden, A. (2001) *The Rise of 'The Rest': Challenges to the West from Late-Industrializing Economies* (Oxford: Oxford University Press)

Aoki, M. (1990) 'Towards and Economic Model of the Japanese Firm', *Journal of Economic Literature*, 28(1):1–27.

Arrow, K.J. (1951) *Social Choices and Individual Values* (New York: Wiley)

Asian Development Bank (ADB) 'Elements of Governance', available at: www.imf.org/external/pubs/ft/exrp/govern/govindex.htm, accessed 17th March 2008

Avineri, S. and De-Shalit, A. (2001) 'Introduction', in Avineri, S. and De-Shalit, A. (eds) *Communitarianism and Individualism* (Oxford: Oxford University Press)

Axelrod, R., Downie, D.L. and Vig, N.J. (2005) (eds) *The Global Environment: Institutions, Law and Policy* (Washington: CQ Press)

Axelrod, R., Vig, N.J. and Shreurs, M.A. (2005) 'The European Union as an Environmental Governance System', in Axelrod, R., Downie, D.L. and Vig, N.J. (eds) *The Global Environment: Institutions, Law and Policy* (Washington: CQ Press)

Baiocchi, G. (2001) 'Participation, Activism and Politics: The Porto Alegre Experiment and Deliberative Democratic Theory', *Politics and Society*, 29:43–72

Baiocchi, G. (2003) 'Emergent Public Spheres: Talking Politics in Participatory Governance', *American Sociological Review*, 68(1):52–74

Baker, S., Kousis, M., Richardson, D. and Young, S. (1997) (eds) *The Politics of Sustainable Development* (London: Routledge)

Bakker, K. (2005) 'Neoliberalising Nature? Market Environmentalism in Water Supply in England and Wales', *Annals of the Association of American Geographers*, 95(3):542–565

Bang, H.P. (2003) (ed.) *Governance as Social and Political Communication* (Manchester: Manchester University Press)

Bardhan, P. and Ray, I. (2006) 'Methodological Approaches to the Question of the Commons', *Economic Development and Cultural Change*, 54(3):655–677

Barry, A. Osborne, T. and Rose, N. (1996) 'Introduction', in Barry, A., Osborne, T. and Rose, N. (eds) *Foucault and Political Reason: Liberalism, Neo-Liberalism and Rationalities of Government* (London: UCL Press Limited)

Barya, J.B. (1993) 'The New Political Conditionalities of Aid: An Independent View from Africa', *IDS Bulletin*, 24(1):16–23

Bastian, S. and Bastian, N. (1996) (eds) *Assessing Participation: A Debate from South Asia* (New Delhi: Konark Publishers Private Ltd)

Bates, R.H. (1988) 'Contra Contractarianism: Some Reflections on the New Institutionalism', *Politics and Society*, 16:387–401

Bates, R.H. (1995) 'Social Dilemmas and Rational Individuals: An Assessment of the New Individualism', in Harriss, J. *et al.* (eds) *The New Institutional Economics and Third World Development* (London: Routledge)

Batterbury, S. and Fernando, J. (2006) 'Rescaling Governance and the Impacts of Political and Environmental Decentralisation', *World Development*, 34(11): 1851–1863

Baumann, P. (1999) 'Democratising Development? Panchayati Raj Institutions in Watershed Development in India', in Farrington, J. *et al.* (ed.) *Participatory Watershed Development: Challenges for the 21st Century* (New Delhi: Oxford University Press)

Baumol, W.J. (1968) 'Entrepreneurship in Economic Theory', *The American Economic Review*, 58(2):64–71

Bebchuck, L. (1999) 'The Rent Protection Theory of Corporate Ownership and Control', *Working Paper, No. 260* (Cambridge, MA: Harvard Law School) Available online http://papers.ssrn.com/sol3/papers.cfm?abstract_id=168990 Accessed 13 March 2008

Becker, G.S. (1983) 'A Theory of Competition Among Pressure Groups for Political Influence', *The Quarterly Journal of Economics*, 98(3):371–400

Bell, S. and A. Park (2006) 'The problematic metagovernance of networks water reform in New South Wales', *Journal of Public Policy*, 26(1):63–83

Benda-Beckmann, F. von (1994) 'Good Governance, Law and Social Reality: Problematic Relationships', *Knowledge and Policy: The International Journal of Knowledge Transfer and Utilisation*, 7(3):55–67

Benda-Beckmann, F. von and Benda-Beckmann, K. von (1991) 'Law in society: From Blindman's Buff to Multilocal Law', *Living Law in the Low Countries*, Special Issue of the Dutch and Belgian Law and Society Journal, *Recht der Werkelijkheid*

Benda-Beckmann, F. von, Benda-Beckmann, K. von and Griffiths, A. (2005) 'Introduction', in Benda-Beckmann, F. von, Benda-Beckmann, K. von and

Griffiths, A. (eds) *Mobile People, Mobile Law: Expanding Legal Relations in a Contracting World* (Aldershot: Ashgate)

Benda-Beckmann, K. von (1981) 'Forum Shopping and Shopping Forums: Dispute Settlement in a Minangkabau Village in West Sumatra', *Journal of Legal Pluralism*, 19:117–159

Bendor, J. (2003) 'Herbert, A. Simon: Political Scientist', *Annual Review of Political Science*, 6:433–471

Bendor, J., A. Glazer and T. Hammond (2001) 'Theories of Delegation', *Annual Review of Political Science*, 4:235–269

Benz, A. and Papadopoulos, Y. (2006) *Governance and Democracy: Comparing National, European and International Experiences* (London: Routledge)

Beresford, A. (2003) 'Foucault's Theory of Governance and the Deterrence of Internet Fraud', *Administration and Society*, 35(1):82–103

Berglorf, E. and von Thaddon, E.L. (1999) 'The Changing Corporate Governance Paradigm: Implications for Transition and Developing Countries', Unpublished Working Paper (Stockholm: Stockholm Institute of Transition Economics)

Berg-Schlosser, D. (2008) 'Determinants of democratic successes and failures in Africa', *European Journal of Political Research*, Online Early Articles Published article online: 31 Jan-2008

Berle, A.A. and G.C. Means (1932) *The Modern Corporation and Private Property*, (New York: Macmillan)

Bertelli, A. (2006) 'The role of political ideology in structural design of new governance agencies', *Public Administration Review* , July/August, 1–13

Besley, T. (2006) *Principled Agents? The Political Economy of Good Government*, (Book manuscript, London School of Economics), available at http://econ.lse.ac.uk/staff/tbesley/index_own.html#book (accessed 24 March 2008)

Besteman, C. (1994) 'Individualisation and the assault on customary tenure in Africa: Title registration programmes and the case of Somalia', *Africa: Journal of the International Africa Institute*, 64(4):484–515

Bevir, M. (2003) 'A Decentred Theory of Governance', in Bang, H.P. (ed.) *Governance as Social and Political Communication* (Manchester: Manchester University Press)

Blair, M.M. (1995) *Ownership and Control: Rethinking Corporate Governance for the Twenty-First Century* (Washington: Brookings)

Bovens, M. (1998) *The Quest for Responsibility: Accountability and Citizenship in Complex Organisations* (Cambridge: Cambridge University Press)

Bovens, M. (2006) Analysing and assessing public accountability. A conceptual framework. European governance papers No.C06-01

Brennan, G. and Hamlin, A. (2000) *Democratic Devices and Desires* (Cambridge: CUP)

Brietmeier, H. (1996) 'International Organisations and the Creation of Environmental Regimes', in Young, O. (ed.) *Global Governance: Drawing Insights from the Environmental Experience* (Cambridge, Massachusetts: MIT Press)

Brock, K., Cornwall, A. and Gaventa, J. (2001) 'Power, Knowledge and Political Spaces in the Framing of Poverty Policy, *IDS Working Paper* No. 143 (Brighton: Institute of Development Studies)

Brown, W. (2005) 'Exploring the association Between Board and Organizational Performance in Nonprofit Organizations', *Nonprofit Management and Leadership*, 15(3):317–339

Bruns, B. and Meinzen-Dick, R. (2005) 'Frameworks for Water Rights: An Overview of Institutional Options', in Bruns, B., Ringler, C. and Meinzen-Dick, R. (eds) *Water Rights Reform: Lessons for Institutional Design* (Washington DC: International Food Policy Research Institute)

Brundtland, G.H. (1987) *Our Common Future: Report of the World Commission on Environment and Development* (Oxford: Oxford University Press)

Bryner, G.C. (2004) 'Global Interdependence', in Durant, R.F., Fiorino, D.J. and O'Leary, R. (eds) *Environmental Governance Reconsidered: Challenges, Choices, Opportunities* (Cambridge: Massachusetts, MIT Press)

Buchanan, J.M. (1975) *The Limits of Liberty: Between Anarchy and the Leviathan* (Chicago: University of Chicago Press)

Bulas, J.M. (2004) 'Implementing Cost Recovery for Environmental Services in Mexico'. Paper presented at World Bank Water Week, Washington, 24–26 February

Bulmer, S. (forthcoming) 'UK and Ireland', B. Kohler-Koch and F. Larat, *A Decade of Research on EU Multi-level Governance* (Aldershot: Edward Elgar)

Burchell, G. (1996) 'Liberal Government and Techniques of the Self', in Barry, A., Osborne, T. and Rose, N. (eds) *Foucault and Political Reason: Liberalism, Neo-Liberalism and Rationalities of Government* (London: UCL Press Limited)

Burman, S. and Harrell-Bond, B.E. (1979) (eds) *The Imposition of Law* (New York: Academic Press)

Buttel, F. (2000) 'Ecological Modernisation as Social Theory', *Geoforum*, 31(1): 57–65

Cabannes, Y. (2004) 'Participatory Budgeting: A Significant Contribution to Participatory Democracy', *Environment and Urbanisation*, 16(1):27–46

Cadbury, A. (1992) *Report of the Committee on the Financial Aspects of Corporate Governance* (London: Gee&Co Ltd)

Cammack, P. (2002) 'The Mother of all Governments: The World Bank's Matrix for Global Governance', in Wilkinson, R. and Hughes, S. (eds), *Global Governance: Critical Perspectives* (London and New York: Routledge)

Canadian International Development Agency (CIDA) (1996) *Human Rights, Democratization and Good Governance: Policy and Objectives for SIDA*, available at www.acdi-cida.gc.ca/CIDAWEB/acdicida.nsf/En/REN-218124821-P93#sec2, accessed 17th March 2008

Carnegie Endowment for International Peace (no date) *Democracy & Rule of Law*, available at www.carnegieendowment.org/programs/global/index.cfm?fa=proj&id=101&proj=zdrl, accessed 17th March 2008

CEEP – Centre for Energy and Environmental Policy, 'Political Ecology', available at www.ceep.udel.edu/politicalecology/index.html, accessed 14 March 2008

Cerny, P. (1996) 'What next for the State?, in Kofman, E. and Youngs, G. (eds) *Globalisation: Theory and Practice* (London: Pinter)

Chandler, A.D. (1977) *The Visible Hand: The Managerial Revolution in American Business* (Cambridge: Harvard University Press)

Chang, Ha-Joon (2002) *Kicking Away the Ladder: Development Strategy in Historical Perspective* (London: Anthem)

Chhotray, V. (2004) 'The Negation of Politics in Participatory Development Projects, Kurnool, India', *Development and Change*, 35(2):327–352

Chhotray, V. (2005) 'Who cares about participation? How a rhetorical state policy is practised incredulously', *Contemporary South Asia*, Volume 14(4):429–446

Chhotray, V. (2007) 'The "Anti-Politics Machine" in India: Depoliticisation through Local Institution Building for Participatory Watershed Development in India', *Journal of Development Studies*, 43(6):1037–1056

Chhotray, V. (2008) 'The Idea of "Anti-Politics": Theoretical Reflections on the Problem of Depoliticisation in Development', John Dunn Workshop, University of Southampton, February

Chhotray, V. and Hulme, D. (2008) Contrasting Visions for Aid and Governance in the 21st Century: White House Millennium Challenge Account versus DFID's Drivers of Change, *World Development*, in press, published online 12th July

Clague, C. (1997) 'The New Institutional Economics and Economic Development', in C. Clague (ed.) *Institutions and Economic Development: Growth and Governance in Less Developed and Post-Socialist Countries* (Maryland: The John Hopkins' University Press, Baltimore)

Clark, J. (1991) *Democratising Development: The Role of Voluntary Organisations* (London: Earthscan Publications)

Coase, R. (1937) 'The Nature of the Firm', *Economica*, 4:386–405

Coase, R. (1960) 'The Problem of Social Cost', *Journal of Law and Economics*, 3:1–44

Coffee, J.C. (1999) 'The Future as History: The Prospects for Global Convergence in Corporate Governance Convergence and its Implications', *Working Paper*, No.144 (New York: Centre for Law and Economic Studies, Columbia University School of Law)

Coffee, J.C. (2001) 'The Rise of Dispersed Ownership: The Roles of Law and the State in the Separation of Ownership and Control', *The Yale Law Journal*, 111(1):1–82

Colclough, C. and Manor, J. (1991) (eds) *States and Markets: Neoliberalism and the Development Policy Debate* (Oxford: Clarendon Press)

Collier, P. & Dollar, D. (1999) Aid Allocation and Poverty Reduction. World Bank, Washington D.C. At http://worldbank.org/research/abcde/washington_11/pdfs/collier.pdf

Commission on Global Governance (1995) *Our Global Neighbourhood* (Oxford: OUP)

Commons, J.R. (1931) 'Institutional economics', *American Economic Review*, 21(4):648–657

Commons, J.R. (1937) *Institutional Economics: Its Place in Political Economy* (New York: Macmillan)

Cooke, B. and Kothari, U. (2000) (eds) *Participation: The New Tyranny?* (London: Zed Books)

Corbridge, S. (2007) 'The (im)possibility of development studies', *Economy and Society*, 36(2):179–211

Cornwall, A. (2002) 'Making Spaces, Changing Places: Situating Participation in Development', *IDS Working Paper* 170 (Brighton: Institute for Development Studies)

Cornwall, A. (2004) 'Spaces for Transformation? Reflections on issues of Power and Difference in Participation in Development', in Hickey, S. and Mohan, G. (eds) *Participation: From Tyranny to Transformation* (London: Zed Books)

Cox, R.W. (1981) 'Social Forces, States and World Orders: Beyond International Relations Theory', *Millenium: Journal of International Relations*', 10(2):126–155

Cox, R.W. (1983) 'Gramsci, Hegemony and International Relations: An Essay in Method', *Millenium: Journal of International Studies*, 12(2):162–175

Cox, R.W. (1996) 'Global *perestroika*', Cox, R.W. with Sinclair, T.J., *Approaches to World Order* (Cambridge: Cambridge University Press)

Cranenburgh, O.V. (1998) 'Increasing State Capacity: What Role for the World Bank?', *IDS Bulletin*, 29(2)

Crick, B. (2000) *In Defence of Politics* (5ᵗʰ edn.) (London: Continuum)

Dahl, R. (1956) *A Preface To Democratic Theory* (Chicago: University of Chicago Press)

Dahl, R. (1971) *Polyarchy: Participation and Opposition* (New York: Yale University Press)

Dailey, G. and Ellison, K. (2002) *The New Economy of Nature* (Washington DC: Island Press)

Daily, C., D. Dalton and A. Cannella, Jr. (2003) 'Corporate Governance: Decades of Dialogue and Data', *Academy of Management Review*, 28(3):371–382

de Sousa Santos, B. (1987) 'Law: A Map of Misreading; Toward a Postmodern Conception of the Law', *Journal of Law and Society*, 14:279

Debreu, G. (1959) *Theory of Value: An Axiomatic Analysis of Economic Equilibrium* (London: Wiley)

Demsetz, H. and K. Lehn (1985) 'The Structure of Corporate Ownership: Causes and Consequences', *The Journal of Political Economy*, 93(6):1155–1177

Dermirguc-Kunt, A. and Maksimovic, V. (1998) 'Law, Finance and Firm Growth', *The Journal of Finance*, 53(6):2107–2137

DeSombre, E. (2005) 'Understanding United States Unilateralism: Domestic Sources of US International Environmental Policy', in Axelrod, R., Downie, D.L. and Vig, N.J. (eds) *The Global Environment: Institutions, Law and Policy* (Washington: CQ Press)

Devarajan, S., Dollar, D. & Holmgren, T. (2001) (eds) *Aid and Reform in Africa*. (Washington DC: World Bank)

DFID (2001) *Making Government Work for Poor People*, available at: www.dfid.gov.uk/pubs/files/tspgovernment.pdf, accessed 17ᵗʰ March 2008

Diamond, L. (2003) 'Universal Democracy', *Policy Review*, 119 (June/July)

Diamond, S. (1973) 'The Rule of Law versus the Order of Custom', in Black, D. and Mileski, M. (eds) *The Social Organisation of Law* (New York: Seminar Press)

DiMaggio, P. and W. Powell (1991) 'Introduction', in W. Powell and P. DiMaggio, (ed.) *The New Institutionalism in Organizational Analysis* pp. 1–38. (Chicago: University Press of Chicago)

DOC Team, Policy Division, DFID (2006) *What does Drivers of Change Mean for DFID: A Draft Approach Paper* (London: DFID)

Doornboos, M. (2000) *Institutionalising Development Policies and Resource Strategies in Eastern Africa and India: Developing Winners and Losers* (London: Macmillan)

Doornboos, M. (2001) 'Good Governance: The Rise and Decline of a Policy Metaphor', *The Journal of Development Studies*, 37(6):93–117

Douglas, I. (1999) 'Globalisation *as* governance: Toward an archaeology of contemporary political reason', in Prakash, A. and Hart, J. (eds) *Globalisation and governance*, (London and New York: Routledge)

Douglas, M. (1982) 'Cultural Bias', in M. Douglas (ed.) *In the Active Voice* (London: Routledge)

Douglass, M. and Marc, G.M. (1990) 'The Search for a Defensible Good: The Emerging Dilemma of Liberalism', in Douglass, M., Mara, G.M. and Richardson, H.S. (eds) *Liberalism and the Good* (London: Routledge)

Dowding, K. (1995) 'Model or Metaphor? A Critical Review of the Policy Networks Approach', *Political Studies*, 43:136–158

Downs, A. (1957) *An Economic Theory of Democracy* (New York: Harper and Row)

Dreyfus, H.L. and Rabinow, P. (1982) *Michel Foucault: Beyond Structuralism and Hermeneutics – With an Afterword by Michel Foucault* (London and New York: Harvester Wheatsheaf)

Drezner, D. (2007) *All Politics is Global. Explaining International Regulatory Regimes* (Princeton: Princeton University Press)

Duffy, R. (2005) 'Global Environmental Governance and the Challenge of Shadow States: The Impact of Illicit Sapphire Mining in Madagascar', *Development and Change*, 36(5):825–843

Dunn, J. (2000) *The Cunning of Unreason: Making Sense of Politics* (London: HarperCollins)

Durant, R.F., Fiorino, D.J. and O'Leary, R. (2004) (eds) *Environmental Governance Reconsidered: Challenges, Choices, Opportunities* (Cambridge, Massachusetts: MIT Press)

Easterly, W. (2006) *The White Man's Burden: Why the West's Efforts to Aid the Rest Have Done So Much Ill and So Little Good* (New York: Penguin Press)

Ehlrich, E. (1913) *Fundamental Principles of the Sociology of Law*, trans. W.L. Moll, (Cambridge: Harvard University Press)

Elster, J. (1979) *Ulysses and the Sirens: Studies in Rationality and Irrationality*, (Cambridge: Cambridge University Press)

Epstein, D. and O'Halloran, S. (1999) *Delegation Powers: A Transaction Cost Politics Approach to Policy Making Under Separate Powers* (Cambridge: Cambridge University Press)

Epstein, D. and O'Halloran, S. (2002) *Delegating Powers* (Cambridge: Cambridge University Press)

Erickson-Blomquist, W.H. and Ostrom, E. (1984) 'Institutional Capacity and the Resolution of a Commons Dilemma', Indiana University Workshop in Political Theory and Policy Analysis (Indiana: Bloomington)

Evans, P. (1996a) 'Introduction: Development Strategies across the Public-Private Divide', *World Development*, 24(6):1033–1077

Evans, P. (1996b) 'Government Action, Social Capital and Development: Reviewing the Evidence on Synergy', *World Development*, 24(6): 1119–1132

Evans, P. (1997) 'The Eclipse of the State? Reflections on Stateness in an Era of Globalisation', *World Politics*, 50(1):62–87

Fama, E. and Jensen, M. (1983) 'Separation of Ownership and Control', *Journal of Law and Economics*, 26:301–325

Ferguson, J. (1990) *The Anti-Politics Machine: 'Development', Depoliticisation and Bureaucratic Power in Lesotho* (Cambridge: Cambridge University Press)

Fischer, F. (2006) 'Participatory Governance as Deliberative Empowerment: The Cultural Politics of Discursive Space', *American Review of Public Administration*, 36(1):19–40

Fitzpatrick, P. (1984) 'Law and Societies', *Osgoode Hall Law Journal*, 22:115

Foucault, M. (1977) *Discipline and Punish* (London: Allen Lane)

Foucault, M. (1980) *Power/Knowledge: Selected Interviews and Other Writings* (New York: Pantheon Books)

Foucault, M. (1982) 'Afterword: The Subject and Power', in H. Dreyfus and P. Rabinow (ed.) *Michel Foucault: Beyond Structuralism and Hermeneutics* (London and New York: Harvester Wheatsheaf)

Foucault, M. (1984) 'Space, Knowledge and Power', in Rabinow, P. (ed.) *The Foucault Reader* (New York: Pantheon Books)

Foucault, M. (1991) 'Governmentality', in G. Burchell, C. Gordon and P. Miller (eds) *The Foucault Effect: Studies in Governmentality*, pp. 87–104 (Chicago: University of Chicago Press)

Foucault, M. (1996) 'The subject of power', in C. Gordon (ed.) *Power/Knowledge: Selected Interviews and Other Writings* (New York: Pantheon)

Frank, D.J., Hironaka, A. and Schofer, E. (2000) 'The Nation-State and the Natural Environment over the Twentieth Century', *American Sociological Review*, 65:96–116

Frederickson, G. (1999) 'The Repositioning of American Public Administration', *P.S. Political Science and Politics*, 32(4):701–711

Freire, P. (1972) *Pedagogy of the Oppressed* (London: Penguin)

Frey, B. (2007) *Motivation Crowding Theory: A New Approach to Behaviour.* Round-table on Behavioural Economics and Public Policy, Melbourne 8–9 August

Fung, A. and Wright, E.O. (2001) 'Deepening Democracy: Innovations in Empowered Participatory Governance', *Politics and Society*, 29(1):5–41

Fung, A. and Wright, E.O. (2003) *Deepening Democracy: Innovations in Empowered Local Governance* (New York: Verso)

Gains, F., John, P. and Stoker, G. (2005) 'Path Dependency and the Reform of English Local Government', *Public Administration*, 83(1):25–45

Galanter, M. (1981) 'Justice in Many Rooms: Courts, Private Ordering and Indigenous Law', *Journal of Legal Pluralism*, 19:1–47

Galanter, M. (1983) *Reading the Landscapes of Disputes: What We Know and What We Don't Know (And Think We Know) About our Allegedly* (Madison: University of Wisconsin Law School)

Gamble, A. (2000) *Politics and Fate* (Cambridge: Polity)

Gaventa, J. (2002) 'Introduction: Exploring Citizenship, Participation and Accountability', *IDS Bulletin*, 33(2):1–11

Gaventa, J. (2004) 'Towards Participatory Governance: Assessing the Transformative Possibilities', in Hickey, S. and Mohan, G. (eds) *Participation: From Tyranny to Transformation* (London: Zed Books)

Geertz, C. (1983) *Local Knowledge: Further Essays in Interpretive Anthropology* (New York: Basic Books)

Germain, R.D. (2002) 'Reforming the International Financial Architecture: The New Political Agenda', in Wilkinson, R. and Hughes, S. (eds) *Global Governance: Critical Perspectives*, (London and New York: Routledge)

Gibbon, P. (1993) 'The World Bank and the New Politics of Aid', in Sorensen, G. (ed.) *Political Conditionality* (London: Frank Cass)

Gills, B. and Rocamora, J. (1992) 'Low Intensity Democracy', *Third World Quarterly*, 13(3):501–523

Gilson, R.J. (1999) *Globalising Corporate Governance: Convergence of Form or Function*, Working Paper No. 174 (The Centre for Law and Economic Studies: Columbia Law School)

Glaeser, E.L. and A. Shleifer (2003) 'The Rise of the Regulatory State', *Journal of Economic Literature*, Vol. XLI (June):401–425

Goldman, M. (2001) 'Constructing an Environmental State: Eco-Governmentality and other Transnational Practices of a "Green" World Bank', *Social Problems*, 48(4):499–523

Goldman, M. (2004) 'Eco-Governmentality and other Transnational Practices of a Green World Bank', in Peet, R. and Watts, M.J. (eds) *Liberation Ecologies: Environment, Development and Social Movements* (London: Routledge)

Goldsmith, S. and Eggers, W.D. (2004) *Governing by Network: The New Shape of the Public Sector* (Washington D.C.: Brookings Institution Press)

Goodin, R.E. (1982) *Political Theory and Public Policy* (London: University of Chicago Press)

Goodin, R. (1996) 'Institutions and their design', in R. Goodin (ed.) *The Theory of Institutional Design*, pp. 1–53 (Cambridge: CUP)

Gordon, C. (1980) 'Afterword', in C. Gordon (ed.) *Power/Knowledge: Selected Interviews and Other Writings* (New York: Pantheon Books)

Goss, S. (2001) *Making Local Governance Work* (London: Macmillan)

Green, J. (1999) 'The Illusion of Green Capitalism', *Green Left Weekly*, Issue 364, 9 June 1999, available online http://www.greenleft.org.au/1999/364/18656, accessed 14 March 2008

Grendstad, G. and Selle, P. (1995) 'Cultural Theory and The New Institutionalism', *Journal of Theoretical Politics*, 7(1):5–27

Griffiths, J. (1986) 'What is Legal Pluralism', *Journal of Legal Pluralism*, 24:1–50

Guillen, M. (1999) 'Corporate Governance and Globalisation: Arguments and Evidence against Convergence', A Working Paper of the Reginald H. Jones Centre (The Wharton School, University of Pennsylvania)

Haas, P.M. (1999) 'Social Constructivism and the Evolution of Multilateral Environmental Governance', in Prakash, A. and Hart, J. (eds) *Globalisation and Governance* (London and New York: Routledge)

Haas, P.M. (2004) 'Addressing the Global governance Deficit', *Global Environmental Politics*, 4(4):1–15

Hadiz, V.R. (2004) 'Decentralisation and Democracy in Indonesia: A Critique of Neo-Institutionalist Perspectives', *Development and Change*, 35(4):697–718

Haggard, S. and Kaufman, R. (1989) 'Economic Adjustment in New Democracies', in Nelson, J. (ed.) *Fragile Coalitions: The Politics of Economic Adjustment* (New Jersey: Transaction Books)

Hagstrom, P. and Chandler, A.D. (1999) 'Perspectives of Firm Dynamics', in Chandler, A.D., Hagstrom, P. and Solvell, O. (eds) *The Dynamic Firm: The Role of Technology, Strategy, Organisation, and Regions*, pp.1–12 (Oxford: Oxford University Press)

Hall, B. and Liebman, J. (1998) 'Are CEOs Really Paid Like Bureaucrats?', *Quarterly Journal of Economics*, 113(August):653–691

Hampson, F.O. (1989–90) 'Climate Change: Building International Coalitions of the Like-Minded', *International Journal*, 45(Winter):36–74

Hardin, G. (1968) 'The Tragedy of the Commons', *Science*, 162:1243–1248

Hardin, R. (1982) *Collective Action* (Baltimore: John Hopkins University Press)

Hardt, M. and Negri, A. (2000) *Empire* (Cambridge, MA: Harvard University Press)

Harrison, G. (1999) 'Clean-ups, Conditionality and Adjustment: Why Institutions Matter in Moazambique', *Review of African Political Economy*, 26(81):323–334

Harrison, G. (2004) *The World Bank and Africa: The Construction of Governance States* (London: Routledge)

Harriss, J., Hunter, J. and Lewis, C.M. (1995) (eds) *The New Institutional Economics and Third World Development* (London: Routledge)

Hart, O. (1995) 'Corporate Governance: Some Theory and Implications', *The Economic Journal*, 105:678–689

Hawthorn, G. (1993) 'How to ask for Good Government', *IDS Bulletin*, 24(1):24–30

Hay, C. (2007) *Why We Hate Politics* (Cambridge: Polity Press)

Heald, D. (2006) 'Varieties of Transparency', in C. Hood and D. Heald (ed.) *Transparency. The Key to Better Governance?*, pp. 25–46 (Oxford: The British Academy/ Oxford University Press)

Healey, J. and Robinson, M. (eds) (1992) *Democracy, Governance and Economic Policy: Sub-Saharan Africa in Comparative Perspective* (London: ODI Development Policy Studies)

Held, D. (1984) 'Central Perspectives on the State', in McLennan, G., Held, D. and Hall, S. (eds) *The Idea of the Modern State* (Philadelphia, PA: Open University Press)

Held, D. (2004) *Global Covenant* (Cambridge: Polity Press)

Heller, P. (2001) 'Moving the State: The Politics of Democratic Decentralisation in Kerala, South Africa and Porto Alegre', *Politics and Society*, 29(1):131–163

Henry, S. (1985) 'Community Justice, Capitalist Society and Human Agency: The Dialectics of Collective Law in the Cooperative', *Law and Society Review*, 19:303

Heritier, A. and Lehmkuhl, D. (2008) 'Introduction. The Shadow of Hierarchy and New Modes of Governance', *Journal of Public Policy*, 28(1):1–17

Herrling, S. and Rose, S. (2007) *Will the Millennium Challenge Account be Caught in the Crosshairs? A Critical Year for Full Funding* (Washington DC: Centre for Global Development)

Heylighen, F. and Joslyn, C. (2001) 'Cybernetics and Second-Order Cybernetics', in R.A. Meyers (ed.) *Encyclopedia of Physical Science & Technology 4* (3rd ed.), pp. 155–170 (New York: Academic Press)

Hill, M. and Hupe, P.L. (2002) *Implementing Public Policy: Governance in Theory and Practice* (London: Sage)

Hillman, A.J. and Dalziel, T. (2003) 'Boards of Directors and Firm Performance: Integrating Agency and Resource Dependence Perspectives', *Academy of Management Review*, 28(3):383–396

Hirschman, A. (1995) *A Propensity to Self-Subversion* (Cambridge, Mass.: Harvard UP)

Hix, S. (1998) 'The Study of the European Union II: The 'New Governance' Agenda and its Rival', *Journal of European Public Policy*, 5(1):38–65

Hodgson, G.M. (2000) 'What is the essence of institutional economics?', *Journal of Economic Issues*, 34(2):317–329

Hood, C. (2000) *The Art of the State. Culture, Rhetoric and Public Management* (Oxford: Oxford University Press)

Hood, C. (2006) 'Transparency in Historical Perspective', in C. Hood and D. Heald (ed.) *Transparency. The Key to Better Governance?*, pp. 3–24 (Oxford: The British Academy/Oxford University Press)

Hood, C., Scott, C., James, O., Jones, G. and Travers, T. (1998) *Regulation Inside Government* (Oxford: Oxford UP)

Hooghe, L. and Marks, G. (2001) *Multi-Level Governance and European Governance* (Lanham: Rowman and Littlefield)

Hoskisson, R.E. and Businitz, L.W. (2001) 'Market Uncertainty and Learning Distance in Corporate Entrepreneurship Entry Mode Choice', in Hitt, M.A., Ireland, R.D., Camp, S.M. and Sexton, D.L. (eds) (Oxford: Blackwell)

Huber, J. and Shipan, C. (2002) *Deliberate Discretion? The Institutional Foundations of Bureaucratic Autonomy* (Cambridge: CUP)

Hyden, G. (1983) *No Shortcuts to Progress* (Berkeley: University of California Press)

Hyden, G. and Michael, B. (eds) (1992) *Governance and Politics in Africa* (Boulder, CO: Lynne Rienner)

Hyden, G., Court, J. and Mease, K. (2004) (eds) *Making Sense of Governance: Empirical Evidence from 16 Countries* (Boulder and London: Lynne Rienner Publishers)

International Monetary Fund (IMF) (1997) 'Good Governance: The IMF's Role', available at www.imf.org/external/pubs/ft/exrp/govern/govindex.htm, accessed 17th March 2008

Isaac, T.M. and Frank, R.W. (2000) *Local Democracy and Development: People's Campaign for Decentralised Planning in Kerala,* (New Delhi: Leftword)

Jenkins, R. (1999) *Democratic Politics and Economic Reform in India* (Cambridge: CUP)

Jensen, M.C. (2001) 'Value Maximisation, Stakeholder Theory, and the Corporate Objective Function', The Monitor Group and Harvard Business School

Jensen, M.C. and Meckling, W. (1976) 'Theory of the Firm: Managerial Behaviour, Agency Costs, and Ownership Structure', *Journal of Financial Economics,* 3:305–360.

Jessop, B. (2000) 'Governance Failure' in G. Stoker (ed.) *New Politics of British Local Governance* (Basingstoke: Macmillan)

Jessop, B. (2003) 'Governance and Meta-Governance: On Reflexivity, Requisite Variety and Requisite Irony', in Bang, H.P. (2003) (ed.) *Governance as Social and Political Communication* (Manchester: Manchester University Press)

Jones, B. (2001) *Politics and the Architecture of Choice* (Chicago: University of Chicago Press)

Johnson, C. (1982) *MITI and the Japanese Miracle: The Growth of Industrial Policy, 1925–1975* (California: Stanford University Press)

Jordan, A., Wurzel, R. and Zito, A. (2005) 'The rise of new policy instruments in comparative perspective: has governance eclipsed government?', *Political Studies,* 53(3):477–496

Kanbur, R. (2002) 'Economics, Social Science and Development', *World Development,* 30(3):477–486

Kang, J.-K., and Shivdasani, A. (1996) 'Does the Japanese System Enhance Shareholder Wealth? Evidence form the Stock-Price Effects of Top Management Turnover', *Review of Financial Studies,* 9(4):1061–1095

Karagiannis, Y. (2007) *Economic Theories and the Science of Inter-Branch Relations,* EUI Working Paper RSAS2007/04 (Florence: Robert Schuman Centre for Advanced Studies, European University Institute)

Kaufmann, D. and Kraay, A. (2007) *Governance Indicators: Where are We, Where should We be Going.* Policy Research Working Paper 4370 (Washington DC: World Bank) at http://siteresources.worldbank.org/INTWBIGOVANTCOR/Resources/wps4370.pdf

Kaviraj, S. (1996) 'Dilemmas of Democratic Development in India', in Leftwich, A. (ed.) *Democracy and Development: Theory and Practice* (Oxford: Polity Press)

Kaviraj, S. and Khilnani, S. (2001) (eds) *Civil Society: History and Possibilities* (Cambridge: Cambridge University Press)

Keohane, R. and Nye, J. (1977) *Power and Interdependence: World Politics in Transition* (Boston: Brown, Little)

Keohane, R.O. (1984) *After Hegemony: Cooperation and Discord in the World Political Economy* (Princeton: Princeton University Press)

Kettl, D.F. (2002) *The Transformation of Governance: Public Administration for Twenty-First Century America* (Baltimore: John Hopkins University Press)

Keynes, J.M. (1933/1950) Keynes, John Maynard (1936/1950) *The General Theory of Employment, Interest, and Money* (New York: Harbinger Books)

Kickert, W.J.M., Klijn, E.H. and Koppenjan, J.F.M. (1999) *Managing Complex Networks: Strategies for Our Public Sector* (London: Sage)

Killick, T. (1998) *Aid and the Political Economy of Policy Change* (London: Routledge)

Kjaer, A.M. (2004) *Governance* (Cambridge: Polity Press)

Klijin, E.-H., J. Koppenjan, K. Termeer (1995) 'Managing Networks in the Public Sector: A Theoretical Study of Management Strategies in Policy Networks', *Public Administration*, 73(Autumn):437–454

Kohler-Koch, B. and Rittberger, B. (2006) 'Review Article: The "Governance Turn" in EU Studies', *Journal of Common Market Studies*, 44(S1):27–49

Kohli, A. (1989) *The State and Poverty in India: The Politics of Reform* (Cambridge: Cambridge University Press)

Kooiman. J. (2003) *Governing as Governance* (London: Sage)

Korten, D.C. (1987) 'Third Generation NGO Strategies: A Key to People-Centred Development', *World Development*, 15(supplement):145–179

Kymlicka, W. (1990) *Contemporary Political Philosophy* (Oxford: Oxford University Press)

Landell-Mills, P. (1992) 'Governance, Cultural Change and Empowerment', *The Journal of Modern African Studies*, 30(4):543–567

La Porta, R., Lopez-de-Silanes, F., Shleifer, A. and Vishny, R. (1997) 'Legal Determinants of External Finance', *Journal of Finance*, 52:1131–1150

La Porta, R., Lopez-de-Silanes, F., Shleifer, A. and Vishny, R. (1998) 'Law and Finance', *Journal of Political Economy*, 106:1113–1155

La Porta, R., Lopez-de-Silanes, F., Shleifer, A. and Vishny, R. (1999) 'Corporate Ownership around the World', *Journal of Finance*, 52:471–517

La Porta, R., Lopez-de-Silanes, F., Shleifer, A. and Vishny, R. (2000) 'Investor Protection and Corporate Governance', *Journal of Financial Economics*, 58(1):3–27

Laclau, E. (1977) *Politics and Ideology in Marxist Theory: Capitalism, Fascism, Populism* (London: NLB)

Laclau, E. and Mouffe, C. (1985) *Hegemony and Socialist Strategy: Towards a Radical Democratic Politics* (London: Verso)

Laffont, J.J. and Martimort, D. (2002) *The Theory of Incentives: The Principal-Agent Model* (Princeton: Princeton University Press)

Lake, D.A. (1999) 'Global Governance: A Relational Contracting Approach', in Prakash, A. and Hart, J. (eds) *Globalisation and Governance* (London and New York: Routledge)

Lancaster, C. (1993) 'Governance and Development: The Views from Washington', *IDS Bulletin*, 24(1):9–15

Lane, Jan-Erik (2006) 'Relevance of the principal-agent framework to public policy and implementation', Unpublished paper available at http://www.spp.nus.edu.sg/docs/wp/wp29.pdf, accessed 13th March 2008

Larson, A. and Ribot, J.C. (2005) *Democratic Decentralisation through a Natural Resource Lens* (Oxford: Routledge Press)

Lazonick, W. (1991) *Business Organization and the Myth of the Market Economy* (Cambridge: Cambridge University Press)

Leftwich, A. (1994) 'Governance, the State and Development', *Development and Change*, 25:363–386

Leftwich, A. (2006) *From the Drivers of Change to the Politics of Development: Refining the Analytical Framework to Understand the Politics of the Places Where We Work* (York: University of York)

Leibenstein, H. (1966) 'Allocative Efficiency vs. X-Efficiency', *American Economic Review*, 56:392–415

Levy, M.A., Young, O.R. and Zurn, M. (1995) 'The Study of International Relations', *European Journal of International Relations*, 1:31–54

Li, T.M. (1999) 'Compromising Power: Development Culture, and Rule in Indonesia', *Cultural Anthropology*, 14(3):295–322

Lipschutz, R.D. and Mayer, J. (1996) *Global Civil Society and Global Environmental Governance: The Politics of Nature from Place to Planet* (Albany: State University of New York Press)

Lockwood, M. (2005) *The State They're In: An Agenda for International Action on Poverty in Africa* (Bourton-on-Dunsmore: ITDG Publishing)

Lyon, T.P. and Maxwell, J.W. (2004) *Corporate Environmentalism and Public Policy* (Cambridge: Cambridge University Press)

Macauley, S. (1963) 'Images of Law in Everyday Life: The Lessons of School, Entertainment and Spectator Sports', *Law and Society Review*, 21:185

Macedo, S. and Others (2005) *Democracy at Risk* (Washington: Brookings)

MacIntyre, A. (1981) *After Virtue: A Study in Moral Theory* (London: Duckworth)

Mackintosh, M. (1992) 'Questioning the State', in Wuyts, M., Mackintosh, M. and Hewitt, T. (eds) (1992) *Development Policy and Public Action* (Oxford: Oxford University Press)

Mackintosh, M. and Roy, R. (1999) (eds) *Economic Decentralisation and Public Management Reform* (UK: Edward Elgar)

Macpherson, C.B. (1973) *Democratic Theory: Essays in Retrieval* (Oxford: Clarendon Press)

Maher, M. and Anderson, T. (1999) 'Corporate Governance: Effects on Firm Performance and Economic Growth', Working Paper (OECD: Paris)

Mallin, C (2003) *Corporate Governance* (Oxford: OUP)

Mamdani, M. (1996) *Citizen and Subject: Contemporary Africa and the Legacy of Late Colonialism* (London: James Curry)

Mann, M. (1997) 'Has Globalisation ended the Rise and Rise of the Modern Nation State?', *Review of International Political Economy*, 4(3):472–496

Mansbridge, J. (1999) 'On the Idea that Participation makes better Citizens', in Elkin, S. and Soltan, K. (eds) *Citizen Competence and Democratic Institutions* (Pennsylvania: Pennsylvania State University Press)

Mansfield, B. (2001) 'Property Regime or Development Policy, Explaining Growth in the US Pacific Groundfish Fishery', *The Professional Geographer*, 53(3):384–397

March, J.G. (1994) *A Primer on Decision Making* (New York: Free Press)

March, J.G. and Olsen, J.P. (1989) *Rediscovering Institutions: The Organizational Basis of Politics* (New York: Free Press)

March, J.G. and Olsen, J.P. (1995) *Democratic Governance* (New York: Free Press)

Marinetto, M. (2003) 'Governing Beyond the Centre: A Critique of the Anglo-Governance School', *Political Studies*, 51(3):592–608

Marsh, D. and Smith, M. (2000) 'Understanding Policy Networks: Towards a Dialectical Approach', *Political Studies*, 48(1):4–21

Martinussen, J. (1998a) 'The Limitations of the World Bank's Conception of the State and the Implications for Institutional Development Strategies', *IDS Bulletin*, Volume 29(2):67–74

Martinussen, J. (1998b) 'Challenges and Opportunities in Danish Development Co-Operation', in Heurlin, B. and Mouritzen, H. (eds) *Danish Foreign Policy Yearbook 1998* (Copenhagen: Danish Institute of International Affairs)

Massell, G. (1968) 'Law as an Instrument of Revolutionary Change in a Traditional Milieu: The Case of Soviet Central Asia', *Law and Society Review*, 2:179

Mawdsley, E. (in press) The Millennium Challenge Account: Neo-liberalism, Poverty and Security. *Review of International Political Economy*

McAfee, K. (1999) 'Selling Nature to Save it? Biodiversity and Green Developmentalism', *Environment and Planning D – Society and Space*, 17(2):133–154

McCarthy, J. (2004) 'Privatising Conditions of Production: Trade Agreements as Neoliberal Environmental Governance', *Geoforum*, 35:327–341

McCarthy, J. and Prudham, S. (2004) 'Neoliberal Nature and the Nature of Neoliberalism', *Geoforum*, 35:275–283

McCubbins, M.D., Noll, R.D. and Weingast, B.R. (1987) 'Administrative Procedures as Instruments of Political Control', *Journal of Law, Economics and Organization*, 3:243–277

McGinnis, M.D. (1999) 'Rent Seeking, Redistribution and Reform in the Governance of Global Markets', in Prakash, A. and Hart, J. (eds) *Globalisation and Governance* (London and New York: Routledge)

McGrew, A.G. (1992) 'Conceptualising Global Politics', in McGrew, A.G. and Lewis, P.G. *et al.*, *Global Politics and the Nation State* (Cambridge: Polity Press)

Meadows, D.H., Meadows D.L, Randers, J. and Behrens, W. (1972) *The Limits to Growth* (London: Earth Island)

Mercer, C. (2003) 'Performing partnership: Civil society and the illusions of good governance in Tanzania', *Political Geography*, 22:741–763

Merry, S.E. (1988) 'Legal Pluralism', *Law and Society Review*, 22(5):869–895

Mitlin, D. (2004) 'Reshaping Local Democracy', *Environment and Urbanisation*, 16(1):3–8

Moe, T.M. (1984) 'New Economics of Organization', *American Journal of Political Science*, 28(4):739–777

Monbiot, G. (2003) *The Age of Consent: A Manifesto for a New World Order* (London: HarperCollins)

Moore, D. (1995) 'Development Discourse as Hegemony', in Moore, D. and Schmitz, G. (eds) *Debating Development Discourses: Institutional and Popular Perspectives* (New York: St. Martin's Press)

Moore, D. (1996) 'Reading Americans on Democracy in Africa: From the CIA to "Good Governance"', in R. Apthorpe and D. Gasper (eds) *Arguing Development Policy: Frames and Discourses*, pp. 123–148 (London: Frank Cass)

Moore, D. (1999) '"Sail on: O Ship of State": Neo-liberalism, Globalisation and the Governance of Africa', *Journal of Peasant Studies*, 27(1):61–96

Moore, M. (1995) *Creating Public Value* (Cambridge, Mass: Harvard)

Moore, M. (1998) 'Toward a Useful Consensus', *IDS Bulletin*, 29(2)

Moore, S.F. (1978) *Law as Process: An Anthropological Approach* (London: Routledge and Kegan Paul, Henley and Boston)

Mosakowski, E. (2002) 'Overcoming Resource Disadvantages in Entrepreneurial Firms: When Less Is More', *Strategic Entrepreneurship: Creating a New Mindset*, in Hitt, M.A., Ireland, R.D., Camp, S.M. and Sexton, D.L. (eds) pp. 106–126 (Oxford: Blackwell)

Mosse, D. (1994) 'Authority, Gender and Knowledge: Theoretical Reflections on the Practice of Participatory Rural Appraisal', *Development and Change*, 26(3):497–525

Mosse, D. (1997) 'The Symbolic Making of Common Property Resources: History, Ecology and Locality in a Tank-Irrigated Landscape in South India', *Development and Change*, 28(3):467–504

Mosse, D. (2000) 'People's Knowledge, Participation and Patronage: Operations and Representations in Rural Development', in Cooke, B. and Kothari, U. (eds) *Participation: The New Tyranny?* (London: Zed Books)

Mosse, D. (2003) *The Rule of Water: Statecraft, Ecologies and Collective Action in South India* (New Delhi: Oxford University Press)

Mosse, D. (2006) 'Collective Action, Common Property and Social Capital in South India: An Anthropological Commentary', *Economic Development and Cultural Change*, 54(3):695–724

Mouffe, C. (1988) 'Hegemony and New Political Subjects': Towards a New Concept of Democracy', in Nelson, C. and Grossberg, L. (eds) *Marxism and the Interpretation of Culture* (Basingstoke: Macmillan Education)

Mueller, D.C. (1979) *Public Choice* (Cambridge: Cambridge University Press)

Murphy, C. (2000) 'Global Governance: Poorly Done and Poorly Understood', *International Affairs*, 76(4):789–803

Nabli, M. and Nugent, J.B. (1989) 'The New Institutional Economics and its Applicability to Development', *World Development*, 17(9):1333–1347

Najam, A. (2005) 'The View from the South: Developing Countries in Global Environmental Politics', in Axelrod, R., Downie, D.L. and Vig, N.J. (eds) *The Global Environment: Institutions, Law and Policy* (Washington: CQ Press)

Newman, J. (2001) *Modernising Governance: New Labour, Policy and Society* (London: Sage)

Nonneman, G. (1996) (ed.) *Political and Economic Liberalisation: Dynamics and Linkages in Comparative Perspective* (Colorado and London: Lyenne Rienner Publishers Inc.)

North, D.C. (1990) *Institutions, Institutional Change and Economic Performance* (Cambridge: Cambridge University Press)

North, D.C. (1995) 'The New Institutional Economics and Third World Development', in J. Harriss *et al.* (eds) *The New Institutional Economics and Third World Development* (London: Routledge)

North, D.C. and Thomas, R.P. (1973) *The Rise of the Western World: A New Economic History* (Cambridge: Cambridge University Press)

O'Neill, O. (2006) 'Transparency and the Ethics of Communication', in C. Hood and D. Heald (ed.) *Transparency. The Key to Better Governance?*, pp. 75–90 (Oxford: The British Academy/Oxford University Press)

O'Malley, P. (1992) 'Risk, Power and Crime Prevention', *Economy and Society*, 21(3):283–299

O'Malley, P. (1996) 'Risk and Responsibility', in Barry, A., Osborne, T. and Rose, N. (eds) *Foucault and Political Reason: Liberalism, Neo-Liberalism and Rationalities of Government* (London: UCL Press Limited)

OECD (1998) *Corporate Governance: Improving Competitiveness and Access to Capital in Global Markets* (Paris: OECD)

OECD (1999) *OECD Principles of Corporate Governance* (Paris: OECD)

Olson, M. (1965) *The Logic of Collective Action* (Cambridge, MA: Harvard University Press)

Olson, M. (1971) *The Logic of Collective Action: Public Goods and the Theory of Groups* (Harvard: Harvard University Press)

Orlandini, B. (2003) 'Consuming "Good Governance" in Thailand', *The European Journal of Development Research*, 15(2):16–43

Osbourne, D. and Gaebler, T. (1992) *Reinventing Government: How the Entrepreneurial Spirit is Transforming the Public Sector* (Reading: Addison-Wesley)

Ostrom, E. (1986) 'Common Property, Reciprocity and Community', *Journal of Economic Issues*, 24(2)

Ostrom, E. (1990) *Governing the Commons: The Evolution of Institutions for Collective Action* (Cambridge: Cambridge University Press)

Ostrom, E. (1999) 'Institutional rational choice: an assessment of the institutional analysis and development framework', in P. Sabatier (ed.) *Theories of the Policy Process*, pp. 35–72 (Boulder, Co.: Westview)

Ostrom, E. (2000) 'Private and Common Property Rights', available at http://encyclo.findlaw.com/2000book.pdf, accessed 14 March 2008

Ostrom, V. (1997) *The Meaning of Democracy and the Vulnerability of Democracies* (Ann Arbor: University of Michigan Press)

Paehlke, R. (2004) 'Sustainability', in Durant, R.F., Fiorino, D.J. and O'Leary, R. (eds) *Environmental Governance Reconsidered: Challenges, Choices, Opportunities* (Cambridge, Massachusetts: MIT Press)

Parris, T.M. (2003) 'Towards a Sustainability Transition: The International Consensus', *Environment*, 45(1):12–22

Payne, A. (2005) 'The Study of Governance in a Global Political Economy', in N. Phillips (ed.) *Globalizing International Political Economy* (Basingstoke: Palgrave Macmillan)

Payne, A. (2007) *Living in a Less Unequal World* (London: IPPR)

Peet, R. and Watts, M. (1996) 'Liberation Ecology: Development, Sustainability and Environment in an Age of Market Triumphalism', in Peet, R. and Watts, M. (eds) *Liberation Ecologies: Environment, Development, Social Movements* (London: Routledge)

Peet, R. and Watts, M.J. (2004) (eds) *Liberation Ecologies: Environment, Development, Social Movements* (London: Routledge)

Perri, 6, Leat, D., Seltzer, K. and Stoker, G. (2002) *Towards Holistic Governance* (Basingstoke: Palgrave)

Perri 6 (2003) 'The governance of technology' Paper for conference on Human Choice and Global Technology (unpublished)

Peters, P. (2004) 'Inequality and Social Conflict over Land in Africa', *Journal of Agrarian Change*, 4(3):269–314

Peterson, J. and Blomberg, E. (1999) *Decision-Making in the European Union* (Basingstoke: Macmillan)

Pierre, J. and Peters, B.G. (2000) *Governance, Politics and the State* (Basingstoke: Palgrave Macmillan)

Pierre, J. and Peters, B.G. (2005) *Governing Complex Societies* (Basingstoke: Palgrave Macmillan)

Pierson, P. (2004) *Politics in Time* (Princeton: Princeton University Press)

Pierson, P. (2000a) 'Increasing Returns, Path Dependence, and the Study of Politics', *American Political Science Review*, 94:251–267

Pierson, P. (2000b) 'Not just what but when: timing and sequencing in political processes', *Studies in American Political Development*, 14:72–92

Pierson, P. (2000c) 'The Limits of Design: Institutional Origins and Change', *Governance*, 13:474–499

Podgorecki, A. (1991) *A Sociological Theory of Law* (Milan: Giuffre Editore)

Pollitt, C. and Bouckaert, G. (2004) *Public Reform Management: A Comparative Analysis* (Oxford: Oxford University Press)

Porter, G., Brown, J.W., Chasek, P.S. (2000) *Global Environmental Politics* (Boulder Colorado: Westview Press)

Pospisil, L. (1971) *Anthropology of Law: A Comparative Theory* (New York: Harper & Row)

Prakash, A. and Hart, J. (1999) (eds) *Globalisation and Governance* (London and New York: Routledge)

Provan and Milward (2001) 'Do Networks Really Work? A Framework for Evaluating Public-Sector Organizational Networks', *Public Administration Review*, 61(4):414–423

Prowse, S. (1992) 'The Structure of Corporate Ownership in Japan', *Journal of Finance*, 47(3):1121–1140

Prowse, S. (1998) 'Corporate Governance in East Asia: A Framework for Analysis', *The World Bank*

Przeworski, A. (1991) *Democracy and Markets* (Cambridge: Cambridge University Press)

Putnam, R. (1993) *Making Democracy Work: Civic Traditions in Modern Italy* (Princeton NJ: Princeton University Press)

Putnam, R. (2000) *Bowling Alone: The Collapse and Revival of the American Community* (New York: Simon and Schuster)

Qian, Y. (1999) 'The Institutional Foundations of China's Market Transition' Paper prepared for *World Bank Annual Conference on Development Economics* (Washington D.C., April 28–30, 1999)

Rabkin, J. (1999) 'Morgen Die Welt: Sharing the World in the EU's Green Vision', Rabkin, J. and Sheehan, J., *Global Greens, Global Governance*, IEA Environment Working Paper 4 (London: The Institute of Economic Affairs)

Rajan, R. and Zingales, L. (2003) 'The Great Reversals: The Politics of Financial Development in the Twentieth Century', *Journal of Financial Economics*, 69:5–50

Rayner, S. (1999) 'Mapping Institutional Diversity for implementing the Lisbon Principles', *Ecological Economics*, 31:259–274

Reno, W. (1995) *Corruption and State Politics in Sierra Leone* (Cambridge: Cambridge University Press)

Reno, W. (1998) *Warlord Politics in African States* (Boulder, CO: Lynne Rienner)

Rhodes, R.A.W. (1997a) *Understanding Governance* (Buckingham: Open University Press)

Rhodes, R.A.W (1997b) 'From Marketization to Diplomacy "It's the Mix that Matters"', *Public Policy and Administration*, 12:31–50

Roe, M.J. (2000) 'Political Foundations for Separating Ownership from Corporate Control', *Stanford Law Review*, 53(3):1–67

Rose, N. (1990) *Governing the Soul: The Shaping of the Private Soul* (London and New York: Routledge)

Rose, N. (1996) 'Governing "advanced" liberal democracies', in Barry, A., Osborne, T. and Rose, N. (eds) *Foucault and Political Reason: Liberalism, Neo-Liberalism and Rationalities of Government* (London: UCL Press Limited)

Rosenau, J. (1990) *Turbulence in World Politics: A Theory of Change and Continuity* (New York: Harvester Wheatsheaf)

Rosenau, J. (1992) 'Governance, Order and Change in World Politics', in Rosenau, J.N. and Czempiel, E.O. (eds) *Governance Without Government: Order and Change in World Politics* (Cambridge: Cambridge University Press)

Rosenau, J. (2000) 'Change, Complexity and Governance in a Globalising Space', in Pierre, J. *Debating Governance* (Oxford: Oxford University Press)

Rousseau, J.J. (1968) *The Social Contract* (Harmondsworth: Penguin)

Runge, C.F. (1981) 'Common property and collective action in economic development', *World Development*, 14(June):623–635

Runge, C.F. (1986) 'Common Property Externalities: Isolation, Assurance and Depletion in a Traditional Grazing Context', *American Journal of Agricultural Economics*, 63(November):595–606

Ruttan, V. and Hayami, Y. (1984) 'Towards a Theory of Induced Institutional Innovation', *Journal of Development Studies*, 20(4):203–223

Salamon, L. (2001) 'The new governance and the tools of public action: an introduction', *Fordham Urban Law Journal*, 28(5):1611–1664

Sandholtz, W. (1999) 'Globalisation and the Evolution of Rules', in Prakash, A. and Hart, J. (eds) *Globalisation and Governance* (London and New York: Routledge)

Savas, E.S (2000) *Privatisation and Public-Private Partnerships* (London: Chatham House)

Saward, M. (2005) 'Governance and the Transformation of Political Representation', in J. Newman (ed.) *Remaking Governance* (Bristol: Policy Press)

Schlager, E. (2004) 'Common-pool Resource Theory', in Durant, R.F., Fiorino, D.J. and O'Leary, R. (eds) *Environmental Governance Reconsidered: Challenges, Choices, Opportunities* (Cambridge MA: MIT Press)

Schneider, V. (2004) 'State Theory, Governance and the Logic of Regulation and Administrative Control', in Warntjen, A. and Wonka, A. (eds) *Governance in Europe* (Baden-Baden: Nomos).

Scholte, J.A. (2005) *Globalization: A Critical Introduction* (Basingstoke: Palgrave Macmillan)

Sen, A. (1999) 'Democracy as a Universal Value', *Journal of Democracy* 10(3):3–17

Sheehan, J. (1999) 'Global Greens: Inside the International Environmental Establishment', in Rabkin, J. and Sheehan, J. *Global Greens, Global Governance*, IEA Environment Working Paper 4 (London: The Institute of Economic Affairs)

Shleifer, A. and Vishny, R. (1997) 'A Survey of Corporate Governance', *The Journal of Finance*, 52(2):737–783

Simon, H. (1945/1997) *Administrative Behaviour* (New York: Free Press)

Simon, H. (1985) 'Human Nature in Politics: The Dialogue of Psychology with Political Science', *The American Political Science Review*, 79(2):293–304

Sinha, S. (1990) *Common Property, Collective Action and Institutional Innovation: An Alternative Framework* (Unpublished Dissertation, Northwestern University, USA).

Skelcher, C., Mathur, N. and Smith, M. (2005) 'The Public Governance of Collaborative Spaces: Discourse, Design and Democracy', *Public Administration*, 83(3):573–596

Sklar, R. and Whitaker, C.S. (1991) *African Politics and Problems in Development* (Boulder and London: Lynne Rienner Publishers)

Smith, G. (2005) *Beyond the Ballot: 57 Democratic Innovations from around the World* (York: Power Inquiry)

Smouts, M.C. (1998) 'The Proper Use of Governance in International Relations', *International Social Science Journal*, 50(155):81–89

Smyth, R., and Lo, D. (2000) 'Theories of the Firm and the Relationship between Different Perspectives on the Division of Labour', *Review of Political Economy*, 12(3):333–349

Sonnenfeld, D. and Mol, A. (2002) 'Globalisation and the Transformation of Environmental Governance, *American Behavioural Scientist*, 45(9):1318–1339

Sorensen, E. (2006) 'Metagovernance: the changing role of politicians in processes of democratic choice', *The American Review of Public Administration*, 36(1):98–114

Sorensen, E. and Torfing, J. (2007) *Theories of Democratic Network Governance* (Basingstoke: Palgrave Macmillan)

Soroos, M. (2005) 'Global Institutions and the Environment: An Evolutionary Perspective', in Axelrod, R., Downie, D.L. and Vig, N.J. (eds) *The Global Environment: Institutions, Law and Policy* (Washington: CQ Press)

Spiertz, H.L.J. (2000) 'Water Rights and Legal Pluralism: Some Basics of a Legal Anthropological Approach', in Bruns, B. and Meinzen-Dick (eds) *Negotiating Water Rights* (London: ITDG Publishing)

Stern, D. (2001) 'The Environmental Kuznets Curve: A Review', in Cleveland, C., Stern, D. and Costanza, R. (eds) *The Economics of Nature and the Nature of Economics* (Northampton, MA: Edward Elgar)

Stern, N. (2006) *Stern Review on the Economics of Climate Change* (London: H.M. Treasury)

Stiefel, M. and Wolfe, M. (1994) *A Voice for the Excluded* (London: Zed Books)

Stiglitz, J. (1998) 'More instruments and broader goals: Moving towards the post-washington consensus', The 1998 Wider Annual Lecture, Helsinki. http://time.dufe.edu.cn/wencong/washingtonconsensus/instrumentsbroadergoals.pdf

Stiglitz, J.E. and Charlton, A.H. (2005) 'A Development-Friendly Prioritisation of Doha Round Proposals', *The World Economy*, 28(3):293–312

Stoker, G. (1995) 'Regime Theory and Urban Politics', in Judge, D., Stoker, G. and Wolman, H. (eds) *Theories of Urban Politics* (USA: Sage)

Stoker, G. (1998) 'Governance as Theory: Five Propositions', *International Social Science Journal*, 50(155):17–28

Stoker, G. (2000a) 'Urban Political Science and the Challenge of Urban Governance', in J. Pierre (ed.) *Debating Governance*, pp. 91–109 (Oxford: Oxford University Press)

Stoker, G. (2000b) *The New Politics of Local Governance* (London: Macmillan)

Stoker, G. (2006a) *Why Politics Matters* (Basingstoke: Palgrave Macmillan)

Stoker (2006b) 'Public Value Management: A New Narrative for Networked Governance?', *American Review of Public Administration*, 36(1):41–57

Strange, S. (1995) 'The Defective State (What Future for the State?)', *Daedalus*, 124(2):55–75

Strange, S. (1996) *The Retreat of the State: The Diffusion of Power in the World Economy* (Cambridge: Cambridge University Press)

Sullivan, H. and Skelcher, C. (2002) *Working Across Boundaries* (Basingstoke: Palgrave Macmillan)

Swedish International Development Agency (SIDR) (2007) *About the Division of Democratic Governance*, available at www.asdi.org/sida/jsp/sida.jsp?d=502&language=en_US, accessed 17th March 2008

Taylor, C. (1979) 'Atomism', in Kontos, A. (ed) *Powers, Possessions and Freedoms: Essays in Honour of CB Macpherson* (Toronto: University of Toronto Press)

Taylor, M. (1982) *Community, Anarchy and Liberty* (Cambridge: Cambridge Univesity Press)

Taylor, M. (1988) 'Rationality and Revolutionary Collective Action' in M. Taylor (ed.) *Rationality and Revolution* (Cambridge: Cambridge University Press)

Taylor, M. (1989) 'Structure, Culture and Action in the Explanation of Social Change', *Politics and Society*, 17:115–162

Taylor, M. (1996) 'When Rationality Fails', in J. Freidman (ed.) *The Rational Choice Controversy*, pp. 223–234. (New Haven: Yale University Press)

Thompson, M., R. Ellis and A. Wildavsky (1990) *Cultural Theory* (Boulder: Westview)

Thomson, J. (1981) 'Public Choice Analysis of Institutional Constraints of Firewood Production Strategies in the West African Sahel', in C. Russell and N. Nicholson (eds) *Public Choice and Rural Development* (Washington DC: Resources for the future)

Tversky, A. and Kahneman, D. (1986) 'Rational Choice and the Framing of Decisions', *Journal of Business*, 59(4) pt. 2:S251–S278

Underhill, G. (2000) 'State, Market and Global Political Economy: Genealogy of an (inter-?) discipline', *International Affairs*, 76(4):805–24

United Nations (2002) *OHCHR and Good Governance*, available at www.unhchr.ch/development/governance-04.html, accessed 17th March 2008

Unsworth, S. (2005) Focusing Aid on Good Governance: Can Foreign Aid Instruments be used to enhance 'Good Governance' in Recipient Countries?, Global Economic Governance Programme (University College: Oxford) Working Paper, Available at www.globaleconomicgovernance.org

Uphoff, N. (1993) 'Grassroots Organisations and NGOs in Rural Development: Opportunities with Diminishing States and Expanding Markets', *World Development*, 21(4):607–622

Veblen, T.B. (1899) *The Theory of the Leisure Class: An Economic Study in the Evolution of Institutions* (New York: Macmillan)

Veblen, T.B. (1919) *The Place of Science in Modern Civilisation and Other Essays* (New York: Huebsch)

Verweij, M. and Thompson, M. (eds) (2006) *Clumsy Solutions for a Complex World* (Basingstoke: Palgrave Macmillan)

Vig, N.J. (2005) 'Introduction: Governing the International Environment', in Axelrod, R., Downie, D.L. and Vig, N.J. (eds) *The Global Environment: Institutions, Law and Policy* (Washington: CQ Press)

Virilio, P. (1995) *The Art of the Motor* (Minneapolis: University of Minnesota Press)

Wade, R. (1987) 'The management of common property resources: Finding a cooperative solution', *World Bank Research Observer*, 2(July):229–234

Wade, R. (1990) *Governing the Market: Economic Theory and the Role of Government in East Asian Industrialisation* (Princeton, N.J.: Princeton University Press)

Warrener, D. (2004) The Drivers of Change Approach. Overseas Development Institute, London: Synthesis Paper 3

Webster, N. (1992) 'Panchayat Raj in West Bengal: Popular Participation for the People or the Party?', *Development and Change*, 23(4):129–163

Wernerfelt, B. (1984) 'A Resource-Based View of the Firm', *Strategic Management Journal*, 5:171–180

Wernerfelt, B. (1997) 'On the Nature and Scope of the Firm: An Adjustment Cost Theory', *The Journal of Business*, 70(4):489–514

Wildavsky, A. (1987) 'Choosing Preferences by Constructing Institutions: A Cultural Theory of Preference Formation', *American Political Science Review*, 81(1):3–22

Wiles, P. (1969) 'A syndrome not a doctrine', in Ionescu, G. and Gellner, E. (eds) *Populism* (London: Macmillan)

Wilkinson, R. (2002) 'Global Governance: A Preliminary Investigation', in Wilkinson, R. and Hughes, S. (eds) *Global Governance: Critical Perspectives* (London and New York: Routledge)

Williams, D. (1996) 'Governance and the Discipline of Development', *European Journal of Development Research*, 8(2):157–177

Williams, D. and Young, T. (1994) 'Governance, the World Bank and Liberal Theory', *Political Studies*, XLII:84–100

Williamson, O.E. (1973) 'Organisational Forms and Internal Efficiency. Markets and Hierarchies: Some Elementary Considerations', *American Economic Review*, 63(2):316–325

Williamson, O.E. (1975) *Markets and Hierarchies: Analysis and Antitrust Implications* (New York: Free Press)

Williamson, O.E. (1979) 'Transaction-cost economics: The governance of contractual relations', *Journal of Law and Economics*, 22(2):233–261

Williamson, O.E. (1985) *The Economic Institutions of Capitalism* (Free Press: New York)

Williamson, O.E. (1996) *The Mechanisms of Governance* (New York: Free Press)

Williamson, O.E. (2002) 'The Theory of the Firm as Governance Structure: From Choice to Contract', *The Journal of Economic Perspectives*, 16(3):171–195

Wilson, J.Q. (1989) *Bureaucracy: What Government Agencies Do and Why They Do It* (New York: Basic Books)

World Bank (1989) *Sub-Saharan Africa: From Crisis to Sustainable Growth* (Washington DC: World Bank)

World Bank (1991) *The Challenges of Poverty: World Development Report* (Washington DC: World Bank)

World Bank (1992) *Governance and Development* (Washington DC: World Bank)

World Bank (1994) *Governance: The World Bank's Experience* (Washington DC: World Bank)

World Bank (1997) *The State in a Changing World* (Washington DC: World Bank)

World Development (2006) Special Issue *Rescaling Governance and the Impacts of Political and Environmental Decentralization*, 34(1):1851–1996

Wuyts, M. (1996) 'Foreign Aid, Structural Adjustment and Public Management: The Mozambican Experience', *Development and Change*, 27(4):717–749

Yahuda, Michael (2001) 'The Potential Significance of a Civil Power: Europe and Cross Strait Relations', reprinted from the *Taipei Journal*, available online http://www.gio.gov.tw/taiwan-website/5-gp/eu/2-6.htm, accessed 14 February 2008

Young, O. (ed.) (1997) *Global Governance: Drawing Insights from the Environmental Experience* (Cambridge, MA: MIT Press)

Zingales, L. (2000) 'In Search of New Foundations', *The Center for Research in Security Prices*, University of Chicago, Graduate School of Business, Working Paper No. 515. Social Science Research Network Electronic Paper Collection: http://papers.ssrn.com/paper.taf?abstract_id=228472

Index